"A personal, practical, and powerful book th; support their transgender child."

—John Sovec, LMFT, author of Out: A Pare...
to Supporting Your LGBTQIA+ Kids Through
Coming Out and Beyond

"This book asks direct and practical questions, and provides diverse and helpful answers, because every parent has a unique experience and a unique child."

—Alex Stitt, LMHC and author of Accepting Gender

"This book answers every single question a new parent has ever asked me—and it doesn't just give one answer, it gives many. Any new parent picking up this book will be informed, reassured, and have a wealth of experience and perspectives at their fingertips."

—Jennifer Shields, healthcare lead at Qtopia and Rainbow
People Health & wellbeing advisor at Pegasus Health

"A compassionate, compelling resource that provides space for many voices and perspectives—though with a common theme running through—listen to your child and love them for who they are."

—Michelle Forcier MD MPH, professor of
Pediatrics, Rhode Island USA

"This book provides your very own trustworthy support team of parents and experienced professionals to answer every question you have had, been too shy or afraid to ask, or didn't know you need to be asking."

—Dara Hoffman-Fox, LPC, author of
You and Your Gender Identity

"Priceless advice from multiple sources, reflecting an open and heartfelt community of trans allies. Touching, honest and all-encompassing."

—Fox Fisher, artist, film-maker and author of
Trans Teen Survival Guide

My Child Told Me They're Trans...
What Do I Do?

from the author

**Everything You Ever Wanted to Know About
Trans (But Were Afraid to Ask)**
Brynn Tannehill
ISBN 978 1 78592 826 0
eISBN 978 1 78450 956 9

of related interest

Beyond Pronouns
The Essential Guide for Parents of Trans Children
Tammy Plunkett
Foreword by Mitchell Plunkett
ISBN 978 1 83997 114 3
eISBN 978 1 83997 113 6

Helping Your Transgender Teen 2nd Edition
A Guide for Parents
Irwin Krieger
ISBN 978 1 78592 801 7
eISBN 978 1 78450 819 7

The A–Z of Gender and Sexuality
From Ace to Ze
Morgan Lev Edward Holleb
ISBN 978 1 78592 342 5
eISBN 978 1 78450 663 6

My Child Told Me They're Trans... What Do I Do?

A Q&A Guide for Parents of Trans Children

Edited by Brynn Tannehill

Jessica Kingsley Publishers
London and Philadelphia

First published in Great Britain in 2023 by Jessica Kingsley Publishers
An imprint of Hodder & Stoughton Ltd
An Hachette Company

1

*The information contained in this book is not intended to replace the services
of trained medical professionals or to be a substitute for medical advice. You
are advised to consult a doctor on any matters relating to your health, and in
particular on any matters that may require diagnosis or medical attention.*

A CIP catalogue record for this title is available from the
British Library and the Library of Congress

ISBN 978 1 83997 277 5
eISBN 978 1 83997 278 2

Printed and bound in Great Britain by Clays Ltd

Jessica Kingsley Publishers' policy is to use papers that are natural, renewable and recyclable
products and made from wood grown in sustainable forests. The logging and manufacturing
processes are expected to conform to the environmental regulations of the country of origin.

Jessica Kingsley Publishers
Carmelite House
50 Victoria Embankment
London EC4Y 0DZ

www.jkp.com

Contents

Acknowledgements

First, I would like to thank all the parents and subject matter experts who participated in this project to make it possible. This is more their book, their stories, and wealth of knowledge than mine: I'm just a glorified project manager here. But I would like to thank a few people in particular. Wayne Maines and Debi Jackson have been friends of mine for years. If they hadn't been so enthusiastic about this project when I proposed it, or volunteered to participate so quickly, I don't think I would have had the momentum to go forward with it. I'd also like to thank Drea Leed, who has been willing to help me edit the book for clarity and content. Finally, thanks to my wife Janis, who stepped up to the plate to fill in crucial gaps in the material. She's been reluctant in the past to wade into the fray, but after all she did to help our son get through transition, and become the amazing young man he is, she decided to share what she has learned, and the book is so much better for it.

Preface

Years ago (around 2013), I started writing about transgender issues and began joining online groups for parents of trans youth. Along the way, I met some of the pioneers in the movement to help trans youth. These included professionals working with the kids, like Darlene Tando. It also included fierce moms and dads such as Debi Jackson and Wayne Maines. I interviewed them, wrote pieces to give the public a better idea of what their experiences and challenges were like, and got to know more about their unique situations.

Fast forward to 2017, when our own son came out as trans. It was a surprise for both me and my wife when he did. It was also a surprise that there were still challenges for us as parents, even in a home that was no stranger to trans issues and had a "Hate Has No Home Here" yard sign. It remained true that when you transition, the world transitions with you. It took some time to get the new name and pronouns right 100 percent of the time, but we were trying, and eventually it all "fitted."

My wife (Janis) joined a lot of the same parent groups I already belonged to. She joined in the discussions and gave advice that was very much reflective of her: thoughtful, compassionate, and as direct as a slice of lemon wrapped around a large gold brick. However, we both noticed that these groups' posts were repetitive: waves of new parents would repeatedly ask the same questions. Often this was because answers disappeared from the board within a few days.

Even worse were parents' questions about things they'd seen on the internet (or had been sent by relatives) that were part of deliberate misinformation campaigns by malicious actors meant to encourage parents to reject the identities of their children, no matter what.

Often, people promoting rejection are given big platforms to spread their message, like in *USA Today*. However, these articles never actually interviewed the adult children of people promoting rejection over affirmation.

But I had.

Most of these young trans people told similar stories of estrangement. I found out that a trans man's adoptive father, who had written about how important it was to reject trans identities, had put his child in a "troubled teen" conversion therapy camp after he came out. This completely broke the father's relationship with his son. Not only is he still trans, but he also hasn't spoken with his adoptive father since he turned 18.

A trans woman, "Natalie," now 22, described how her mother sent her to a conversion therapist after she came out at 15. She was told by her mother, and the conversion therapist, that she would just have to learn to live with her body until she was 18. After Natalie's mental health and relationship with her parents continued to decline, Natalie was told by her mother that she'd made an appointment with a gender clinic, but that there was a two-year waiting list. However, when she got to the appointment two weeks after her 18th birthday, she found out from the doctor that there was no waiting list—it had all been a lie to delay her from transitioning. This completely broke her relationship with her family. She told me that she can never forgive them, and that any relationship she has today is "performative" to keep the money for college flowing. Natalie described the experience: "I was metaphorically jumping up and down and waving and yelling 'Help me! Help me!' and getting silence."

What stuck with me the most was Leelah Alcorn, a trans girl in Ohio who was subjected to conversion therapy, and whose parents never acknowledged her identity. She killed herself in late-December 2014 by stepping onto a highway in front of oncoming traffic. At the time, we lived about 20 minutes away from where this happened. It drove home the point though, that when it comes to taking care of trans youth, this is a fight for their lives.

Conversely, the parents featured in this book, who have supported and affirmed their children, have had a very different experience.

When we sent our son off to university in Canada, we all cried. He couldn't wait to come home for Christmas and play Dungeons and Dragons with the rest of the family. Wayne Maines' daughter Nicole was the first transgender person to play a superhero on television and talks with him all the time. The parents who answered the questions in this book all have positive, ongoing relationships with their children, even as adults.

All of this led me to conclude that a book with answers to "frequently asked questions by parents of trans youth," by parents of trans youth and the professionals who work with these kids on a daily basis, was a desperately needed resource. It won't address every situation, but it will cover the most common issues from a variety of perspectives. Every parent's situation is different, and the parents in this book each had their own take on how to address the challenges they faced along the way.

The parents in this book are also using their real names, unlike many of the people online who recommend rejecting the identity of trans children. Similarly, the subject matter experts (SMEs) helping to answer these questions have all worked with transgender people as part of their practice, or even ministry. Conversely, most of the people promoting rejection of the identities of trans youth have never treated trans youth.

This book presents the answers to frequently asked questions, with experts' answers first to give a theoretical basis, and then parents' answers to help you put it into practice. Many of the parents discuss mistakes they made and things they would have done differently. Sometimes they disagree on the specifics, but that's okay. The goal is to help give parents the tools they need to get through what can be a difficult time.

Lastly, if you take nothing else from this book, take this: believe your child. Affirm and support their feelings, wherever they're at in the moment. Don't be a gatekeeper and don't lay the burden of your own feelings on them. They love you and don't want to hurt you. It took a lot of courage and trust to be willing to come out to you and tell you what's up. Don't break the faith with them by making them regret coming out. For them, it was a moment of extreme vulnerability and trust, and as parents we want to make sure that they continue to trust us that much again in the future.

If you keep these things as your guiding star, the details will work themselves out.

Brynn Tannehill
February 16, 2022

Chapter 1

Parent and Subject Matter Expert (SME) Biographies

Marsha Aizumi is the proud mother of a transgender son. She has shared her story of moving from shame, sadness, and fear to unconditional love and acceptance with schools, corporations, and organizations in the US and Asia. Marsha currently serves on the PFLAG National President's Council and is a former PFLAG National Board Member. She is co-founder of the PFLAG San Gabriel Valley Asian Pacific Islander (SGV API) chapter, the first API-focused chapter in PFLAG's history. Her book, *Two Spirits, One Heart*, written with Aiden, is a heartfelt story about a mother and son finding their way back to each other, then using their visibility and voice to bring greater awareness, support, and hope to the LGBTQ community and their families.

Clara Baker lives in Southwest Harbor, Maine, with her spouse and four children. She grew up listening to *Free to Be You and Me* and reading her mother's *Ms.* Magazines. Like many daughters of second-wave feminists, Clara experienced the contradictions of growing up with an activist who made the personal political. In college, she founded the NOW (National Organization for Women) chapter on her college campus, and in graduate school she was fascinated by Judith Butler and feminist semiotic theory. When her child socially transitioned at the age of three, Clara organized community events about trans experience, served on her local chapter of GLSEN (Gay, Lesbian, & Straight Education Network), and advocated for trans kids in schools.

Janna Barkin is an author, educator, and mother. Her youngest child is transgender. She currently supports transgender youth and their families as a facilitator of parent support groups, workshop presenter, speaker, and parent coach. Her 2017 book, *He's Always Been My Son*, was a number one bestseller on Amazon and continues to be a valuable resource. Janna hopes that sharing her story about raising her transgender child and what she has learned along the way will foster more compassion, understanding, and acceptance in our society.

Dr. Sebastian M. Barr (he/him) is a licensed psychologist and clinician-researcher. He received his PhD in Counseling Psychology from the University of Louisville and completed his training at Cambridge Health Alliance under the auspices of Harvard Medical School. His research, which focuses on the mental health and well-being of the trans community, has been published in peer-reviewed journals and honored with multiple awards including the Transgender Research Award from the American Psychological Association's Society for the Psychology of Sexual Orientation and Gender Diversity. Additionally, Dr. Barr has robust experience providing psychotherapy to members of the trans community and their loved ones, and often works as a consultant and trainer in this area. He has co-authored multiple textbook chapters focusing on aspects of gender-affirming care for clinicians. Additionally, Dr. Barr is a proud transgender man.

Noah Berlatsky is a journalist and critic based in Chicago who often writes about social justice. He has been writing about trans issues for some years, but his 17-year-old daughter (she/her) only came out as trans in 2020. Not long after she did, Noah's wife (she/her) came out as non-binary. Both Noah and his wife were knowledgeable about trans issues before their daughter came out, and that put them in a good place to advocate for her. There have obviously been stumbles and challenges, but he is excited to share their experiences with others.

Amy Cannava, EdS, NCSP is in her 19th year of practice as a school psychologist and is the recipient of the 2019 National Association of School Psychologists (NASP) Presidential Award in recognition of Exceptional Service to Children and School Psychology. For the last decade, she has specialized in LGBTQ youth, which resulted in her being appointed as the Chair of NASP's LGBTQI2-S Committee. Amy is a recognized and frequently requested speaker at local and national conferences. She has authored book chapters for NASP on LGBTQ youth, worked with The Trevor Project, GLSEN, Gender Spectrum, the Human Rights Campaign (HRC), PBS Frontline, HBO, and Project Thrive representing NASP. A former crisis counselor for The Trevor Project, Amy remains inspired and appropriately challenged by the youth she serves, who motivate her to continue bettering the world. She is the proud mother of a transgender son.

Luchina Fisher is an award-winning writer and filmmaker. Her feature directorial debut *Mama Gloria* premiered at the Chicago International Film Festival and BFI Flare London, received numerous awards, and made its broadcast debut on World Channel and PBS (where it is currently streaming). Luchina began her career as a journalist and has written for *People*, the *Miami Herald*, *The New York Times, O, The Oprah Magazine* and ABCNews.com. In 2018, Luchina wrote an essay for *Good Morning America* about her daughter Gia and the support she received from their small town after transitioning at age 13. The family's story has since been featured on *Megyn Kelly Today* and *CBS This Morning* and in *The New York Times, People,* and *USA Today*. Luchina is a member of the Human Rights Campaign's Parents for Transgender Equality Council and is active in The GenderCool Project, where her daughter Gia was a founding Champion and now serves on the board.

Master Sergeant Nathan Glickler is an active-duty member of the US Air Force and parent of a transgender daughter. Having been stationed at various bases in the US and overseas during his 19 years of military service, he understands the way differences in afforded rights can hurt transgender children. He has served under administrations which have upheld those rights and those that have assaulted them. His most recent change in assignment was accomplished with the express purpose of moving to a location where he could secure medical services for his daughter. Currently, he lives in Maryland with his wife, and three of his children (the fourth is also on active duty).

Dr. Matt Goldenberg (he/him/his) is a licensed psychologist serving the Gender Clinic at Seattle Children's Hospital. He has been a trainer, clinician, and activist working in gender equity since 1999. Matt has operated a dynamic private practice and is a popular speaker. Matt is married and has two children. Among other hobbies, Matt enjoys reading, walks with his beloved dog, and exploring the Pacific Northwest. Though throughout childhood Matt hoped to become a famous comedian, listening to people's stories and finding our common ties in the mysteries we write is close enough.

Rachel Gonzalez is an advocate, parent, and ally in the movement for transgender equality. Rachel has testified multiple times at the Texas Capitol, was an integral part of blocking Texas's anti-transgender bathroom bill in 2017 and continues to push for trans equality across Texas and around the country. Rachel maintains a local and national media presence, a platform she uses to defend the rights of the transgender community. As a member of the Human Rights Campaign's National Parents for Transgender Equality Council, Rachel provides input to HRC's national strategy and has participated in roundtable discussions with the Congressional Transgender Equality Task Force in Washington, DC. A fourth-generation native Texan, Rachel is based in Dallas where she lives with her husband, three children, and three dogs.

Dr. Paria Hassouri is a pediatrician, mother of three, writer, and transgender rights activist. She graduated from the University of Pittsburgh School of Medicine and completed her residency training at the Cleveland Clinic Foundation. Her personal essays have been published in multiple sites, including *The New York Times*, *The Washington Post*, the *Los Angeles Times*, and *The Huffington Post*, and she has presented stories on stage through *Expressing Motherhood*. When her middle child came out as transgender at the age of 13, she was completely blindsided by it, despite being a pediatrician who had already been in practice for 15 years. Her memoir, *Found in Transition: A Mother's Evolution during her Child's Gender Change*, chronicles her journey from anger, denial, and grief to acceptance and advocacy. She practices at Cedars Sinai Medical Center, where she most recently started the Pediatric and Adolescent Gender Wellness Clinic, helping other families navigate their youth's transition.

Pastor Chester Hitchcock is a retired Seventh-Day Adventist Pastor. He received his BA in Theology from Columbia Union College (Washington Adventist University) and has completed coursework towards a Master's in Pastoral Ministry from Andrews University, Berrien Springs, Michigan. Pastor Chester lives in Medina, Ohio, with his wife, Michelle, where they enjoy bird watching, taking nature walks, gardening, and finding ways to serve the Lord.

Jo Ivester (she/her) is an LGBTQ and civil rights advocate. Using stories from her two award-winning memoirs—*The Outskirts of Hope* and *Once a Girl, Always a Boy*—Jo encourages people to broaden their awareness of racial relations and of what it means to be transgender. She serves on the boards of Equality Texas, the Anti-Defamation League of Austin, and the Ground Floor Theater. She has a BS from the Massachusetts Institute of Technology and an MBA from Stanford University.

Debi Jackson is the mother of two children, including Avery, who is transgender. Avery socially transitioned at the age of four and is now 14. Debi grew up as a Southern Baptist conservative Republican in the Deep South and has had to wrestle with relationships with family and friends to boldly support her daughter. In the last decade, she has become a global champion for transgender children and their families, works with educators across the country through the National Education Association to support trans kids in schools, and focuses on political issues as a founding member of the Human Rights Campaign's Parents for Transgender Equality Council.

Clara Lee is a Korean parent of a bi/queer son with trans experience. She is the founder of the API Rainbow Parents of PFLAG New York City (NYC) chapter, a group providing support for LGBTQ individuals and families of Asian heritage. She is currently serving on the PFLAG NYC Board of Directors. She is also a co-founder of Korean American Rainbow Parents, a network of Korean parents and families with LGBTQ loved ones. Clara is passionate about supporting and advocating for LGBTQ youth, specifically to prevent bullying, suicide and homelessness. She also believes in the importance of improving LGBTQ equality in API homelands and faith groups to create better acceptance of LGBTQ individuals within the API communities. She has conducted and spoken at many workshops and events across the US, Japan, and Korea on such topics.

Dr. Wayne M. Maines' family's story was told in the book *Becoming Nicole: The Transformation of an American Family*. This *New York Times* bestseller book has now been published in China, Spain, Germany, and the United Kingdom. Wayne is an Air Force veteran, a parent, an avid outdoorsman who has a Bachelor's degree from Cornell University and Doctor of Education degree from West Virginia University. Wayne is the Vice President of Safety and Operations at Austin Community College in Austin, Texas, helping support students and staff create a climate for success. He has conducted LGBTQ training for the FBI, the Department of Justice, Harvard Medical School, the Pennsylvania Juvenile Court Judges' Commission, and others across the nation.

Cristy Mereles is a licensed clinical social worker (LCSW) and has been active in the transgender community since 2011. Cristy works with families and individuals of all ages. Cristy provides ongoing therapy, consultations, community education and advocacy through her private practice in San Diego, California. Her focus is to help her clients deconstruct how they have come to understand gender so that they may relearn gender in a way that is inclusive and affirming. Cristy's goal is to walk alongside her clients as they move forward in their journey, recognizing that change can be intimidating but necessary when striving to be the best possible version of yourself.

DeShanna Neal is a queer mother of four and graduate of Wilmington University with an MS in Applied Family Science. Since sharing their story of raising a transgender child, they have been a public figure for families of LGBTQ children in Wilmington, Delaware, for several years. They battled Delaware Medicaid for pediatric transgender services after their own transgender child was denied and, after an eight-month fight, won. They changed policy for all transgender and non-binary youth in the state. They were the co-organizer and creator of New Castle County's first ever LGBTQ Youth Pride Festival, as well as Delaware's first Drag Queen Story Hour. They have also co-authored a children's picture book, *My Rainbow*, with their daughter Trinity Neal. Now, they have created their new non-profit for Delaware's often ignored LGBTQ communities to ensure they too have a place at the table.

Dr. Danielle O'Banion (she/her) is a board-certified family physician who works in primary care and has a particular expertise in sexual health and gender-affirming medical care for people of all ages. She received her MD from Louisiana State University School of Medicine and completed her residency in Family Medicine at Cambridge Health Alliance under the auspices of Tufts University School of Medicine. Dr. O'Banion has cared for many trans young people and their families as they navigate unique gender journeys. She was previously an active member of Fenway Health Institute's Transgender Health Echo, providing training and consultation on gender-affirming healthcare to providers around the country. Additionally, Dr. O'Banion speaks frequently with providers and trainees on gender-affirmation in medical settings and has co-authored a textbook chapter in this area.

Jennifer See is a mom to four children, ages 13–19. Her spouse came out as transgender and began transitioning in 2011, and their oldest child came out as transgender at age 12. Together, for over 20 years, the family has been navigating the paths of LGBTQ and disability-rights advocacy as well as political and community organizing. Jennifer has advocated for trans children at rallies in Washington, DC, and has met with legislators and policy-makers, sharing her family's stories and concerns. In 2010, Jennifer received the Volunteer of the Year award from the Foundation for Ichthyosis and Related Skin Types for her community advocacy and education efforts within a disability rights community. Professionally, Jennifer has worked as a college, high school and middle school educator, and most recently was part of the Virginia Department of Health's COVID-19 tracing, mitigation, and education efforts.

Jennifer Solomon is a community advocate and ally for LGBTQ youth and families. In 2017, she founded the PFLAG South Miami Chapter. She is on the executive board of the Miami Coalition for Queer Youth which meets quarterly with the superintendent to ensure that policies are in place districtwide to protect LGBTQ youth in the school settings. In the past, Jennifer has successfully lobbied in Tallahassee against the harmful anti-trans youth legislation in the state of Florida. Through numerous speaking engagements and various media events, Jennifer has shared her family's journey in raising a gender non-conforming child. Jennifer was appointed by the Human Rights Campaign to serve on the Parents for Transgender Equality Council, allowing her to elevate her voice to the national level. Jennifer works tirelessly, empowering families to embrace and support their loved ones. She is committed to creating a society where all children can live as their authentic selves.

Kelly Storck is a licensed clinical social worker with 25 years of clinical experience, extensive professional development in the gender care field and nearly 15 years in gender care work with clients. She currently offers therapeutic support to individuals within her private practice located in St. Louis, Missouri. Kelly's professional focus is providing affirming gender care and advocating for the rights of transgender people. All of Kelly's work aims to help support the greater health, well-being, and liberty of people of all genders. Kelly is also the author of *The Gender Identity Workbook for Kids*, an educational activity book for trans, non-binary and gender-questioning children.

Darlene Tando is a licensed clinical social worker and has a private practice in San Diego where she has been working with transgender youth and adults since 2006. Darlene provides consultations and ongoing therapy for gender-expansive/transgender children, adolescents, and adults. Darlene writes a gender blog (www.Darlene TandoGenderBlog.com) about all things gender-related. Darlene is a proponent of the Informed Consent model and believes the individual is the "expert" on their own gender identity. She believes it is her role to support the individual and family in making the journey easier. Darlene has also authored the book *The Conscious Parent's Guide to Gender Identity: A Mindful Approach to Embracing Your Child's Authentic Self*.

Janis Tannehill is originally from British Columbia, Canada. While her background is in environmental science and she holds degrees in biology and business, she has devoted most of her time to her three children, supporting their school, scouting, sporting, music, and theatre efforts. Her son came out five years ago at the age of 14 and is now attending university in Quebec. Janis lives in Virginia with her extended/chosen family.

Lizette Trujillo is a Tucson small business owner and community advocate for transgender youth and families. She spends much of her time volunteering for the Southern Arizona Gender Alliance, where she and her spouse facilitate a local support group for families of transgender, gender creative/non-conforming youth called Families Transformed. She also co-facilitates a support group for Latinx-/Spanish-speaking families for the national organization Trans Families, which is part of Gender Diversity. Her local efforts have brought her national attention and she now serves as a member of the Human Rights Campaign's Parents for Transgender Equality Council. Lizette is a proud mother to a 14-year-old transgender son, and enjoys being a mother above all else. You can hear about her experience, the experiences of others, and the importance of allyship on the podcast she co-hosts with Dr. Drew Cronyn called *I Stand by You with Lizette and Drew*.

Chapter 2

Getting Started

When a child comes out as trans, it seems as if parents' first reactions are almost inevitably to go online for answers. The first stop is usually a group for parents of trans youth on the internet. Their first question is almost universally: "My kid came out. What should I do now?" From there they go through a lot of common questions: how did this happen? Why? What are the next immediate steps for me and my child?

The short answer is to listen to, love, believe, accept, and support your child. They're going through a lot. So are you, but you can't let your child see that, since it probably took a lot to come out to you in the first place. What comes next, and at what pace, will in great part be determined by what your child wants as they explore their gender and expand their comfort zone. This chapter shares the advice of subject matter experts who have seen this a hundred times over. It also shares how parents have handled it, along with what they would do differently if they had to do it all over again.

My child just came out to me as trans. What should I do?

Kelly Storck (LCSW): For most kids, sharing this with parents likely comes after significant soul-searching, struggles for self-acceptance, and dizzying fears of rejection. The fact that your child came to you is evidence of two very important and wonderful things: first, that you have raised a kid who loves themselves enough to do the hard work of being true to who they are, and second, that they are now honoring their relationship with you by affording you the opportunity to know them more deeply. Take a moment and celebrate that they trusted you enough to do this. Then make sure your kid knows you are glad they came to you and that you care about their experience.

Fear and discrimination are very powerful experiences. Trans kids are often most afraid that people, including the parents they depend on, will no longer love them. No exploration or disclosure of gender should ever be grounds for the withholding or withdrawal of your love. Do what you can to assure your child that you love them and that your love is not tied to their gender identity. Resist the urge to ask too many probing questions or run through all your anxiety-filled concerns right away. There are times and places for your questions and worries but it is not during these early, vulnerable moments with your kid. Let your early responses reflect the things your kid needs most in these early experiences—to be seen, heard, believed, honored, and loved just as they are.

Subsequent steps can include finding affirming resources to help you understand your child's experience and what things you can do to best support them. There are many amazing resources—articles, books, blogs, documentaries, organizations, groups, and so on—ready to bring you the wisdom and support you seek. Many parents also find it immensely helpful to connect with other parents of gender-exploring or trans kids. Look for local or online support communities that can put you in touch with others, such as PFLAG.

Marsha Aizumi: When my child came out to me as trans, it was actually his second coming out. Five years previously, he had come out as lesbian. These are some things that I did that were so helpful when Aiden came out as lesbian, then trans:

1. I went to PFLAG to get support.
2. I read books and did a lot of research to understand what being LGBTQ meant.
3. I found another mother who had a child about the same age who had transitioned from male. Over a lunch with her I was able to ask a lot of questions. It lessened my fear from the horrible stories that were playing in my head.
4. I educated myself but did not agree with everything I read. It

might have applied to other families, but I realized in some cases that it was not right for our family. I chose what worked best for my family.

5. I told my child that I wanted to talk about a lot of things I didn't understand. And my questions were not meant to block what he wanted to do but understand his transition process and feel like a good mother supporting him. This kept our communication lines open.

6. I told my child often that I loved him, I asked him to be patient with me, and apologized when I made mistakes. This kept our hearts open to each other.

I think the most important things I did to keep my relationship with my son strong, trusting, and transparent were numbers 5 and 6. In the beginning, all my questions seemed to end up prompting tension between us. I think he was afraid that I would not support what he wanted to do. But once he understood that I was just trying to wrap my head around transitioning, so that I could support him and feel like a good mother, our communication became easier and more honest.

And knowing that I loved him gave him the assurance that he would always belong in our family. Apologizing when I made mistakes let him know it was okay if he made mistakes too. It was challenging in the beginning as we were trying to find our way, but today my son and I are closer than ever. Aiden trusts me and I trust him. It is the kind of relationship I want with my child.

Janna Barkin: From the moment they are born, and even way before a child is conceived, we develop an image of who our children will be. We may even daydream about our future children right down to their names, their gender, the things they will do, the adventures they will have, even the hand-me-downs they will wear. But of course, there are many variations of being human that challenge our notion of who our children will be. We are all asked as parents to adjust and adapt. Some of these adjustments are easier to make than others.

1. *Be loving.* Love your child. Being trans is just one more beautiful way of being human. All children deserve to be loved

unconditionally. It's a sure sign they trust you when a child tells you something so very personal.

2. *Be approachable.* Regardless of your child's gender identity, remind them that you are there for them. "You can tell me anything. You can text me, send me an email. You can draw a picture. You can talk to me in whatever way works for you." Respond in a way that keeps the door open.

3. *Be patient.* Have patience with your child—and with yourself. Your child is probably many steps ahead of you. They have probably been thinking about this for much longer than they have let on. It's okay to take time to process this new information and learn more about it.

4. *Be curious.* Keep an open mind. It's okay to not know the answers. You can ask your child, "Can you tell me more about that?" or, "How do you feel about that?"

5. *Be supported.* Seek out knowledgeable, gender-informed support. There are support groups both locally and online. Find a good therapist—not just for your child, but especially for you as you tread this new path. There is a wealth of information available online and elsewhere.

Being transgender is not a "lifestyle choice"; rather, it is just one more beautiful, normal variation of being human. Having the support of family is the number one way to prevent depression and suicide among transgender youth. Every child deserves to be loved and supported unconditionally.

Noah Berlatsky: There is a lot of stigma surrounding trans identities. A child who is trans is going to have real concerns about their emotional and even physical safety if they come out. In that context, coming out as trans is a really courageous thing to do. If your child comes out to you as trans, it is an expression of trust and love. You should feel proud and honored. And you should tell them you are proud and honored! Tell them you love them too. Ask them what their pronouns are, and what their preferred name is. Do your best to use those going forward.

You may have a lot of other questions and concerns—will they want hormone therapy, how will other family members react, will they need a new wardrobe of clothes? But try to focus on expressing love and support. There's plenty of time to work out all the ramifications, but the first thing your child needs to know is that they are safe and that you love them and are proud of them. You can work everything out from there.

Nathan Glickler: Be supportive. Children need to be loved and accepted, and not treated as if there is something wrong with them. Their sense of self-worth is strongly influenced by what they are told. Take all your assumptions about what gender dysphoria is and throw them out the window; look for supportive, factual information. Understand that you can influence who your child is (a good person or not, accepting or not, etc.) but not "what" they are. Your focus as a parent should be on making them feel comfortable with what and who they are and understanding that there isn't something wrong with them.

Wayne Maines: My first hope is that you will not do much at all, except say that you love them and that you will support them in any way possible. I hope you will remind them that your home will always be a safe place.

Then you need to start your own journey of discovery. Read everything you can, reach out to your local LGBTQ community so that they can help you help your child. Safety will take on a new meaning. Friendships may need to be adjusted and family relationships might change for the better or worse. How often, how fast, and how long may depend on your child's age. At each stage of your child's life, your game plan will need to change.

This said, I want to turn the tables and talk about coming out from a young adult's perspective. I have travelled across the nation talking to middle school, high school, and college students. At the end of each lecture, I field these same questions: "Mr. Maines, I just came out to my parents and they do not understand" or "Mr. Maines, I came out to my mother, but I am really afraid of what my father will do." Last, "Mr. Maines, I wish you were my dad."

Every time I am asked these questions, I take a deep breath and say to them, the first thing you must do is be safe, knowing that often these kids are thrown out of their homes, or worse. Then I tell them that they have been thinking about who they are for a long time and having just sprung this on their parents they will need time to process what they heard. I tell them their parents love them, but are scared and need time to learn more about what being transgender means. I also explain that everyone will learn at their own pace. I explain that I had my own struggles, but I always, always loved my daughter and any misgivings I had with accepting who she is were based on my own shortcomings. Once I did that, I was able to really help her and together we have become a team that has been helping families across the nation. In my case, it has mostly been fathers.

Now, back to the original question. You must explore your own weaknesses, and any beliefs that may obstruct your ability to help your child on their journey. I cannot tell you in this short answer what you must do or what challenges might be ahead, but I know you will need to learn some simple rules. Do not try to label your child, or friends; do not flinch when you meet friends who at first glance make you uncomfortable, and, most importantly, figure out why you are uncomfortable. Learn their language and use it. Start to develop a plan that includes a variety of professionals so they can help you get where you need to be physically and emotionally.

Who do you need? A family practice physician who has experience in treating transgender/non-binary children, a local LGBTQ mentor, and a school resource person who has the proper training to help establish a safe school environment. Last, something that I did not have, a counselor for you and your partner to help you navigate the many potential roadblocks ahead. You will survive this. My family survived this, and you will too.

Janis Tannehill: Believe them. Love your kid.

The soft sell is that people are all different and we all deserve to live our truth. Gender variance is something that is not a conscious choice, not anyone's fault, and can't be helped. The best thing you can do is to use the name and pronouns they ask you to use. If you come at this from an angle that you are in this together as a family, it will be so much better for everyone in the long run.

Educate yourself—sex, gender, gender expression, orientation and sexuality are all different things and a change in one does not necessarily mean a change in another. None of them is black and white, either. Gender expression, like orientation, can be on a continuum or sliding scale.

Know your rights. Every state is different and has different laws, especially as exclusionary ones are being passed daily. The Transgender Law Center is an excellent place to start, since you need to know which states will allow transgender healthcare and surgery, legal name changes, changes to birth certificates, affirmative psychological care, and which states prohibit these things. Figure out what the policies and best practices in your school district are; just because the best practice may be to use a student's preferred as opposed to legal name doesn't mean it is official policy (e.g., old name still in the yearbook, on the teachers roll) and doesn't mean that a teacher or administrator would be punished in any way for using the wrong name or gender.

Seek expert help. PFLAG is a national parent organization and may be a good place to start. Search for gender clinics in your area for medical care and as a good place for psychological referral. Don't go this alone.

The hard sell is this: over 40 percent of gender variant people attempt suicide at some point in their lives. The number one predictor that a transgender person will attempt suicide is lack of family support. Forty percent. 4. 0. That number should stagger you to your soul. That is not a gamble I am willing to take with my child's life. If you are okay with an almost fifty-fifty chance that your kid could die due to a lack of your support, then you need to rethink your right to be a parent.

I have one fundamental job as parent: to keep my kid alive. Every decision I have made, every expert I have consulted, every parent meeting at the school I have had to get ugly at, every piece of clothing bought, prescription filled and appointment made has been for one purpose and one purpose only, to keep my kid alive. Have I evolved as a parent since my kid came out, changing into a parent who is not just about helping my kid survive, but thrive? Yes, of course, and I am happy and relieved and so damn proud that he has done so amazingly well. But in the early days it was a battle for survival. We are entering a war, people, we are fighting for our children's lives. Failure is not an option.

What if this is a phase?

Darlene Tando (LCSW): This is a natural concern for many parents. After all, parents often see their children go through several different phases in their lives, so it's understandable why this may be initially seen as just another one. Additionally, a child who has struggled with unnamed/unidentified gender dysphoria may pursue many different interests and go through many different "phases" as a part of seeking happiness. Often, it isn't until the gender identity piece is discovered that the child can rest in the knowledge of who they are and what they want. Authentically feeling like another gender is not usually a phase. Although it may seem to have come on suddenly (and studies show most trans youth grapple with their gender for years before they come out), this does not mean it will suddenly go away.[1] It may intensify the need for intervention, because once it is consciously understood, the need to act on it can be quite urgent.

Gender expression and gender identity are two separate things. The way a youth may express or perform their gender may change and evolve over time, and the way they express it may represent a "phase" of sorts. However, gender identity is typically more consistent and remains more stable especially once a youth is able to identify their truth. Regardless, supporting and affirming how your child is expressing themselves/identifying themselves is the best practice, no matter how long it may last.

Cristy Mereles (LCSW): Looking at this with the fear of "what if this is a phase" is not helpful. What your child needs is to see that you trust them to know themselves and that you trust them to explore who they are and even possibly try on new things about themselves in the process. The bigger message is "I have your back." Letting your child know that they are their own best expert and that you love and support them regardless of their gender, gender expression, or other details about who they are is a huge gift. If you can give your child this gift they will return your investment tenfold in the form

---

1   Bauer, G. R., Lawson, M. L., & Metzger, D. L. (2021). Do clinical data from transgender adolescents support the phenomenon of "rapid onset gender dysphoria"? *The Journal of Pediatrics*, 243, 224–227. https://doi.org/10.1016/j.jpeds.2021.11.020

of self-esteem and peace as they move through their life. To the pediatrician who says, "What if this is a phase?" say, "So what if this is a phase! I am here to show my child respect as they explore who they are and I expect that you will do the same."

Janna Barkin: Is gender expansive behavior or identifying as trans or non-binary just a passing fad or phase? Could it be? Sure. How do we know? A fad is something that comes and goes quickly while a trend is a direction or pattern that continues over an extended period.

The only way to know is to explore the possibilities. There are many ways to explore gender and gender expression that are not permanent. For our child, it was spikey hair cuts and "boy" style underwear in kindergarten, playing baseball (not softball) in elementary school, and breast binding in middle school. It wasn't always easy for us as parents to go along with our child's choices. We could tell by the look in his eyes when we were going in the right direction. Somehow we had the sense to trust that he knew who he was.

Research has revealed that the number one factor trans youth feel leads to their happiness and self-acceptance is parental support.[2] Sadly, to the contrary, trans and gender-expansive youth without family support have been shown to be in the highest risk pools for depression, anxiety, and suicide. These are sobering statistics. Children who do not express gender in stereotypical ways need parents who are knowledgeable, flexible, and patient.

When a child is given the space and support needed, they will find what is true for them over time. In contrast, if a child does not feel safe to express what is true or does not have anyone to help them understand what they are experiencing, they may keep the information to themselves. The inner feelings do not go away, they just get stuffed down or hidden from view.

And what if it *does* turn out to be a fad for your child? You will know soon enough, and your child will learn that you were there for them, no matter what. It's a parenting win.

---

2   Travers, R., Bauer, G., Pyne, J., Bardley, K., Gale, L., & Papdimitriou, M. (2012). *Impact of Strong Parental Support for Trans Youth*. Ontario: Trans PULSE. Accessed 11/10/2021 at http://transpulseproject.ca/wp-content/uploads/2012/10/Impacts-of-Strong-Parental-Support-for-Trans-Youth-vFINAL.pdf

Noah Berlatsky: Coming out as trans is a major and difficult decision. Young people who come out are *extremely* aware that doing so puts their relationships with parents, friends, and others in jeopardy, and makes them a target for prejudice. We'd told our daughter repeatedly that we supported trans people, and would support her if she was trans. But she was still really nervous about coming out, because she was worried about how it would affect her acting career, how it would affect her relationships with other family members, how it would affect her relationship with herself. Coming out is scary!

No one comes out as trans lightly. If your child tells you they are trans, they are only doing so after a huge amount of thought and soul-searching. Don't dismiss the work they've put in, or the trust they're showing you by telling you who they are.

It's also true that gender identity is complicated, and as people grow they may change some aspects of how they identify or see themselves. They might change pronouns or may change their name a few times. They might detransition (often this is because social pressure has forced them back into the closet, but not always). Everyone grows and changes over time and everyone questions who they are and who they want to be at some point. But it's insulting to treat trans identity as a "phase" or to suggest that trans people are just trying to be trendy.

Wayne Maines: My first response to this question is to let your child grow and they will tell you who they are. They will start to show you at an early age, through play, dress choices, and other actions, and when they are able, they will tell you with such innocence that you will really begin to know. The next step is to gather a team of professionals, doctors, mental health professionals, and LGBTQ specialists.

Jennifer See: Frankly, it doesn't matter. This is who your child is telling you they are. If you have a cisgender child tell you that they are Elsa or Elmo, you don't correct them and tell them, "No, you're Sarah." Most parents just roll with it. If it's a phase, Elsa disappears and Sarah returns. If your 11-year-old hates their name and decides to be Lauren and not Sarah; okay, you roll with it. Lauren may be Lauren for a few years or the rest of their life. It is their identity and who they want to be. Why should we deny this to a child who tells you they are Matthew and not Sarah? No matter what, time will tell you if it is a phase or your child's reality, and in the meantime, the best way to show that you love them and believe them is to accept them where they are. Use the name and pronoun they request. Ask that others do the same. Make sure you are the person they trust with their most essential emotional needs.

The thing about trans kids is that they are still children. They want to please the people around them. Peer pressure and parent pressure might cause them to tell you what you want to hear, not what they feel about themselves. It can sometimes take years to figure out what your specific child needs. Some kids will tell you at a young age that they are not the gender you thought they were. Others, like mine, don't identify that they are transgender until puberty starts and the flood of hormones sets off anxiety and unhappiness. Some kids may not have the vocabulary yet to tell you what is going on and may not work it out until after puberty.

Jennifer Solomon: There is no one in the world who knows your child more than you do so listening to your parental instinct is important. When you have concerns about the health and well-being of your child you should bring these up to your pediatrician. It is to be hoped that they are educated on gender and can provide you with reassurance and resources for you to use as a guide to promote an affirming home environment for your child. Unfortunately, this is not always the case. Doctors can have unconscious biases that cloud their professional views. A suggestion that your child is in a phase can further confuse you and make you doubt your parenting. As your child's advocate and ally it is important for you to do your own research and be up to date on the latest guidelines so that you can be sure the advice you may get is in fact the truth. When in doubt, find a healthcare practitioner who is recommended by other parents of LGBTQ youth. Remember, even if your child is simply exploring and eventually conforms more towards their birth gender, there is no harm in teaching them that you are supportive and loving. We know the statistics of children who are raised in environments that ignore or don't support them. I like to think that my child will be a wonderful unique person whether I support him or not, but by being supportive I get to be along for his amazing journey. Phases come and go but the heart and soul of our beautiful children are precious and should be treated with care.

Janis Tannehill: Sports are a phase. Becoming an artist or an astronaut is a phase. Wanting to take a class in championship baton twirling (true story) is a phase. We all have a garage full of sporting equipment or a box full of watercolor painting supplies in the basement from the latest passing interest. For every other phase, we know in our hearts it won't last but what do we do? We pay for the lessons, get the equipment, buy the t-shirt, drive to practice, show up to shows and games. We hope for good outcomes in that maybe this will become a long-term interest, starring role, or sports scholarship, although we know in our heart of hearts the whole thing might end up in mothballs.

So what if your kid questioning their gender is just a phase? Seek out professional help both medical and psychological. Educate yourself. Sex, gender, gender expression, sexuality, biology are all different things. Help find a community for yourself (PFLAG) and for your kid (Queer TikTok is a thing). Go to a gay pride parade to find support and celebration. Buy a Mama Bear T-shirt. Show up for your kid. This might sound like "fake it til you make it" but if that is what it takes for you to support your kid, then do it. And when you are still buying "Queer AF" merch for your kid years down the road then you will know it's not a phase, this is who they are.

What if they change their minds?

Darlene Tando (LCSW): This is a very common, very intense, fear of many parents. Sadly, outdated and skewed research studies have given the impression that most trans youth do at some point "change their minds." This is misinformation and has caused harm to many trans kids. More recent studies have indicated that the "myth of trans regret" is far less common than people worry it is.[3]

---

3   https://epath.eu/wp-content/uploads/2019/04/Boof-of-abstracts-EPATH2019.pdf

Sometimes the fear of their child changing their mind causes parents to delay access to needed interventions. It can be really tough not having any guarantee regarding outcomes. As the author Laurie Frankel[4] states in the book *This Is How It Always Is*, parents never truly have guarantees that they are making the best choice for their kids. All they can do is use the information available to them to make the most informed, conscientious, and loving choice in the present moment. Affirming a child and taking steps to decrease their dysphoria is the recommended best practice from those of us doing the work with trans youth.

One thing to think about is something I like to refer to as "cisgender projection." This means that cisgender folks tend to look at gender transition from their lens of *already* being comfortable in their assigned and authentic gender, which are aligned. Making changes in others' perception of their gender, as well as any bodily changes, seems like a scary and unwelcome undertaking. What they may fail to understand is that for transgender folk (youth and adults alike), these changes will help them feel *more* aligned with their own authentic gender. Such a welcome and dysphoria-relieving intervention is unlikely to cause regret.

Clara Baker: When we were thinking about facilitating our three-year-old child's social transition, a voice in my head kept asking, "What if he changes his mind?" Initially, I knew very little about trans experience. I remember wondering if we would *turn him into* a boy if we let him wear boy clothes. I also wondered what others would think if he changed his mind. Would family and people in our community judge us and think we had acted hastily and led him in the wrong direction?

Our child had been "insistent, consistent, and persistent" about communicating that he was a boy. "I boy" were some of his first words, and by the time he was three he was having daily meltdowns about his body and gender experience. I looked for answers, and the people and experts I trusted encouraged me to lean into what he was saying. The catch phrase was "follow your child's lead." But with a

---

4   Frankel, L. (2017). *This Is How It Always Is.* New York, NY: Flatiron Books.

three-year-old, this advice was frustrating. He wasn't going to *ask* us to use he/him pronouns, for example, but he was telling us he was a boy, so *should* we use the pronouns that agreed with his identity?

Changing his pronouns and name seemed like a radical act and, yet, from what I was reading, the consequences of *not* facilitating a child's gender experience could be tragic. People of trans experience are afflicted by suicide attempts at a rate four times higher than the general population. In one article I found, a psychologist determined that the earlier an individual transitioned, the better the chances of forming secure lifelong attachments. In effect, ignoring the child's communications could impact their ability to have healthy relationships. With these terrifying pieces of information, we set aside our fears about the future—our fears about what might happen if he changed his mind or what people might think—and decided to live in the present with our child.

Our son is 12 now, and we chuckle about the misconception that gender experience and expression are constant. Our child has remained consistent in his desire to block female hormones and use "he/him" pronouns, but his gender experience is anything but binary. At some point, our family—parents and siblings included—shifted to the stance that we all reserve the right to change our gender presentation. We celebrate creativity and no longer interpret gender expression as gender identity. Our son might choose to wear makeup and that does not make him less of a boy. Yes, he will undoubtedly change. All our minds have changed, our sense of ourselves and our gender possibilities have changed. We are forever growing, reimagining, and exploring—day to day, moment to moment, year to year.

Clara Lee: When my child came out as a trans boy at 14 years old, he needed permission from his parents to go through the necessary medical and legal transition because he was under age. Through PFLAG support meetings I learned about how to best support my child but I was still afraid of giving parental permission, especially since medical transition would impact so much of his future life and his own physical safety. And what if he changed his mind and blamed his parents for making such a life-changing decision?

One day in the support meeting, I saw a mother crying her

heart out because her young adult trans son didn't want her to be at hospital while he was going through the top surgery. As a mom, she wanted to take care of her child and she felt hurt for not being needed by her child due to various reasons. That was an eye-opening moment for me: if I don't support my child to transition, he'll go away to do the necessary transition when he turns 18 and never come back. In Korean culture, many parents have a very narrow definition of success and happiness for their child and I realized my fear for his future happiness was based on my own misguided perceptions of LGBTQ people and their lives.

I could not predict if my child would change his mind but I knew I'd rather be part of his journey than not have him in my life, no matter what decision he would make in the future. Those realizations helped shift my mind and heart. I decided to put aside my fear of unknowns and focus on what my son needed at that time.

Paria Hassouri: Worrying about the trans identity being a phase or possible detransition had me paralyzed with indecision and inaction for months, as I'm sure it may for many other parents as well. How do I let a teenager, who changes their fashion style or musical taste on a monthly basis, medically transition, when hormone therapy has some irreversible effects? Ultimately, several factors made the difference.

First, I decided that I was not going to be responsible for this decision, and that I was going to seek guidance from the experts in the field. If my child had a therapist whose specialty is working with transgender youth, and I was taking my child to a doctor who had been providing care for trans youth for 20 years, then I would have to rely on them to tell me what the best decision was. For a micro-managing parent like me who needs to be in control of everything, this was both difficult and very easy. It provided a sense of relief. I could always tell her that I took her to the best in the field and followed their advice. The other thing that helped was to decide that rather than worrying about a possible 2 to 3 percent detransition rate and parenting with fear about the future, I was going to parent with love based on the teen in front of me that day.

I had to ask myself what was appropriate to keep this child in front of me today thriving. Holding her back would only cause further depression. And the last thing was to come to terms with the fact that there is never 100 percent certainty about anything in life. I heard a very wise physician say, "If you're waiting for 100 percent certainty to allow your child to transition, that may never come." All you can do is truly see the child in front of you today, let go of fear and hesitation, and do what you need to do to help them thrive.

DeShanna Neal: "I'm done as a girl now, mommy. I'm a boy." This statement was made by my then four-year-old son, Thane. As a mother of four whose oldest came out as transgender when she was also four, and knowing that gender identity is established by age three, imagine my surprise when my youngest child declared this after living through life as a girl for a full year![5] My first question was whether or not I knew anything about gender identity, especially after all these years of parenting a transgender child. However, I recognized that while education on gender is constant, my oldest child's journey differed vastly from my youngest.

My primary question, "How will I explain this to everyone?", caused me initial anxiety because, well, the idea that transitioning is a phase could come up and pose a larger issue for us. I over-analyzed every possible scenario to the point of nausea. I literally made myself ill at the thought of my son being my son after living as my daughter for a year. So by the time the day came I told family, friends, and educators to no longer use female pronouns for Thane, I had broken out into hives. My little preschooler asked me why I was "so worried." I explained that I feared others would be upset with the change. I wasn't completely sure he'd understand what I meant, but he surprised me and stated: "Why will people be upset? I was happy as a girl and now I'll be happy again as a boy. If they are my friends they will not be upset."

So there it was, out of the mouths of babes. The best part was that no one seemed angered by his change, which gave me the same confidence that all would be fine. No harm was done, he kept all his

---

5   Mayo Clinic (2021). Children and gender identity: Supporting your child. Accessed 06/07/2022 at www.mayoclinic.org/healthy-lifestyle/childrens-health/in-depth/children-and-gender-identity/art-20266811

friends, and I learned that when a child is free to find their fit, they grow more secure in their own self and help their peers see that being happy and confident is the best part of growing up!

Janis Tannehill: People use this argument to deny hormonal or surgical intervention early, ideally before puberty has its way. The question really is: what if I make a mistake and my kid hates me for it? Realistically, our kids hate us more when we deny them something than when we give them something they ask for.

The Australian Family Court examined the desistance narrative using the largest sample of transgender youth ever. The Royal Children's Hospital Gender Service in Victoria began treating transgender youth in 2003 and had taken in 701 patients for assessment as of 2017. The court found that 96 percent of all youth who received a diagnosis of gender dysphoria from 2003 to 2017 continued to identify as transgender or gender diverse into late adolescence. No patient who had commenced treatment (blockers) had sought to transition back to their birth assigned sex.[6]

I am in a unique situation in that I have seen medical transition to female and to male. There is very little done with hormones and surgery that cannot be undone with more hormones and surgery. However, how much surgery (and the costs thereof) do you want your child to go through as an adult to undo the wrong puberty? More importantly, how much psychological pain and anguish could be avoided by medical intervention? The truth is, the younger a person is when they transition, the easier it is on their body and mind.

My child never showed signs of being trans before coming out. Is this normal?

Dr. Matt Goldenberg: Some parents and caregivers feel confused or surprised when their child comes out as trans or gender diverse, and often will re-examine the past for signs that they may have missed or

---

6   Family Court of Australia Re: Kelvin (2017). FamCAFC 258. Accessed 02/01/2022 at www.humanrights.gov.au/sites/default/files/Re%2BKelvin%2B30%2BNovember %2B2017.pdf

misinterpreted. Old memories might look different in this light—did they really love that birthday gift? Is this why they were so emphatic about that character? Were there times when they cried and couldn't describe why? Many parents find that they need to relearn what their child needs. When parents cannot relearn what their child needs, they deny their child's needs altogether. There is no greater lesson in love than letting go. It allows space in our hands for the new.

It is common for families to try and understand their child through the closest association they may have to gender-diverse experiences. For instance, a parent or caregiver may have trans friends or co-workers, may have seen trans characters in the media, or may be trans themselves. Using that person as their primary comparison, parents and caregivers may be unable to see their child in the other person's experience. However, each person's transition and the pathways they walked to begin transition are unique.

It is also common for parents and caregivers to learn about their child's identity after the child forms language, a structure for beginning to share their identity, and personal exploration. In a paper by Dr. Natacha Kennedy in 2020, the acquisition of relevant language is named an epiphany.[7] Prior to the epiphany, there is a period termed "tacit deferral," which people often describe as a sense of difference that they feel consistently but cannot really describe. As people gain access to language that broadens human gender possibilities, an internal structure that can better hold our experiences begins to build. There is the epiphany, often a long string of knots. Each knot is not too striking on its own but when held together, they start to tell a story of who we are.

Kennedy goes on to describe that discursive deferral follows epiphany, characterized by the difficult questions of *whether* to come out, *how* to come out, *why* it would be of use to come out, and to *whom*. Finally, the person has their coming out process, itself not a linear line with a clear beginning or end. As it goes for many LGBTQ people, coming out occurs over a lifetime. When your child comes out to you, they are inviting you into a deeply intimate conversation.

---

7   Kennedy, N. (2020). Deferral: The sociology of young trans people's epiphanies and coming out. *Journal of LGBT Youth, 19*(1), 55–75.

Don't be afraid to take your child's outstretched hand; if you can summon the courage and lean into vulnerability, you and your child will find a way together.

Nathan Glickler: It is absolutely normal. Vulnerability is difficult. Fear of being judged, of being denied because someone disagrees is very real. Think of all the things you could never tell someone—that's what your child is likely grappling with before they open up to you.

Paria Hassouri: My child, designated male at birth, came out as a transgender girl at the age of 13 and six months. I was completely blindsided by it. I didn't believe her. I'm a pediatrician, and I'd already been in practice for over 15 years when she came out. How was it possible that as a pediatrician and her mother, I would miss this? As far as I knew, she had *no* signs. I wracked my brain for weeks, combing over her childhood and trying to think of any single time she did something or said something that may have been a clue that I missed. I couldn't come up with anything.

One time, she had asked me around age eight or nine why boys and girls couldn't be friends, and I had said that they could be. When I prodded further to see why she was asking, it was because she wanted to invite a friend who was a girl over for a birthday sleepover, and everyone else invited was a boy. I told her she could invite her. Other than that single instance, I can't remember any gender-related question ever. She played with trains and cars and Lego and video games. She never resisted a haircut, wore t-shirts and shorts happily, and never really showed an interest in any of her younger sister's belongings.

She did have some difficulty making friends, she was often lonely. But there was never any indication that gender was the underlying reason for her loneliness or social difficulty. I kept grilling her, "Did you always know and just keep it hidden and now you're telling me?" That would have been easier for me to accept, but she kept saying, "No, Mom, I didn't know. I've just figured this out." Later, I went on a quest to try to figure out why some kids present so clearly at three or four, and others present later. This is too complicated to answer succinctly, but for some people, when the entire world tells them they are a certain gender, then they believe it. They live it until they can't live it anymore. I'm glad she figured it out at 13 instead of 30 or 60. I'm glad she decided that she had to tell me and live her truth. Yes, it's normal. And it is more common that you think.

Janis Tannehill: My oldest was coming into freshman year when they came out as transgender. While for him it wasn't an "all or nothing" decision but rather a part of a process, for the rest of us his coming out was a distinct event. It may seem like this is a sudden development or comes out of nowhere to us, the outside parent observer, but behind the scenes your child has been struggling for a while, trying to come to terms with who they are, what it means for them, finding the language to express it, and then plucking up the courage to tell those who are the most powerful people in their lives: their parents. By the time they tell you, it has been months or even years in the making. And they have been processing this mostly alone. It is new to you, but not to them.

We were just stunned that we didn't somehow see this coming. Sometimes coming out seems like an explosive decompression to us. For your child, this has probably been the most terrifying, shameful secret that have ever had to keep; we are just seeing what happens when they can't hide it anymore.

How can I tell if my child is really trans?

Darlene Tando (LCSW): In life, many of us find ourselves wishing there was some sort of guarantee for the outcome of things. Wouldn't that make life a lot more manageable? Something life teaches us over the course of time is that there are no guarantees about anything. We make decisions and invest and pursue things that don't have guarantees all the time.

However, when it comes to our children, this is the scariest thing of all. Having concrete answers, or feeling confident in knowing what an outcome will be, often decreases anxiety, and that is something all parents seek. Part of this journey of being an affirming parent is being able to tolerate the uncertainty, the unknowns, and the lack of guarantees. While it's hard to avoid living in the past or the future, the present is where we have our power. When your child tells you who they are, believe them. Affirm them. There is no litmus test to see if your child is "really" trans, but if they assert a different gender identity than the one they were assigned, that is what is most important. If they express a discomfort with being associated with their gender assigned at birth, and an alignment with a gender that was different from what they were assigned, affirm them. More will be revealed over time as they explore, so in the present moment rest easy that affirming and believing are your two most powerful gifts to your child.

Noah Berlatsky: The person who best knows if your child is trans is your child! So if they tell you they are trans, that is an extremely strong indication that they are trans. Trans people are constantly labeled as inauthentic and have to prove they are the gender they say they are. Their behaviour, their dress, and their bodies are under hostile scrutiny. But behaviors, dress, and bodies vary widely across genders and across individuals of each gender. My daughter sometimes wears dresses and sometimes doesn't; I don't like to watch sports; my wife loves Led Zeppelin. What does this tell you about our genders? Not much!

There's no secret sign that someone is a man or a woman or non-binary or cisgender or trans. You know your own gender because you're in your own body and your own head. So, again, the best way to tell if your child is really trans is to listen when they tell you who they are.

Nathan Glickler: Believe them first and foremost, but a diagnosis is often helpful. However, you can often see the signs. The key words are persistent, consistent, and insistent, and that is what a medical and mental health professional will look for when making the diagnosis. In the end though, let that decision be up to your child. There is a whole spectrum of identities and maybe they think they are one but discover through experience and your support that they are actually another. Let them be free to find out, and support them in their journey.

Paria Hassouri: It would be so great if there was a blood test that would tell us if our kids are definitely transgender or not. Even a checklist of signs and symptoms of being transgender would be great, but there is no such thing. What I have learned from seeing so many gender-diverse youths is that there is not one way to be trans, and there is no way to definitively know. There is no 100 percent certain test.

Here is what you can probably know with certainty: instead of asking "How can I tell if my child is really trans?", ask yourself, "Is my child happy and thriving, or is my child in distress?" If your child is happy and thriving, doing well in school, going out with friends, involved in activities and life, then there is no need for you to do anything. You don't need to take your child to therapists or doctors. But if your child is in distress, then all you can do is listen to them and figure out how you can address this distress today. How can you get your child out of distress?

As parents, sometimes we think that we should have all the answers and we should know our children when it comes to something as fundamental as their gender. But the truth is, gender diversity is not something any of us were taught in any parenting class. Listen to your kid, and if they are in distress, find the right therapists and doctors with experience in treating trans youth. Together, make the best decisions you can based on the child in front of you today. There is no one-size-fits-all test.

Wayne Maines: You need time and good observation skills, and to take notes and listen. Gather your team of professionals, family and friends whom you trust, and find groups like the Parents of Transgender Children Facebook Group. Talk to your family physician and locate the nearest gender clinic. They will have qualified doctors and mental health professionals to help you. Every child is different and every transgender child's needs require a unique treatment plan.

Janis Tannehill: The key words are insistent, consistent, and persistent. With psychological and medical professionals, with school, at home and with his peer group, my son was insistent on his gender identity, name and pronouns, and relatively consistent in his presentation. He was persistent in working towards being accepted on the boys' sports team by the school district and in his desire for medical intervention in the form of hormones. The gender psychologist finally had to say to me, "Look, this is real, this is happening. You're here so you obviously want what is best for your kid. You can be scared of the future, you can worry, but this is happening."

My child wants to use they/them pronouns. How should I handle this? It's really hard for me grammatically.

Darlene Tando (LCSW): It's hard for many people, at first. It's especially hard to use different pronouns for your own child. Feeling as if the pronouns are grammatically "incorrect" makes it much harder for many people. However, there's nothing grammatically incorrect about it at all. It's called the "singular they." It's been around for centuries, and you likely use it all the time without knowing it. You might say something like "they dropped off the package on the front porch" when it was just one person doing so. Saying "they" is just a way of removing gender from the reference.

It may be hard for you to remove gender from the reference of your child, but this may be precisely what they need from you, and why they are asking for they/them pronouns. It can be helpful to try to understand the dysphoria or other feelings that come up for your child if you use gendered pronouns, and this will reinforce your use of they/them as a compassionate thing to do.

Clara Baker: When your child asks you to refer to them using they/them pronouns, you should do so. Period, the end. You should not tell them that you are sad about a perceived "loss" of the child you thought they were. You should not complain that it is confusing to use a plural pronoun for an individual. What you should do is practice the pronouns in your own time. Meditate on your child and talk to yourself about that child with the pronoun they have requested. When you mess up, say sorry, correct yourself, and move on. Every single time. If you make a mistake and your child does not correct you, do not interpret their silence to mean that they have changed their mind about using a different pronoun. They love you and are looking for permission to be who they are. It was hard to ask the first time; do not make them ask again. They will let you know if they change their mind.

Nathan Glickler: This is actually simple. Set down your pride and ask your child to correct you every time you slip up—even if it means interrupting you. Don't require them to preface with anything apologetic or to even be super polite about it. Let them be a little forceful and respond appropriately, then restate the phrase/pronoun after they correct you, and thank them—this way they will know you support them and they will feel empowered.

Wayne Maines: I remember one time when we were going to the movies and I said, "Does they want to go with us?" My daughter said, "Daddy, that is not proper English." I laughed and said, did I not get credit for trying? Everyone had a good laugh. They are just words, please use them to reinforce that you love and want to help your child whenever possible.

Janis Tannehill: Try abandoning they/them altogether and use a different word as an intermediary to retrain your brain to use the new name and pronouns. Pronouns of all types and name changes can be difficult. I was screwing it up, using "she" constantly and I knew it was really bothering and hurting my kid. I had to make the conscious decision to not use a proper name or singular pronouns for six months to reset my brain. Strangely, the most useful thing to come out of time we spent living in Florida was picking up the word "y'all." It is far more difficult and awkward than it sounds. I used a nickname from babyhood (Bug) and they/them/y'all as a way to get to the chosen proper name and "he" pronouns. It sucked and I sounded like an idiot to my own ear, but I did it and it worked.

My child is still "into" toys and interests associated with their sex assigned at birth. What does this mean?

Darlene Tando (LCSW): Children who identify as any gender can be keen on any kind of toys or interests. Transgender and cisgender children alike should not be pigeon-holed into feeling that they should like any particular type of thing, especially when society has deemed it is for a specific group. Toys and interests fall under the category of gender expression, not gender identity. The way a person performs gender or the interests they may have are considered part of gender expression and may or may not align with what is "expected" for their gender identity. Children who are trans feminine may have a more masculine gender expression, and some trans masculine folks may have more feminine interests. It's all a part of the beautiful spectrum of possibilities.

Clara Baker: Your child's toys and interests do not reflect their gender identity. My child who was assigned female at birth and now identifies as a boy was the only one of his siblings, including two sisters, who played with a doll. If he had to choose between kicking a ball and reading a book, he would go for the book. Early on in his transition, I was anxious for his strengths and interests to be aligned with typically masculine-presenting behaviors. I feared that his gender presentation wouldn't be persuasive enough to other people, that people would doubt his "boyness."

There was a moment when he was four or five years and he had begun to fight with toy swords and walk with an exaggeratedly tough-guy demeanor. I commented to his uncle that I thought my son worried about whether he was masculine enough, to which my brother-in-law replied, "He's in the club. Welcome to the male experience." The idea that anxiety about being manly enough wasn't just my son's problem, but a defining experience for many men laid bare my bias and the bigger problem in our culture.

We are all minimized if we adhere to social norms that limit our choices and behaviors. Trans youth advocate Jenn Burleton talks about the irony that men are placed in a very small box in terms of what qualifies as masculine behavior. Everything outside that frame is "feminine" and distasteful—especially so if it appears in men. As tempting as it is to read your child's interests as evidence of their gender, it is best to interpret them as a healthy reflection of their creativity and expansive curiosity about themselves.

Nathan Glickler: It means nothing. Gender norms are harmful. They are an illusion and have led to a number of societal and mental health issues. Follow what Lego said about gender in the 1970s: "A lot of boys like doll houses. They're more human than spaceships. A lot of girls prefer spaceships. They're more exciting than doll houses. The most important thing is to put the right material in their hands and let them create whatever appeals to them."[8]

Debi Jackson: If your child is still "into" toys or interests after telling you they are trans or non-binary or even transitioning, it means your child likes those toys and interests—simple as that. Toys and interests aren't naturally gendered, but our society has determined that certain things—colors, toys or games, school subjects, and careers—are "masculine" or "feminine" in their own right. These societal determinations are why it's important to understand and recognize the difference between gender, gender expression, and gender roles.

Our gender is who we know we are, whether that fits in our binary system of male/female, whether it's outside the binary as bi-gender, non-binary, agender, genderfluid, or if it's something else. Gender expression is how we present ourselves to the world through things like our hair, clothing, mannerisms, and voice. Gender roles can be literal or emotional. For example, we used to expect men to be doctors and women to be nurses (some people still have that expectation), and men to be protectors and breadwinners with women taking on the role of nurturer and homemaker.

It's important to note that these "rules" we have aren't universal and vary from society to society. They also don't usually make a lot of sense if you stop to think about them. It's traditionally been a girl's role in a home to cook while boys were expected to do other kinds of chores. But we expect chefs to be men because we see that as a leadership role. That means those boys had to be in the kitchen learning to cook first. See how those rules are confusing?

Your child has already shown you or told you that their sex

---

8   Bologna, C. (2014). "Letter from Lego to parents in the '70s makes an important point about gender." HuffPost, 24 Nov. 2014. Accessed 06/07/2022 at www.huffpost.com/entry/lego-letter-from-the-70s_n_6212362

assigned at birth and their gender don't match. Resist the temptation to impose arbitrary and outdated ideas of what toys and interests they should now enjoy. They are already forging their own path, and that path will be more interesting if it curves and swerves and goes off-road a bit. Avery has always had more "traditionally masculine" interests, like martial arts, parkour, and playing video games. I don't see those as "boy things" but others in our lives certainly have. So we explain that she's a "tomboy trans girl" and it helps people realize that a lot of kids actually break these gender rules. If ours do, it's not a big deal.

Wayne Maines: For the most part, from ages two to ten my children played with all types of toys, but Nicole always came back to "girl toys." Toy use, dress, and role models are just a few of many indictors that may help you establish your child's gender identity. At this stage, like many dads I was not on the team yet. Every time I watched Nicole play with "male toys" or play baseball, I thought we needed to back off on our transition plan, she is not transgender. Of course, I was wrong in so many ways. You need to watch and listen to your kids and they will reveal who they are.

At what age do people figure out that they are transgender?

Darlene Tando (LCSW): People can come into conscious awareness of being transgender at any age. When and how their authentic gender identity comes into their conscious understanding is influenced by a variety of factors. The stronger their dysphoria, the sooner they may seek to understand their discomfort, and become aware of who they are authentically. Similarly, if their gender expression is censored by others, this creates a greater discomfort and may lead to exploring reasons for this sooner. Children who are allowed to express themselves authentically may not have reason to strongly question their identity until later.

It also depends on what the individual is exposed to. Often, there is a catalyst that can lead to an awakening of sorts. For example, if one is hungry but not consciously aware of it yet, smelling or seeing a food may cause the hunger to come into their conscious awareness. The food did not create hunger, it simply allowed the individual to become aware of it. Such is the case with gender identity; when one becomes aware of the possibility that someone can have a different authentic gender identity than the one they were assigned at birth, something can trigger this awareness. Sometimes it's learning about or meeting transgender people, sometimes it's mainstream media, and so on.

Dr. Matt Goldenberg: Researchers believe that gender identity, the core and innate gendered sense of who we are, develops at a young age. All humans share a task of telling the story of who we are throughout our lifetime, and gender expression and gender identity are important ways of doing this. We know that having access to words that can help us understand who we are is essential, but the meaning of those words and how they are framed within our homes and cultures is also key. For instance, in some families, the word "transgender" refers to a person who knows who they are and is authentic and generous with sharing who they are with others. In other families, the word "transgender" is associated with mental illness, a trend, or an off-limits topic. Likewise in some communities, the word "transgender" may be associated with outsiders, the unwanted, or enemies. In contrasting communities, the word "transgender" may be associated with a friend, family, or a leader. We may be less likely to self-refer with words that carry negative stigma to limit conflict or to create safety. Hence, we understand that there may be a distinction between when a person figures out they are transgender and when they choose to share it with others.

Kristina Olson and Selina Gülgöz (2017) have contributed significant work to the research field of gender development in children.[9] A key finding from a longitudinal study of children who have socially transitioned, named the TransYouth Project, shows that the development of gender in transgender children is like the development of gender in cisgender children. This is an important finding for several reasons, such as understanding that all children have relatable

9   Olson, K. R. & Gülgöz, S. (2017). Early findings from the TransYouth Project: Gender development in transgender children. *Child Development Perspectives, 12*: 93–97. https://doi.org/10.1111/cdep.12268

experiences with each other and that transgender children are not unique in their intuitive and cohesive sense of self. The research also supports our understanding that transgender children are authentic in stating who they are, and they should not be subject to interrogating questions about how they know and what informed their sense of self.

Clara Baker: People figure out that they are transgender at all ages. We each have a unique experience of self. Our personalities, our environment, and families all affect the way we know ourselves and our comfort level communicating that knowledge to others. My son was telling us who he was before he could speak. He put on his brother's clothes and threw tantrums when we changed him into dresses. He jabbed his finger at the pictures in books of princes with long hair and asked "Girl?" "Boy?" When he first spoke, he was clear: "I boy." We watched and listened without shaming or silencing his truth, and he was able to be who he is from an early age.

People would ask, "How can he know when he is so young?" Many of us aligned with a gender at a similar age. Whether the clarity comes for an individual at two years or at 70 years of age, it is most important that loved ones are willing to listen and learn.

Nathan Glickler: Children often know there is something off at a very early age—studies indicate transgender children know as early as three—but they don't necessarily understand what it is. It happens more often as they get older that they see an example and it clicks, "that's me!" You will find that you recall behaviors and comments they made from a very early age that line up with them coming out once they discovered what it was they were feeling and felt comfortable being vulnerable and opening up to you.

Paria Hassouri: I used to think that all people know their gender in early childhood. In addition to being the mother of a transgender child, I'm a pediatrician, and in my pediatric residency training, we were taught that "a child should be able to tell you if they are a boy or a girl by age three." While I understood that gender diversity may be a little confusing for a kid and present a little later, I thought that surely by six or seven at the latest, a child would know if they are transgender. So when my teenager came out at 13 and six months and said, "I just figured this out in the last six months," I thought that she was just a confused attention-seeking teenager. I thought she was confusing sexuality with gender and didn't realize she could be a gay boy who wears makeup for fun sometimes.

Now I know that 50 percent or more gender-diverse people may not present until puberty or later. I learned that you can present in childhood, peri-puberty, or late adolescence into adulthood. People have varied life experiences and access to information and processing of information, and, therefore, they can figure out that they are transgender at any age.

Our AFAB (assigned female at birth) child came out after puberty. I'm worried they want to transition just because they don't like menstruating and having breasts. How do I make sure this isn't the case?

Darlene Tando (LCSW): Gender dysphoria is so much more than just not "liking" parts of puberty. For many, going through a puberty that does not align with their authentic gender identity feels like a complete betrayal by their body. It signifies turning into a person they do not feel they are, and dreading every change as a reflection of something that is not truly them. The best thing you can do is try to understand (as best you can) what your child's dysphoria feels like, what creates the most dysphoria, and what would lessen it. If your child identifies as a girl and goes through female puberty but doesn't like parts of it, that is one thing. It is an entirely different thing to be male/trans masculine and have to go through female puberty!

Marsha Aizumi: I had the same worries about my AFAB child making decisions that were irreversible. I thought what if I support them to do something that they will regret later? I had so many mixed feelings. I understood that many parts of hormone replacement therapy (HRT) are not reversible and that scared me. Having top surgery, which is always a risk anyway, scared me. And then having a hysterectomy made me sad that they would never be able to have children in the future if a bad decision was made.

I finally asked my child if we could spend the afternoon together, just talking about my concerns. He knew my questions were to understand and not to block what he wanted to do. This was a very important point I made in the beginning. Aiden wanted to spend the day organizing his room. As we sorted things to be donated, thrown out, or kept, we just talked in a relaxed fashion. My hope was I would feel close to 100 percent comfortable with all his decisions to transition.

By nearly the end of the day, I did not have enough information to feel that comfortable. Finally, I asked Aiden, "How do you know for sure that this is the right thing for you to do?" He stopped for a moment and then slowly began to speak, "I know I may never find someone who will love me as a guy. And I know I may end up alone in this world if I transition. But knowing this fact, I would do it anyway...as long as I could be the man that I feel inside. I would give up love to be who I am."

This was the moment that I knew for sure that my son must transition and whatever I could do to support him I would do. I also believed if he felt my love and the love of his family, he would believe he was worthy of love himself. Today he has been married for eight years. He and his wife own their own home, both have wonderful jobs, and a life filled with good friends. He is living as his true self, and he is loved.

I don't know if you can ever be 100 percent certain, but for me, it was important to keep the lines of communication open and listen to my child. I also received comfort, knowing that if my child wanted to transition back, they could get breast implants and adopt children. I was 99 percent sure that this was the right thing for Aiden but having a backup plan for the 1 percent made me feel more confident.

Janis Tannehill: Let's unpack that. Breasts and menstruation came along as a result of hormonal changes at puberty. Sure, we know intellectually looking at the female members of our family that the boob fairy is coming, but until it actually arrives, we really don't know what we are in for. Some of us get far more than we bargained for but most of us feel somewhat at home in the skin we are in and treat these changes as embarrassing or a minor inconvenience. Transgender people don't. Their body has betrayed them and developed in a way they didn't expect or were really hoping wouldn't happen. Your body not matching what you have as a self-image in your mind is very distressing. Dysphoria is a symptom of being transgender. Hating menstruating and having breasts because they are not a part of your self-image plan is being transgender.

Seek out experts, as they will act as gatekeepers to transition and will figure out if it is body dysphoria or the inconveniences of puberty driving the bus. This is why transgender-affirming psychological care is so essential.

My child has not come out to me, but I think they may be trans. What should I do?

Darlene Tando (LCSW): This is tricky. Sometimes, if parents ask about it, the child can feel pressured to come out before they are ready. Other times, kids wish their parents would have asked or checked in about this before they had to come out themselves. Do your best to act on what you know about your child's temperament. You can make comments and statements about gender identity that show you understand what it is (and how it's different from anatomy, sexuality, etc.). The more informed you seem, the safer it will likely feel to come out to you. You can also gently communicate to your child that you have noticed certain things and are open to a discussion whenever they are ready. (This can be done in the form of a note, so they do not feel pressured to respond in the moment. You can even invite a note in return.)

Noah Berlatsky: Our daughter started wearing dresses in public before she told us she was trans (though after she'd told us she was queer.) We'd already made it clear many times over the years that we'd love and support her if she was trans. But we didn't push it; we figured she'd tell us in her own time if there was something to tell us. And she did.

Obviously, you're concerned about your child and want to talk about what's happening with them and what they're experiencing. But coming out as trans is often difficult and scary, and pushing kids before they're ready will likely as not just increase stress. The best thing to do is to be supportive of their gender expression and exploration, whatever that may be, and to give them space to access resources and support. Do not, for example, police their internet use or try to determine if they're looking at websites about trans issues. Don't try to cut them off from trans friends. Be patient and supportive. That's the best approach regardless of whether your child is trans or not.

Nathan Glickler: They will tell you when they are ready, but you can help them along. You can give indications that you are supportive without asking them specifically. Mention a story you read about a kid who came out and the reactions they got and comment that it's wonderful they got the support they needed or that they deserved more. Treat people across the entire LGBTQ spectrum with respect openly and without reservation and let them and others see you doing it. Show your child by your example that you believe that all people, regardless of orientation, identity, and so on are deserving of love and respect.

Even then, they may still be nervous. My son came out as bisexual to my wife, who is also bisexual (and he knew this), and there was still a part of him that was worried. If and when your child does come out, ask them point blank, "Okay, what do you need from me? How can I support you?"

Jo Ivester: Our son Jeremy, who at the time we viewed as our daughter, dressed boyishly, preferred his hair short, hung out with his friends as one of the guys, seemed uncomfortable with his body, didn't take care of himself physically, and talked about wanting top surgery. Everything we'd read shouted out, "Your kid is transgender!" But that's not what Jeremy said. He called himself a tomboy and said he had gender dysphoria, adding that if he could just have a more masculine-looking chest, the dysphoria would go away and he'd be happier. He denied—even to himself—that there was any possibility that he was trans.

I believed him because I thought it important to follow my son's lead. And, if I'm being honest with myself, I wanted it to be true; I didn't want my son to be different from most others and have to face the challenges that would inevitably come with being unlike everyone else we knew. My husband, having buried himself in the medical literature, wasn't so sure.

From an early age, all of Jeremy's heroes were men, mostly sports figures. As a toddler, he would say that he was going to grow up to be like Daddy. What we didn't know was that as he got into his tweener years, he went to sleep every night wishing that he'd wake up as a boy. Or that when he pictured himself growing old, it was as a man. None of us was able to put two and two together and recognize that Jeremy was trans.

This was over a decade ago, so we didn't know anybody who was trans, and nor did the teachers, counselors, or physicians in his life ever suggest it as a possibility. If we'd had a knowledgeable support network, teachers who introduced Jeremy and us to books with transgender characters, or a pediatrician who saw the possibilities, we could have talked openly with him about what he was feeling and encouraged him to explore the possibilities. We already frequently spoke of our love for him, but we could have added that we would love and accept him no matter what his gender identity was.

I believe we were right to follow Jeremy's lead, but my biggest regret as a parent is that because we were clueless and thus didn't encourage his growth as a transgender man, he lost out on his childhood and teen years, for he didn't become his true self until he was in his twenties.

DeShanna Neal: Too long, didn't read; follow their lead while showing that you will always support them.

In many cases, children will find a way to tell their parents. An example of this is from a friend of mine whose child told her he was trans as they drove up to the school drop-off site. From that point, the child was ready to start transitioning immediately. The same occurred with my oldest, Trinity. Once she knew she had my support and acceptance, social transition happened within a week. So, I thought I was an expert on transgender kids, but I sure was wrong!

My third born, Hyperion, has always been my gentle and quietly spoken child. Filled with deep self-awareness and never afraid to ask the hard questions, her gender expression was always pretty creative. I guess for me, my first inkling of Hype possibly being transgender came from her suddenly asking me about mom and dad bodies, having babies, and if she could one day be a mom despite being assigned male at birth. I would answer these questions to the best of my ability, making certain my answers were always as inclusive as possible. Some days she would ask if she could be a mom for a day and carried a baby doll and purse wherever she went.

Freedom of expression is a constant mantra in my household so I never felt concerned about Hyperion's behaviors. For me, it was the continuing conversations around gender, bodies, and gender norms that made me wonder if my child was transgender. Having experienced this all before, I knew what I needed to do: follow my child's lead. I used a few resources that I had from friends of trans kids to help guide a natural conversation, but overall, there was no rush. Finally, three years after her first question, Hyperion came to me (on Christmas Eve, of course!) and said, "Mom, please don't be mad. I'm really a girl."

I nodded and smiled. I didn't say, "I knew it!" or "What took you so long?", I simply hugged her and told her I could never be mad. I would always love her. A few days later, she got to talk with her big sister, Trinity about all things trans. Since that day, I have been, and still continue to be, a happy mom of two cisgender boys and two transgender girls.

Janis Tannehill: Kids knowing they are in a safe space will help them to come out. Simple acts of compassion like not making gay jokes or using being gay or trans as the punchline counts for a lot. Representation counts for a lot. LGBTQ media is becoming more commonplace so watching *I Am Jazz* on TV might open up a discussion.

My child came out after their friend did. Could this be because of that?

Darlene Tando (LCSW): Often, there is a catalyst that can lead to an awakening of sorts. Sometimes it's finding out what it means to be transgender, sometimes it's mainstream media, and so on. For some, it's meeting someone who has lived trans experience. This can bring their own authentic gender into conscious awareness, and the understanding of the misalignment between their assigned gender and who they really are. The other person didn't cause this, of course. They were merely the catalyst in bringing this understanding to the forefront of their mind.

Dr. Matt Goldenberg: In my practice, 1 have never had parents approach me and wonder if their child is stating that they are cis only because of social influence. That is curious because the benefits of being cis are bountiful, and there are likely more cis people to influence our children than there are trans people. Imagine for a moment that your child does not sustain their transgender identity. What harm do you imagine might occur from validating and affirming their exploration while it's going on? Sometimes it can be helpful to reflect on what our deeper fears are, and to consider if supporting a gender-explorative child will actually cause any harm.

If your child knows and can articulate what it is like to feel different from others, then you have an empathetic child. This is socially beneficial, and indeed a foundation for success in many areas of life. Celebrate that your child can see themselves in others and can see others in themselves. What we know about humans is that we all influence each other throughout our lifetime. We are naturally a herd species, and many of us seek ways to ensure that we are able to stay near others and not be faced with isolation.

The Pew Research Center shows that individuals born after 1996, known as Gen Z, are more likely to expect multiple options on forms for gender. They are the most educated, most racially diverse, and most progressive generation of Americans studied. They are also digital natives, meaning they cannot a recall a time without the internet. For children raised in the information age, there are endless influences on how they see themselves and others, and those who do not have an abundance of influence may have to sacrifice quite a lot to ensure their child stays unaware.

Sansfacon and colleagues noted in their 2020 study that for some youth, finding information about other transgender people delayed their coming out because what they read about did not align with their own experiences so far.[10] Others described how they shifted between being very vocal about their gendered experiences and being much quieter about them. Importantly, their internal experience of their gender did not change; rather, it was how much they discussed their gender, and with whom.

Noah Berlatsky: Our daughter had a circle of trans friends for years before she came out. This is pretty typical. Young people who are thinking about gender identity and sexuality and feel alienated from cisgender heterosexual peers often seek out other people who have similar concerns and interests.

Trans friends are a huge gift and resource for trans kids. Trans kids teach each other, most importantly, that if they come out, not everyone will reject them—there's a community there to embrace them. Your child may have been inspired to come out by their friend. They may have taken courage from their friend coming out. Their friend may have helped them find out who they are and helped them tell you about it. But their friend didn't make them trans.

Nathan Glickler: Perhaps, but not in a bandwagon sense. Many people come out after they see someone else do so because it is empowering. "They were strong enough, and I can be too." Be supportive and don't dismiss it.

Janis Tannehill: Gender-variant kids and teens do tend to seek each other out, like any other group, so some may have the chance to try

---

10 Sansfaçon, A. P., Medico, D., Suerich-Gulick, F., & Temple Newhook, J. (2020). "I knew that I wasn't cis, I knew that, but I didn't know exactly": Gender identity development, expression and affirmation in youth who access gender affirming medical care. *International Journal of Transgender Health*, 21(3), 307–320. doi: 10.1080/26895269.2020.1756551

out pronouns, names, gender expression and styles on each other. This support network is a valuable source for putting the language together to express their feelings and to practice coming out to each other. While it may seem as if kids are "following the trend" or "coming out because their friend did," they have been on parallel but individual journeys. They are using each other as bellwethers: you came out to your parents and nothing horrible happened, I should hopefully get the same results. Depending on many factors (strength of support network, perceived outcome with parents, cultural or religious background), this getting ready to come out may take months or years or may never happen. Coming out close together in time should not be seen as "jumping on the bandwagon" but rather an indicator of a strong support network.

After going to college my child came out as LGBTQ. Did the school cause this?

Darlene Tando (LCSW): No person or entity can cause someone to be LGBTQ. Your child was, is, and will continue to be who they are based on a beautiful combination of inherent factors. Often, an individual will be LGBTQ but not have the language or the awareness to understand that part of themselves or how to connect to it, much less how to communicate it to others. When an individual goes to college, their world is expanded in many ways. They learn more, and not just regarding academics. They may meet people from more diverse backgrounds that reveal to them more possibilities of existence than they knew before. They may start to see all the intricate ways people identify with their sexuality and gender identity, and some of these things may resonate personally with them. This can have the impact of a type of "Ah-ha!" moment when aspects of the self come into conscious awareness. These aspects are not created by any external entity but can certainly be impactful when it comes to the individual discovering new things about themselves. The college environment may be an open, diverse, affirming space where your child has felt more freedom to be who they are, and they now want to share that with you.

Did the colors of the rainbow exist before people created words to describe each color? Yes. It is the same with identities. They exist first, and then they can be described in a way that not only makes sense to the individual but allows them to be understood by others, as well as connect to others who share similar experiences.

Marsha Aizumi: I can't count number of times that I have heard Asian families make this comment about wishing that their child had never come to the United States to attend college. Many first-generation immigrants say they regret their child was accepted to a progressive US college or university because they came out afterwards. Many Asian families do not understand that it is not a choice for our children to be LGBTQ. These parents believe that their children are making a "lifestyle" choice, because they have come in contact with LGBTQ individuals at the college they are attending. Or I have heard parents say their children have caught the American disease. This makes sense to them, since LGBTQ depictions in movies, TV, books and other media feature white or western faces and families.

I see that changing today though. More organizations and companies are showing people from communities of color when they depict the LGBTQ community. And more and more parents from communities of color are becoming visible and using their voice to express their love for their LGBTQ children. We can't change the narrative if we are silent. Silence allows people to make up stories in their heads. And silence can be viewed as shame. But we can show our love and support for our children by visibly showing up and speaking out. We can also show our love by educating other parents that this is not a phase or lifestyle choice. My son has chosen to live in truth and courage. And as his mother, I have a choice to make as well. I will always choose you, Aiden.

Janis Tannehill: Oh honey, they always were, they were just waiting to be adults and out of your house to come out because they knew they wouldn't be accepted. College is where people figure themselves out or find communities and people to give them the language that they didn't previously have to explain who and what they are. Since your kid is now an adult, the choice is now what kind of relationship do you want to have with them? Now that they have had a taste of freedom and know there are ways to support themselves and never return home, you are dealing with an adult who can cut you out of their lives if you do not choose to be a part of their journey.

Chapter 3

Feelings as a Parent

One of the best pieces of advice given to me and my spouse when I came out and began transitioning is that when you transition, the world transitions with you. Transition can be emotionally difficult for everyone. Many parents go through some, or all, of the stages of dealing with a life-changing event: namely, denial and isolation; anger; bargaining; depression; and acceptance. Often, parents don't know how they're supposed to feel, or don't feel comfortable expressing these things. One of the best pieces of advice is that even supportive parents can use a therapist to support their emotional needs. However, it's important to remember that if your transgender child sees you struggling, they may feel guilt or shame over having been honest enough to tell you about what they are experiencing.

You want to keep the lines of communication between you and your child open, but you need to take care of yourself emotionally as well. This chapter shares expert advice on how to handle some of the most emotionally difficult parts of transition for parents. It also includes advice from parents who have gone through the process and have emerged with healthy young adults and even healthier relationships with them. Each of these parents found their own ways to process and deal with these issues, and it is hoped that some of these approaches will work for you as well.

Is it okay for me to mourn the child I feel I lost?

Dr. Matt Goldenberg: Mourning is an active process in which a person expresses sorrow for someone that they have lost, typically through death. Parents can experience a sense of loss, though they often struggle to articulate who or what they believe they have lost. There in front of you is still your beautiful child, smart and funny, and worthy, and you have so many memories together.

The outside shapes of all our children change, this is the product of growth. And just as most parents do, we learn to let go because our children teach us that letting go means having room in your arms for something new. This new shape of your child may not be known to you yet, and that is frightening. It is okay to talk about this with adults you trust, whether that be a clergy member, a friend, or a therapist. Having the support you need to acknowledge the journey you and your family are on may help parents understand what is theirs to carry on their own and what they should share with their children.

Clara Baker: It is always okay to have feelings, but it is in the best interest of your child and your relationship with your child not to share your perceived feelings of loss when they transition. I am imagining a youth, vulnerable to the adults in their lives, looking for love and approval. When they communicate their truth, they are scared, but also excited about the possibility of living a life that reflects their reality. This is a moment to celebrate, to reassure the child. How it plays out is crucial for the health of the child and the health of the caregiver-child relationship.

In *Far from the Tree*, author Andrew Solomon speaks to the experience of not sharing a trans experience with one's child. This can be isolating for the child and can present a sense of loss for the parent. It is not that the child is "lost" to the parent; it is that the parent doesn't know how to best help the child in this experience. The parent can be quite literally "at a loss." Feel this scary feeling of not knowing how to help your child, and then get to work educating yourself and reaching out for the resources to support them.

Noah Berlatsky: You're going to feel how you feel, and it's okay to be concerned or sad about lost possibilities. Our daughter is a very talented actor, and when she came out, we were all (including her) worried about how being trans might limit her career or prevent her from getting the roles she might have had.

I'd keep in mind, though, that you haven't lost a child! Your child is still there; they just are telling you that they're someone a bit different from who you thought they were. You (hopefully!) wouldn't think your child had died if they told you they wanted to be a poet rather than a doctor (or vice versa).

I'd also be careful about making your child's transition about your own worries or sadness. Coming out and transitioning is a difficult thing considering the stigma trans people face; your child is very aware of that and is no doubt dealing with their own anxiety and fears. Telling them you are upset about their transition, or that you feel they're lost to you in some way, or that they've failed to live up to your expectations—none of that is going to be very helpful to them. If you are really struggling, you should consider talking to a trans-friendly therapist who can work through your emotions in a way that doesn't burden your child.

Paria Hassouri: My answer to this question may not be popular among some people, but I absolutely think it is okay and probably necessary to allow yourself to mourn the child that you feel you lost. Of course, we do not lose a child as the parent of a trans person, but we do lose what we thought our child was, and the vision that we created for that child since we took that very first pregnancy test. I think it would be hard to move on and come to full acceptance without acknowledging the emotions that we are feeling and allowing ourselves to feel them. At the same time, we have to protect our children. Do not say this to your child. Only express it to your therapist, spouse, friend, or loved one, or a support group. It's not your child's burden to bear.

Mourning the vision you had for your child and supporting your child are not mutually exclusive. You can do both. Any feelings you have that you don't acknowledge will only catch up with you later. One of my regrets about the time when my child was transitioning is that I did not find a therapist for myself. My daughter was seeing a gender therapist, but I didn't see one. I was fortunate enough to have a husband, family, and friends who were supportive and there for me. I joined a support group of other families going through the same thing, which was invaluable. But I still would have benefited from seeing a therapist myself. The most supportive family and friends are still not therapists. Take care of yourself at the same time as you are taking care of your child.

Lizette Trujillo: A few weeks ago, my 14-year-old transgender son ran into my room visibly upset and exclaimed, "Not all parents feel this way, right?" He then placed his phone screen in front of my face and showed me a TikTok that another mother had made where she shared a compilation of old photos of her transgender child pre-social transition and discussed the sadness she felt at times. I looked at my son's face, and watched the emotions of sadness, disappointment, and anger wash across it. My son said, "He didn't die. He is still here, and he gets to be himself. Why would that make her sad!" We had a long talk about this issue of "grief" that is so often discussed in parent support spaces. We talked a lot about the ways that "grief" gets confused and conflated with the loss of privilege, loss of relationships, and loss of civil protections. While my son understood the underlying reasons for this; he still felt that it was wrong, and hurtful. I have to say that I agree with him.

Soon after our talk, I reached out to my friend Rachel to further discuss this concept of "grief" and "loss" that she and I often talk about, and we decided to explore this very difficult topic. I hope this book helps you look inward and see that marginalization and societal bias at their core are created and meant to produce stigma and fear. It is what allows these ideas and worries to take root. It is our innate understanding that the world is not safe for people who are perceived as different, but it is also an opportunity for parents to envision a world in which our transgender, non-binary, and gender-diverse children and loved ones are finally free, affirmed, and protected.

Rachel Gonzalez: There is a seemingly unwavering societal pressure to put people, especially kids, in easily identifiable boxes or assign markers with which to interpret how a person should be treated. It is no secret that those pressures infiltrate every aspect of our lives, including parenting. Few parents can say that they don't imagine a life for their child as they grow and move into adulthood. We all want the very best we can provide for our children. Unfortunately, that often comes with our own gender role expectations. When our children no longer fit into the life we've imagined, it can be difficult. Expressing your grief where your child can see it is a detriment to transgender and non-binary children's well-being and growth. As Lizette notes in recounting her son's confusion and sadness, whether it is your child or another transgender or non-binary child who witnesses your grief over the child you thought you had, a trans or non-binary person might feel guilt, shame, or fear that their parents resent them, do not fully embrace them, or are unhappy that they decided to share and live their truth as a transgender or non-binary individual.

As parents, we are given this amazing gift and opportunity to support our children in the way that they need, not the way that we want them to need us. Giving our children the resources and opportunity to thrive in the life they know they are meant to lead is an amazing privilege. Is it fair to link that longing for a life free of turmoil to a preconceived idea of who our kids are? Absolutely not. It's time that we flip the narrative, own the loss of relationships, safety, and privilege, and celebrate our kids. They have an opportunity to express their happiest, most alive, and authentic selves, so let's focus on honoring and loving them for being brave enough to share their truth with us and the world.

Wayne Maines: When Nicole started middle school, we moved Kelly and the kids to Portland, Maine, and I stayed behind in Orono. For the next five and a half years I rode the bus to Portland, Maine to see them. During the bus rides, I wrote in my journal. It was helpful and important that I put down how I was feeling because I was not the type of guy who shared his feelings.

Journal entry, 2008:

In the beginning when Nicole was coming out at home and to our family, I truly was remorseful. Every once in a while, when I see an old photo or something on television that reminds me of Wyatt, I have to control my emotions.[1] I dared not talk about it with Kelly

---

1   Not all trans people want their birth name/deadname disclosed. Wayne shares it here in this book with Nicole's permission.

for fear she would think the worst. I did not want her to think I was not on board. With time, I knew it would become easier to deal with watching my son transform into a girl. A year after Wyatt became Nicole, I saw a picture of Wyatt smiling and playing with his friends in the second grade and I still felt the emotional pain. It used to be difficult to accept the loss of my son and to this day some memory of Wyatt will grab me and gently tug at my heart, but I do not mourn this loss anymore, because I realize I never had the son to lose, I only lost the dream of growing old with two sons. Now I dream of growing old with my daughter and son and everything is as it should be.

I have gained a daughter, a beautiful, funny, loud, and loving daughter. Just the other day we were at the grocery store and we got out of the van. Nicole grabbed my hand and we held hands all through the store. That physical and emotional bond from holding hands may seem like a simple gesture to others, but for me it provides validation that we are father and daughter. Jonas is a little man now; he will no longer hold my hand in public. He does not allow me to kiss him goodnight any more. I look forward to Nicole holding my hand for years to come and relish having the opportunity to still kiss her and hug her. I have lost some things, lost a few dreams, but I have gained so much more. So "the boys" have been quietly tucked away in my memories. The phrase is almost forgotten in our home. For family and friends, it is still hard. They sometimes slip and say, "We can't wait to see you and the boys." They quickly say they are sorry or their own kids correct them. It happens less and less. Sometimes I lie in bed at night and wonder if in my old age, if I might revert back to these early years and talk about the boys? Will I forget about Nicole and remember Wyatt? Will I hurt my daughter's feelings?"

I have talked to Nicole about my old age fears, and we make jokes about it. She says, "You can't remember anything now, why do you think I will be surprised 20 years from now?"

Janis Tannehill: My journey with my trans kid has been an exercise in the stages of grief. Like our kids, one size does not fit all when it comes to where we are on our own journeys and some stages are easier or more difficult than others. You are the adult here and you will keep it together for your kids—do not take it out on them and don't let them see you break. Grief is real and deserves all the feels, just don't get stuck there. I went through all the classic stages of grief:

Disbelief and shock

When my kid first came out to me, I knew something was up. We spent a lot of time together and he has always been a chatterbox. The summer before freshman year he was in an all-girls' social justice project. I knew he was struggling trying to fit in with his peer group, having difficulty communicating effectively with them, and generally feeling like an outsider. In a car-door-slamming fit he yelled, "Maybe I'm just a guy!" Nah. Teenage girls are just difficult to negotiate, I don't care who you are, being a teenager is rough. Besides, he just bought a pair of second-hand hooker heels (ex-goth, Gen X parent-approved) for back to school. Just words.

When he put the words together ("I've been using a boy's name and male pronouns at school. I'm pretty sure I'm trans. I'm a guy") and came out to me in the fall it obviously wasn't real. I am lucky in that I know transgender people, though. I spent hours on the phone with the youngest, coolest, trans dude (Landon) I know whose response was "No shit, yeah?" I'm sure he gave me the best, most detailed list of what to do next that he wished his parents could do for him, but I was in a haze. What I do remember is that he talked me through the shock at least. What it boiled down to was, your kid is your kid, and you will love them. You'll get through this together.

But what about the Tardis dress you just had to have for homecoming? What about the nail polish? What about the hooker heels?! A year later, I asked him about the shoes, and he told me, "Denial isn't just for parents, Mom. Nail polish is cool, and so are bow ties, but those shoes were impossible."

Denial

I'm a scientist by nature, so when in doubt I consult the experts. There were no books on kids; adult memoirs, sure, but trans and gender-variant kids were just barely starting to become mainstream. Psychologists could surely tell me if this was really happening or not, right? The ADHD (attention deficit hyperactivity disorder) psychologist was the first to admit he was outside his wheelhouse. One pediatrician wouldn't even talk about it, another came out and admitted that the whole of pediatrics was abysmally behind the curve in its training. I got lucky that the local gender clinic, a hellish one-hour-plus slog through DC traffic, was just starting to see teens.

I was hoping that working through gender dysphoria with the psychologist would not necessarily cure things, but I would perhaps end up with a non-binary, butchy girl. I could sell that to the grand-parents. It would certainly be an easier road medically. But this was not my journey to make.

Guilt and pain

How could this possibly be happening to my kid? How scared and confused must they be? How horrible every day at school must be for them being called the wrong name, being bullied, being harassed? How could I not have seen this coming and helped them come to terms with it? What the hell did I do wrong to cause this? My kid is a part of the most hated subgroup of people around the world. How do I fix this?

I tried blaming the faulty genetics of the other parent because nothing like this had ever happened in my family before. Well, it never happened in theirs either, so that was a dead end. I tried finding answers and found some interesting lines of research in pre-natal development and the nature versus nurture of faulty genes.[2]

The truth is: it's no one's fault, least of all our kids'. I felt so guilty for my child's pain, whose pain I would gladly take on as my own. I wish I had taken him at his word sooner. I wish I had allowed transition to happen quicker. Was I being the adult and a good gate-keeper, or was I just being in selfish denial? However, the guilt got me moving. I worked just that much harder to make sure he made all the appointments and got all the medication he needed.

---

2   Roselli, C. E. (2018). Neurobiology of gender identity and sexual orientation. *Journal of Neuroendocrinology, 30*(7), e12562. https://doi.org/10.1111/jne.12562

Bargaining

Then things got really bad for my kid. First-time heartbreak followed by a misdiagnosed concussion along with gender-based bullying at school led to my kid being hospitalized for five days right before Christmas sophomore year. Nothing is really accomplished in a psych ward except for giving your kid a safe place to get meds on board. When a medical professional tells you to hide the forks and thumbtacks, you know there is something really messed up. It says something that, of the ten kids on the ward, five were gender non-conforming.

Don't get me wrong, I would give anything for my kid not to be trans simply because there is so much hate in the world. But I needed to keep my kid alive more. The doc says you needs these meds? Take them. The kid says they need surgery and the gender psychologist and doc agree? Do it. I didn't not spend my time trying to push the trans back in the bottle. He's here, he's queer, and it's not his or anyone else's fault. The days of hoping for a butchy non-binary girl were over. I wasn't bargaining for him to not be transgender; I was bargaining with the crippling depression and anxiety for his life.

Anger

My kid was in pain and that pissed me off. Some parents take their anger out on their kid (how dare you do this to your family/my perception of self/God). Me, I took my anger out on the world. Mama Bear shirt in full effect. The school caught it in the face every single time a teacher misgendered him, every time his old name showed up on correspondence, and every time his special needs protocols were ignored. They learned not to mess with me pretty quickly. The government could go straight to hell—I pounded more than my fair share of the pavement working to get the intolerant bigot on the school board fired. Human Rights Campaign, The Trevor Project, GLSEN...take my money! I fought with insurance every, single, damn time he needed more meds. Anyone I knew who wasn't immediately on board got cut out of my life. My tolerance for people online evaporated. Trans jokes? Nope. Your family is intolerant? Cut them off. Your spouse isn't on board? Leave them. You need time to process? Do it quicker. Yes, I became one of *those* people.

Granted, some of these things needed to be done. My friends, acquaintances, and family members who still couldn't figure out that pronouns were causing my kid real upset needed to be put at a distance. The local school and school board needed to do better for transgender and gender-variant kids. (They finally have a trans inclusive policy for the district, despite the hateful people brought in from out-of-district to spew their hate at school board meetings.) The insurance company is still broken, but I learned to get my way.

Now that he is 18, extended out-of-state family can't touch him or call child protective services on us. I took a good long break from being online as I was part of the problem and not the solution—getting down in the mud to wrestle with the pigs only gets you dirty, and doesn't help the people who are genuine in their desire to do right by their kids but just don't know how yet.

Be angry—our kids are called hateful names by the media, they are denied access to the friggin' bathroom and healthcare in some states. But channel that anger towards those causes that will make life for our kids better.

Depression

Channeling my efforts towards causes that make the world a slightly better place for transgender and gender-variant youth has helped.

On and off I have spiraled hard. At times I have been so abysmally sad and felt like such an abject failure as a parent. I would get the kids off to school and then just go back to bed more often than I would like to admit because the world just hurt too much. I missed my daughter and all the hopes for the future bound up in that. I was so disappointed in myself for tying so much worth and loss of experiences to something as socially constructed as gender. Every time he would use the term "deadname" for his old name it cut like a knife.

Acceptance

So my daughter became my son. Like learning a new language, eventually I got to the point where I looked at him and didn't have to translate the old name and pronouns into the new ones—it just happens automatically. It has taken a really long time to be able to say "my son" and for it to feel natural, for "son" to have a whole new list of connotations based on who he is and how he presents now.

About six months after my son had top surgery, I asked him how he was feeling when he looked in the mirror. He said he "feels at peace" with where he is medically. Gender and orientation and medication were not the topic of every single conversation. It was weird how it kind of faded away as other more pressing teenager things took its place: Covid-19, senior year, sports, boys, university, graduation. My acceptance of my kid being transgender was not the issue. I think I made that leap early when I figured out I wanted a live son more than a dead daughter. My son's acceptance of himself was the real healing moment for me.

It really is as true for youth as it is for adults that once you get to the point in transition—whether it be social, medical, or both—where you feel whole, the gender dysphoria falls away. My kid now has always been my kid. We just need to fix the honest mistakes of giving him the wrong name and dressing him up in the wrong clothes. Accepting and affirming your transgender kid will lead to good outcomes. He's healthy, confident, attending a great university, getting good grades, and has a ton of friends. He's leading the sort of life any parent would want their child to have.

Lizette Trujillo: As a first generation, Mexican American woman (coming off the heels of the 2016 election) the chants of "build that wall" and "Mexicans are blah, blah, blah…" were a stark reminder of the discrimination and bias that continues to persist in our country. As a child, and even as an adult, I had often been asked, "What are *you*" or, "But where are you *really* from"? as if my being American was impossible. It was this awareness of further stigma and marginalization that kept me up at night, when our son came out to us in August 2015. Understanding this made me feel protective and *guilty* that I had not affirmed my son when we first began to see his gender-expansive behavior, at two-and-a-half years old.

I knew the world was already hard for people who were perceived as different, and I had made my son feel this way so many times over the years by not affirming him. I share this because I want to give people a little background as I write about this moment that I shared with my son in spring 2016.

I wish I could remember the details of this moment, or at least have recorded it. My son was eight, and we were a few months into social transition. There was so much happening all at once; and yet through all that chaos, all I wanted to do was protect my tiny human from what I feared was headed our way.

What I recall is that we were sitting in my bedroom, and my son was asking me to explain why his peers perpetually teased another student for having a learning disability. He told me that he thought them mean for doing this every day. He wanted to understand "why." I felt that it was important for me to explain to my son the difference between having empathy and having sympathy for someone. Once I had defined the difference between the two, I told him that it was important that we always treat people with respect and empathy.

My son looked at me and said, "Mom, I think God made me this way on purpose...so I could *be* empathy and *teach* empathy"! My eight-year-old had stated something so profound, and yet so simple. His ability to see what made him different from others as a gift was empowering and impactful. It pushed me towards advocacy, and although I didn't realize it at that time, shaped so much of my work today. I think of this moment often and remind myself of his words when I feel fearful or angry.

To *be* and to *teach* empathy. As humans, we forget how much we absorb from our surroundings. This is how bias takes root. We grow up aware of what society perceives as different, or wrong. We learn to treat those around us who fall into these categories with contempt, judgement, or fear. If we are part of those categories, we learn to internalize these perceptions and feel ashamed or try to hide them. Some even try to assimilate to belong, and yet my eight-year-old son was able to see past this. He was able to understand that his experience and understanding allowed him to see someone else without judgment.

I often think, would we even use the word "mourning" when referring to our children if we had not been socialized to see them as different? I choose to work towards a world where our differences are gifts! My son expanded my heart, forced me to let go of my own personal expectations, to confront my own biases, and taught me what it means to love fully. He taught me what it means be authentic in a world that tells you it is wrong to do so. He empowered me to push for equality and taught me to fight for a better tomorrow. It is the gift that our transgender/non-binary children give all of us, and I hope you embrace that part of your journey too.

What should I do with all the pictures and mementos of my child pre-transition?

Kelly Storck (LCSW): There are a lot of ways people can feel about the visibility of their life pre-transition and those feelings can change over time. As with most things, it's best to let your loved one lead the way here. Acknowledging that you understand that they may need you to change things around the house can be a wonderful way to show your child that you affirm their gender and are eager to consider their needs. Not all trans people struggle with reminders of their lives pre-transition—some still embrace that little self—but it's also understandable that other people do need their feelings and privacy protected. Assure your child that you care about them more than any family artifacts and that making your home a warm, safe, and affirming place is your priority. You can start building a new collection of photos and personalized items that affirm your child's gender and name (if it has changed). You may also want to consider having your favorite old photos edited to reflect their gender as you know it now, and updating gendered childhood mementos with some artistic renovations.

Marsha Aizumi: What I have done with all the pictures and mementos of my child pre-transition is this: I asked Aiden which pictures and mementos he wanted me to keep up, and which ones he would like me to put away. Most of the photos and mementos were placed in storage, but he allowed me to display some items.

A few years later, I asked my son again, which photos I could keep up and which to take down. Interestingly, he asked me to put away additional photos, so I realized that with the passing years, his comfort level with certain memories changed. I currently have three photos remaining that are pre-transition. One is a small photo of him with his brother that sits on our living room mantle. The second is a photo in a collage which was given to our family as a Christmas present and is hung in our hallway. Finally, the last photo is actually one of my favorite memories with our family on the golf course. Except for the photo collage, all pre-transition photos remaining show Aiden in pants. I asked Aiden recently about the three pre-transition photos that are still being displayed and he said that he is fine with all of them.

To be honest, taking down the photos for the first time, I went through a grieving process. It felt as if I was burying my child and he wanted to forget the 20 years we had had together. But then, I thought: how do I want Aiden to feel when he comes to see me? And I knew that I wanted him to feel totally supported as our son. Taking down any photos that made him uncomfortable would be sending that message. In the end, I tried to process my feelings, and balance how I felt with how he would feel. And if I had any uncertainty about what I should do, I would always choose what would make my son feel the most loved. I still use that process today.

Noah Berlatsky: Probably the best thing to do is to ask your child whether they'd like to have the pictures and mementos put away or not. You might also ask your child about how they feel about online pictures and social media posts. Our daughter hasn't been much concerned with that...but then, we don't have many pictures of her pre-transition online or around the house. Different kids are going to have different preferences; you won't know unless you talk to them.

Nathan Glickler: There's not necessarily anything wrong with keeping them; you do, however, need to be aware that seeing themselves as what they were may be somewhat hurtful to your child. Have a talk with them about it and see how they feel. If they are uncomfortable with these things being on display, you can show them you care and keep the pictures so you can view them whenever you like by putting them in an album somewhere. It doesn't need to be an either/or sort of deal.

Debi Jackson: A lot of parents wonder what to do with photos or other mementos that show their child pre-transition. My answer is always, "What does your child want?" That answer might vary significantly depending on how old your child is. Regarding photos, our daughter Avery was fine with old photos of her at first. Since she socially transitioned at four, we didn't have a lot of them on display. But as kids that age usually think their parents are infallible, she thought it was "hilarious" that we had made such a big mistake in ever thinking she was a boy. She loved being able to point to a photo of her at age two or three and laughing at our ridiculousness. But a couple of years later when we had a new group of friends (because our old friends had abandoned us for supporting her), she was worried that if anyone came to our house and saw those pictures, they would start asking questions and she would be outed. We all know that trans people should be able to determine if, when, where, and how they disclose to others, and having photos up would potentially out her without her being in control. That wasn't acceptable to any of us. So, we put the photos away in drawers and boxes so that she could decide later if she ever wanted to see them or to have others see them.

With mementos like Christmas ornaments and stockings, we tried to replace them as quickly as possible. There's often nothing more painful for a transgender child than seeing their parent get super sentimental at pulling out a stocking with their birth name on it and tearing up. Holidays are inherently emotional because of all the memories we associate with them. But they can also be super affirming if you take the chance to surprise your child with a new special item with their new name on it.

If you have a hard time putting all of these special items away, it's okay to have a keepsake box in a private space like your bedroom or home office that you can pull out from time to time. But be careful about treating it like a shrine! Looking at those items too often and dwelling on the past can make it harder for you to move forward in supporting your child as their authentic self.

Wayne Maines: There is a time to remove them because they are reminders of the past. They can also "out" your child in an innocent way. Kids would come to our house and ask who that was in the photo with Jonas. That was a defining moment for us to make a change.

Janis Tannehill: Family pictures are a delicate subject. Most transgender people find old, pre-transition pictures of themselves quite jarring and they can trigger feelings of dysphoria. Clothing and hairstyles in children are highly gendered, so it is impossible to mistake the pictures of the kid with long hair and wearing a pink tutu as being another person.

I had to put all the pictures away in a box, still in the frames, in the basement. I haven't revisited them in a while. Some people have had great results with getting some baby pictures redone in sepia tones or black and white and I may look into this in the future.

Some things were easy. The Christmas stocking was kind of generic, so I just had to replace the embroidered name with the new one. Some things are more difficult and may have to continue to live in the box they are in. I am in the process of going through Christmas decorations that have been in hiding for years—I'll put the kitten in a tutu ornaments collectors set in a box and let my son figure out what he wants to do with it when he is ready.

New pictures can be equally as touchy. Family pictures were "forbidden" for my teen mid-transition. He was so self-conscious of his body and hated the way he looked. Most clothes were chosen to hide his body and any requests to wear something besides a hoodie resulted in fights. What few pictures of him I have at the time show dour expressions and a hunched-over posture. I hated seeing him so miserable. I am almost glad we don't have family pictures from that time because they would just hurt both him and me to look at.

Post-surgery pictures, however, are stunning. He is happy and at home in his body. He is stylish and brave, handsome and strong. Graduation pictures are of a proud young man with a dancer's posture and hope for the future. The pictures finally match the kid. Ornaments on the rainbow light tree with trans flags and "love is love" slogans match as well.

In short, I am the one who is stuck in the past. Maybe I need to have a Buddhist moment and "be here now" while letting the past go.

Lizette Trujillo: I walked into my office one evening and I noticed that every single photo of my son pre-social transition had been turned around or laid flat so that no one could see them. I walked around the house and realized that this had been done to all the photos within his reach. I went to his room and asked him if he had done this and why? He put his head down and said quietly, "Mom, people will think I'm weird if they see the pictures from before. They won't believe that I'm me." I told him that his feelings were valid, and I asked him if he wanted to help me put the photos away. He said, "Yes," and so we held hands as we walked through the house and pulled down every photo of him pre-social transition. He looked up at me and gave me the biggest smile as we did this, and I returned that same happy smile. I did my best to not cry. We put the photos away in an envelope, and eventually the photos were placed in a box labeled "Daniel's Memories." It was not until we had put the photos away (and Daniel happily went back to his room to play) that I allowed myself a moment to cry. I did not feel grief, loss, or sadness that these photos were gone! What I felt was a deep sadness that my child understood that there were some people who did not believe him or see him for the boy that he was. I felt sad that my nine-year-old son had already contemplated that people might think him "weird" or reject him. My heart broke knowing that he already understood what it felt like to be unseen, or have his boyhood and humanity questioned. He was only nine years old, and he should have felt loved, valued, seen, *believed*, and supported. He is now 14 and keeps the box in his room. He looks back at the pictures with fondness, and what I hope he remembers most from that day is that I listened, and that I affirmed him.

I spent so long choosing my child's name and it hurts to hear it called a "deadname." What does that mean and what else can we call it?

Cristy Mereles (LCSW): Birth name and former name are also ways to refer to a deadname. Some people use these terms interchangeably; other people have a strong reason why they use one word over the others. With my clients, this is something I ask directly about so that I can stay respectful with my words as we work together.

Many parents experience emotional pain on realizing a name that they spent so long choosing is being discarded in such a way. It is amazing what a strong hold a name can have. It is possible to view a child's name as one of many symbols of their gender journey. As such, when it comes to letting go of their name it can feel so much more than just letting go of words. A name is one of many places where parents begin to attach gender, hopes, and dreams to their child. Parents begin dreaming of who their child will be and what their child will do long before they are born. Letting go of a name is, in part, letting go of these hopes and dreams. Letting go of a name is also symbolic of embracing new possibilities for their child, along with embracing their gender, and realizing that their child has arrived with their own identity, hopes, and dreams for themselves.

I have seen parents progress from feeling hurt when hearing their child's birth name to feeling bittersweet to reporting a dry mouth when in a situation where they are required to say it for some reason in reference to their child. In the end, for most parents, a birth name becomes too painful to say out loud in reference to their child. Letting go of a child's former name is part of the process of learning to love and accept the child in front of you rather than the image of the child you projected and imagined you would have.

Paria Hassouri: Letting go of the name I gave my child at birth sometimes felt harder to me than letting go of the old gender. For the longest time, I could not get myself to call it her deadname. I usually call it her birth name, although hearing the term deadname does not make me cringe the way it used to. Like everything, that term starts to have less significance, just as the birth name itself does. My husband and I had spent months trying to come up with a name for her when I was pregnant. We wrote lists and ranked the names and compared our lists, and her birth name ended up being a compromise name that we could agree on. But as soon as she was born and we started calling her that name, I fell in love with it. It seemed perfect for her. When it came to choosing her new name, there was a lot of disagreement again. We are an Iranian-American family, and we all have Iranian names. I had carefully chosen each of my three children's names, each having a special significance and meaning and a way for us to declare our identity and hold on to some part of our culture.

Having my daughter pick an American name felt as if she wasn't just changing her gender but denying this other part of her identity that was important to our family. In the end, we compromised on the new name as well. Now, her name, Ava, seems to suit her perfectly. I used to think about her birth name all the time. I still sometimes do, but less so with time. And while I will still talk about her old name or birth name or name given to her at birth, the term deadname doesn't bother me when used by others anymore. Her name is dead, but she is not.

Wayne Maines: "Deadname" has a place in homes. It is important that this name not be spoken unless permission is given. I would never use my child's deadname without her permission. However, I have her permission and I use her deadname often to frame a story.

Somewhere around the age of six Nicole started seriously talking about changing her name. The first time I heard her talk about a name change, she said she wanted to change her name to Raven. Raven was a character in one of her favorite television shows. I looked at her and said, "Raven, that's not a real name, that's a TV name." I did not say anything else, but I was thinking how much I loved her name.

One summer day, our neighbor's son came over to play. My son said, "Do you want to play Ninjas? Wyatt's new name is Nikki." He said, "Okay. Nikki, can I have that sword?" I laughed and went over to his house to tell his parents about the name change. The name change was very hard for me.[3] It took months for me to even say the name Nicole. I did everything I could to avoid using her chosen name. I remember thinking this is stupid, but I could not help it. As time passed, her new name became natural for me.

---

3 Not all trans people want their birth name/deadname disclosed. Wayne shares it here in this book with Nicole's permission.

Janis Tannehill: I hate the term deadname with a blinding passion. It is so rude and disrespectful. My transgender kid is my oldest and his first name was agonized over, chosen with deliberate care and homage to his most loved and respected great grandmothers, a beautiful, classic, aristocratic family name. Poor kid had a lot to live up to before he was even out of the womb. His treatment of the name with such distain was hurtful to me.

The person I gave the name to isn't dead, and the name I gave them was well thought out and given as a gift with intention and purpose. The name, like my child, is not dead. The name is a strong name, a beautiful name; it just doesn't fit my strong, beautiful child anymore. It has taken me three years to be able to say that. This is the acceptance journey I have had to take and things that I've had to work out for myself.

Once I separated my own feelings from the situation and saw it for what it was, I understood my kid more, and my feelings on the subject shifted. Refusing to use a transgender person's chosen name has been described by some in the community as an act of violence. We do not perpetuate violence on those we love, on children who are counting on us to be their biggest cheerleaders. Refusing to use a transgender person's name because you refuse to believe them or because you don't support "those kinds of people" or because you simply wish it to not be true is an act of emotional violence.

Why am I uncomfortable about my own child?

Darlene Tando (LCSW): It's important to try to separate your feelings about your child from your feelings about their gender. Your child has a soul to which you have likely been attached since the moment they joined your family. That soul is not changing; thankfully, it is not going anywhere. Your personal understanding of their gender is what is having to change. This adjustment can be extremely uncomfortable, and that's okay. It is important to show loving kindness to yourself and accept your natural response to your child's authentic gender and transition. The most important thing is to make sure your behavior is loving and affirming, no matter how difficult your internal struggle. Get support; talk to other adults about this. Talk to your partner, friends, family members, maybe a therapist. Just don't talk to your child about it. Your child is undergoing their own emotional struggles and it is not their job to help you work through yours. I can tell you that the initial discomfort is usually temporary. Your heart and brain will adjust to understanding and connecting to your child in their authentic gender. Be patient and take good care of yourself during this time.

Another thing to think about is that due to societal conditioning, you may have an internal feeling about "gender rules." These rules are something that get implanted in us from a very young age. We are often conditioned to look at gender as binary, and to think that there are only certain things that are appropriate for each gender. Even as we evolve and come to understand that gender is not binary and there really are no "rules" when it comes to gender expression, your gut may tell you differently when you see your child engaging in gender non-conforming or unexpected gender expression different from their gender assigned at birth. You may feel as though your child is "breaking" some sort of rule. This may be some of the source of your discomfort. Again, be kind to yourself and talk yourself through it. Your child is not breaking any rules. Your child is simply being themselves, and you are there to be a loving witness to their journey.

Clara Baker: Sometimes I'm uncomfortable with my child because I am overwhelmed about how to help them, and I can't tolerate not being able to fix their dysphoria. Early on, when my child was still very young, I was unnerved when he was unhappy about his body. At three, he would cry about not having a body like his father and brother. He refused to wear underwear or fitting clothes because it reminded him of "what is there and what isn't there." After his first day of kindergarten, I caught him looking at himself with disgust, slump-shouldered in the mirror, and he said, "I look like a girl." These moments would leave me full of despair that I couldn't take away his sadness. I vacillated between absorbing his pain and trying to ignore it—neither of which was helpful.

Eventually, in my reading, I came across the idea that our children's dysphoria—their sadness, anger, and discomfort—is the information we need to support them on their journey. If a child wasn't having these feelings, we wouldn't know how important it was to facilitate their transition. The dysphoria equaled the depth of their need to be who they are. I came to be grateful that my child was communicating it to us, whether verbally or non-verbally. I stopped regarding his discomfort, his dysphoria, as the enemy, but rather as evidence of his truth, which we were fortunate to know.

He's 12 now, his hormone blockers aren't working perfectly and, as his cisgender peers' bodies begin to change, he is in a stasis that doesn't feel right either. I don't know for sure when, or if, the discomfort will abate. Perhaps with testosterone? But I know that when he is communicating his dysphoria to me, he is communicating his clarity about his experience. I can offer another round of blood work to be tested, we can look for a binder online, and in the meantime, I can be present with him and know that he is on the right path.

Wayne Maines: At age four Nicole asked me, "Daddy, why can't I wear a dress?" I had no answer. This question and the others that followed started my journey, a journey of understanding and acceptance.

When people began targeting Nicole, I was faced with a new line of questioning, one that required I examine my ability to help her and protect her. I was ill-prepared to answer the very first question. Looking at me with tears in her eyes she asked, "Daddy, what did I do wrong?" I answered the question immediately. "You have done nothing wrong," was all I could say, because I did not know how to proceed or how to make the pain go away. That night, lying in bed, I reflected on the past few years and the road that was before us. The next day we talked to the kids and reminded them of who we are and that we will always protect them.

With our backs to the wall, we started to fight back, to demonstrate to Nicole and her brother that we would not be bullied. We learned that our family life, and the decisions we made, would have a major impact outside our home. Everything we do continues to be a balancing act, that requires considering our children's well-being and a need to promote positive change. We are very hopeful that someday Nicole will not be recognized as a transgender girl or transgender woman, just another person making her way in the world. To drive this message home, we continue to listen to Nicole, try to observe signs of concern, learn from others, and strive to develop ways to help everyone understand and accept our daughter and others like her.

The process was not always easy. I learn best by experience. Through this experience, I started to understand a world that includes transgender children. Understanding lead to further acceptance and then advocacy. Acceptance was the first significant step required for me to become an active participant, one who was on the same page helping Kelly and Nicole. I hope that providing a peek into our world may help others understand and accept new concepts and the needs of transgender children. I hope this book might help fathers who struggle with helping their children and their wives, so that they can begin to effectively communicate that all children need love, support, protection, and equal rights, no matter what the perceived differences or challenges are at home, at school, and in the community.

I quickly learned by experience that transgender children and adults face harassment and discrimination on a daily basis. It appears that even after our great nation has strived to promote human rights worldwide, my daughter and others like her continue to experience injustice at home. Nicole unknowingly at age nine became part of a new civil rights movement. She stepped forward and said in her own way, I want the same basic rights as my classmates. I am very proud of how she and her brother have supported this cause. As I look back, I realize what courage it took for Kelly to step forward when I was still wavering on the sidelines. This new movement is in its infancy; it requires education, acceptance, and fair legislative action to recognize and protect transgender people.

I am hopeful for change. Equal rights for transgender people may not come until our society reaches a level of understanding and acceptance that demands change. For us, the understanding and acceptance started at home, in our school, and in our community. Working with our school and community, we changed the hearts and minds of the people who interacted with Nicole and our family.

Unfortunately, much of that progress was reversed when others became fearful of a nine-year-old girl. Nicole has suffered dearly because of these fears. Transgender children in Maine and through-out the United States are under siege and live in hiding. These children deserve better. They deserve unconditional love and support from their parents, family, friends, and schools. They deserve the protection of our state leaders. Transgender children deserve the same level of safety and same basic human rights that their friends and their parents often take for granted. If each of us does our part, other children, like Nicole, will not have to say, "Daddy, what did I do wrong?"

Today I announce that I am the proud father of identical twins; one is a boy and one is a girl. I am pretty sure there are not many dads who can make that statement, but maybe in the future we will hear from other dads who feel the same way. It took me a long time to publicly announce that statement. To help my daughter and others, I needed to open up and discuss my family's story. My story is about Wyatt, a cute, loving little baby boy who helped me realize that he is really my daughter (Nicole).[4] With time, I came to learn that she was never my son.

Throughout this book, I will interchange names from Wyatt to Nicole and will revert back to Wyatt when the timeframe is appropriate, and I am doing this now with Nicole's permission. When I started my journal, it was very difficult not to use Nicole's name for every example. Even though I was focusing on stories about Wyatt, I naturally speak and write about Nicole. I know this may be hard for you to understand and it is hard to explain, but after reading this book maybe you can begin to accept what I just described.

As I became more comfortable talking to others, I quickly realized that there is a big difference in how dads and other men think about, act about, and accept transgender children. The mothers and other women I have talked to have been much more open, honest, and supportive. I hope my stories and the few facts provided might make it easier for men to keep reading and to keep asking questions, and will nudge them in the right direction.

---

4 Not all trans people want their birth name/deadname disclosed. Wayne shares it here in this book with Nicole's permission.

Did I do something to make my child trans?

Dr. Matt Goldenberg: Trans adults, all of whom were once trans children, have existed across generations. When your child comes out as transgender, they are claiming association in a beautiful and rich culture with traditions, language, holidays, and leaders. There is no known biological, psychological, social, or evolutionary singular cause of a person being transgender. What we do know is that parents who are raising gender-diverse children have an opportunity to create a bond with them by meeting them with compassion, curiosity, and positive affirmations. If your child has shared with you or others that they are trans, you as a parent have helped raise a wise and clear-sighted individual who wants to be understood and seen as who they are. What a gift you have given the world with this amazing child of yours!

Gender identity likely has a multitude of origins, including culture, biology, environmental factors, and access to language. Even biological causes of gender identity are not simplistic. They are likely tied to our endocrine system, genetics, and neuroanatomy.[5] Our gender identity is informed by many factors. We do not choose our gender identity. Nor do parents, providers, or other children have the ability to choose a gender identity on behalf of another person.

Much has been written, contradicting actual scientific evidence, suggesting that transgender children are inauthentic and primarily victims of social influence.[6] As a psychologist, I find it rather curious that cisgender children are not suspected of being victims of social influence, and are not seen to be at similar risk of only believing they are cisgender because that's what their peers are saying. After all, if transgender youth were coming out in larger numbers simply to gain access to social memberships, there would be much more benefit to joining the cis community and to be on the benefitting side of cissexism rather than face chronic and catastrophic marginalization.

---

5   Saraswat, A., Weinand, J. D., & Safer, J. D. (2015). Evidence supporting the biologic nature of gender identity. *Endocrine Practice, 21*(2), 199–204.

6   Gülgöz, S., Glazier, J. J., Enright, E. A., Alonso, D. J., *et al.* (2019). Similarity in transgender and cisgender children's gender development. *Proceedings of the National Academy of Sciences, 116*(49), 24480–24485. doi: 10.1073/pnas.1909367116

In parenting, your children may come to you with many "why" questions. Children have an innate curiosity about how things work and why, and they also have questions about who they are. Parents are a key factor in building resilience against shame, and the skills that are needed to grow healthy and happy adults. There are a lot of reasons to be proud of being a transgender person, and that is the conversation to focus on. Further, there are a lot of reasons to be proud of parenting a transgender person, and that is another conversation to have.

Noah Berlatsky: Nope, you did not make them trans. Trans people have existed basically forever in every society and culture, just like gays, lesbians, and left-handed people. There are probably some biological causes, and some cultural causes (people are much less likely to identify as or admit to being trans if there's a lot of stigma attached). But basically, being trans is just one way people are human. There's nothing you can do to make your child trans, just as there's nothing you can do to make them stop being trans.

Parents can do a lot to make their child feel comfortable *coming out* as trans, though. And they should! Ideally, as a parent you should let your kids know that being trans is natural and normal and good, and that if your kids are trans, you will support them. If your child eventually feels comfortable telling you they're trans, then you've done something right.

Nathan Glickler: No. The causes of gender dysphoria are still not clearly understood, but any number of genetic, hormonal, and environmental factors may have an impact on it. You can think of it as having a male, female, fluid, or genderless brain in a body that doesn't match. We are incredibly complex creatures; we have a minimum of 100 trillion neural connections in our brains and we are composed of trillions of cells. There are a great many things about what makes us who and what we are that we likely will never understand.

From a religious standpoint, if you believe we are created by the divine, then the divine made your child transgender. You should rest easy knowing that, if you believe the divine to be infallible, it was the right decision.

Wayne Maines: This question is common but in a different format. Often it is the father accusing the mother of doing something to make their child transgender.

When Nicole was younger, three to five years of age, I was frustrated and angry that my child wanted to be a girl. When I am angry my coping mechanism is to internalize the anger and try to develop strategies to solve the problem. In this case it was a never-ending cycle of harm, for me, my child, and my family. In the end, I learned that it was not Nicole's problem, it was mine. Once I admitted this, it was much easier to develop solutions to help Nicole and our family. It has been much harder to develop solutions to improve how society addresses transgender children.

I am still embarrassed that I was not able to recognize and act on my feelings when my family needed my help early in the process. It is okay to have the feelings, but you need to talk about them to work through the change process. It is not a weakness to have these feelings or doubts; everyone has them to some degree. The weakness is not acting on them. The best thing you can do is to be open and honest with your child about being transgender.

Jennifer See: Absolutely not. Nobody knows what causes someone to be trans, but what we do know is that it doesn't happen from outside influence. You can't force a kid be an extrovert. You can't force them to like trains if they like building blocks. You can't force a child to like being a cheerleader or a bookworm or anything else. If you can't push a kid into something as simple as a preferred toy or interest, how could you possibly influence something as innate as identity?

I keep messing up with my child's new name and pronouns. I don't mean to, and it's really hard, but they feel hurt by it. What should I do?

Dr. Matt Goldenberg: When you misgender someone, be mindful that your authority and importance towards that person influences how they may react. For instance, when misgendered by an unimportant stranger, a person may brush it off or choose to respond more directly.

Correcting someone who has misgendered them requires an evaluation of how safe it is, and some awareness of whether the environment is conducive to a correction. If the misgendered person decides that it's a good environment for correction, they may need to decide if it will be good or bad for their relationship with the person they're correcting. This is a lot of guessing, and the person also needs to decide if they have the emotional energy to correct the error. If a person has been misgendered repeatedly either by the same person or during a short period of time, they may feel exhausted by being perceived incorrectly and misunderstood.

To ease this, the person who did the misgendering should acknowledge that it occurred. A quick apology, and an explanation of how they will continue to learn and work on it, may be enough.

To help parents integrate this new language, consider using reinforcement. For instance, let family or friends know, "I am working on using the right pronouns for my child. Can you help me by reminding me if you hear me make a mistake? I am still learning, and I would love for you to support us."

Just as it takes time to get used to new names, pronouns can be very difficult to integrate as well. Younger children may enjoy a family project to create name plates for their room, or sewing initials onto their backpack, or even making bracelets with names and pronouns. Older youth may prefer to wear a pronoun pin or necklace or ask a sibling or family member to help remind others who are having a hard time using the new name and pronoun.

Be kind to yourself. The name and pronoun you have used in the past with your child likely has cultural or personal significance. When you can use the correct name and pronoun with more regularity, the positive feedback from your child will reinforce your changed behaviors and increase the positive feelings associated with doing so.

Clara Baker: The challenge in getting new pronouns right is not simply retraining your brain to use a different word in referring to your child. The challenge is your willingness (or lack thereof) to know your child as a different gender. Wayne Maines, a contributor in this volume, once said that when he misused pronouns for his child, he knew he had to dig deeper. For me, this has meant looking more closely at my biases and unpacking the messages 1 received about gender as a child. It involves feeling my resistance and fear and letting go of what 1 thought 1 knew. Ultimately, it means prioritizing my child's experience.

When you mess up your child's new name and pronouns, try responding like you do when you trip over someone's foot. When you trip over someone's foot you do not ignore that you banged their foot. You also do not make a big deal of it with an excessive apology. You do not go on about it, looking for reassurance that it is okay that you stepped on their foot. When you misgender your child, acknowledge that it happened, apologize, and let it go. Next time, try harder to watch your feet.

Janna Barkin: Practice! Adjusting to new pronouns takes practice. Our brains are wired over time. It takes effort to change patterns. Need some motivation? The Trevor Project's 2020 Survey of LGBTQ youth found that when parents use the correct pronoun for their child, their child can have much higher levels of health and well-being compared to those who did not have their pronouns respected.[7]

Our brains are also very good at creating new patterns, especially when we practice. Here are some suggestions:

- Write a letter about what you like about the person, or what you like to do with the person, using new pronouns.
- Write sentences with the new pronoun (like we did on a chalkboard when we were kids).
- When you think about the person to yourself, practice using correct pronouns.
- Create a "pronoun jar"—like a swear jar—where you put a dollar into the jar every time you make a mistake, then donate the money to a local LGBTQ organization.

---

7   *The Trevor Project National Survey on LGBTQ+ Mental Health 2020.* (2020). Los Angeles, CA: The Trevor Project. Accessed 11/11/2021 at www.thetrevorproject.org/wp-content/uploads/2020/07/The-Trevor-Project-National-Survey-Results-2020.pdf

- If the person has given permission, talk about them with friends. Sometimes it is easier to practice with strangers; speak fondly of the person using the new pronoun.
- Practice the new pronouns with a close friend or family member, agree to support each other in using the new pronouns. Some parents create a friendly competition among themselves. Have fun with it.
- Change the person's name and add the correct pronouns to your phone.
- Take new photos and display them around the house. Practice saying the person's correct name and pronouns to yourself as you look at the photos.

Yes, it can be hard to make these changes. As a parent, I now understand it was even harder for my child to be living his experience in a world that was, and still is, learning about gender diversity and what it means to be transgender.

How will you practice?

Nathan Glickler: Apologize when you mess up and repeat whatever you said with the correct name and pronoun. Thank your child for correcting you and ask them to keep doing so to help you be supportive. Tell them you love them and respect them and want them to feel accepted for who and what they are. Don't express that it is difficult; this makes it sound as if they are inconveniencing you.

Clara Lee: Two of the first social transitions for my son were to change his name and pronouns. He asked others to use both. I was still struggling to accept my son's new identity but thought I was doing my best by trying to use his new name and pronouns, although I often made mistakes. It was a hard time for everyone at home, with fights every so often. I told my son to give us some time and space to get our heads around it, but what I didn't realize was how hard it must have been for him when his parents did not take him seriously about his desire to be treated as a boy by correctly using a new boy name and pronoun.

One day during a family vacation, which I thought was going well, almost like the times before his coming out, we again got into a big fight. He didn't think we were doing our best because we kept on messing up his new name and made it sound like a girl's name. His new name contained a "z" character, which is a really hard sound to pronounce for many Korean immigrants like me who came to the US in my teenage years. And it must have sounded like a girl's name when I said it.

I explained how hard it was for Koreans to pronounce a word with the "z" character and wished it was as simple as Tom, Mike, or John. He then asked, "What name would you have given me if you had given a birth to a baby boy?" When he heard the name we prepared, he thought about it for a few seconds and said, "Okay, I like it." And that name became his legal name. This incident was a turning point for me in feeling as if I was part of his journey. It was no longer about new name and pronoun struggle. It was about recognizing my child as a son from birth, a gender he was born with but he was then incorrectly assigned as a girl.

Jennifer See: You have a long history of knowing your child by a name. You have memories of them dressed as their birth gender, memories of birthday parties and time spent with grandma. The change is tough because it's not like meeting a stranger for the first time. For me, it took a good six months to cement the new name, new pronoun, and new way of talking about my child or my lifemate. I used to say, "my boys" and "my husband." During their transitions, I didn't go straight to "my wife" or "my daughter." I had to adjust my thinking. "My spouse" came before "my wife." "My oldest" and "my children" came before "my daughter." And their names both came long before the pronouns did.

If you make a mistake, correct yourself. Apologize. Let your child know that you are trying to make the effort to rethink a lifetime of memories. One of the biggest struggles we had was that even once the name and pronoun were pretty well cemented, the day she didn't do her homework or she left a mess for me to clean up and I got angry about it, the old name would pop out unexpectedly.

When you see your person every single day, eventually it becomes natural. You create new memories with your child in their new identity. The hardest part is that the pictures and memories are still there from pre-transition. How do you refer to your four-year-old dressed as a princess for Halloween? If you have a child who identifies as female, you might see Logan, but that same child is now Sarah. It is really easy to say Logan...he...when talking about the past, but that can create unhappiness. Some kids get really upset that they had a previous name and identity. Others just accept that they were once Logan but are now Sarah. It is not easy, but my own experience has been that the most supportive way to talk about my daughter is always as my daughter, with the new name, she/her/hers pronouns, and never with the old name or male pronouns.

When I run into an elementary teacher who only knew the former identity and asks how Sarah is, I just let them know that there have been some changes and that they are going by Logan now, Logan's in the band, doing karate, whatever. In situations like that, most people tend to roll with it, and it's no different than if I had told them I'd got married and changed my last name. They are more interested in how your child is doing than the name issues.

As an example of how natural this has become, here are two incidents from our home. One day our nine-year-old came running into the kitchen yelling, "Mom! Mom!" My spouse responded first. My son gave my spouse a withering look and said, "No, not you. The other mom!" And another day, our toddler yelled from the bathroom that they needed assistance with wiping. My spouse looks at me and says, "Well, you're the one that wanted kids." And I said, "Well, you're the one that wanted to be mom." My spouse just shook her head and went to help our toddler.

Janis Tannehill: So here's my pro-tip for any of you parents or family members who find themselves in the position of having a transgender person in their lives: try using a nickname (that doesn't hurt your child's feelings) for as many months as it takes for their new name to feel as if it can roll off your tongue. By giving yourself a little bit of space and time away from their old name and as you watch them become this new person they were meant to be, their new name will fit. It took me six months of not referring to my kid by anything other than nicknames for me to reset my brain.

How do I explain my child to my co-workers?

Darlene Tando (LCSW): Try to look at it as sharing about your child, rather than having to "explain" them. Of course, if your child has already transitioned, there is no need to tell your co-workers about their trans experience. However, if they knew your child previously and you need to inform them of different pronouns, and so on, here are a couple tips to keep in your back pocket. "Actually" is a great way to interject or lead into the conversation. For example, if they ask you about your "daughter," you could say "Actually..." This is a great way to pause the conversation and let them know you are going to provide them with correct information. It also can buy you a couple seconds to decide how you want to say it. "Actually, we recently found out he's my son! His pronouns are [**] and he's going by the name [**]." If you share this assertively with positive energy, your co-workers will read that from you.

Marsha Aizumi: When my child transitioned to male, I did not have to explain their transition to my co-workers, because Aiden attended the same network of charter schools I worked for and an email went out. The corporate office sent an email to the leaders of all departments and the sister companies about using "Aiden" and "he/him/his" pronouns instead of his previous name and feminine pronouns. Nobody asked me any questions, and there was no big announcement at my company. It was more that I informally talked to individuals to let them know about the transition, which most of them had probably heard about already.

My co-workers were wonderful and when I had to take two weeks of personal time off to support Aiden's top surgery, they all stepped up to help in whatever way they could. I never felt compelled to hide any information from my co-workers, because I felt their support and the support from leadership. I know that this may not always be the case, so each parent must decide for themselves how much to disclose and how much to keep private. I was very privileged to work for a company that wanted to support not only my family, but individuals in the LGBTQ community.

Luchina Fisher: First of all, you don't owe your co-workers an explanation about your child. Half the time, they won't even remember your child's gender anyway. So by the time your child socially transitions, your co-workers may be thinking that was your child's gender all along. But while you're in the midst of trying to figure out what's going on with your child, that's probably not the best time to share with co-workers who may have little or no knowledge about trans or non-binary people themselves. You may find that your co-workers judge your parenting or dismiss your child's behavior as a phase, as happened to me when I opened up one day to a group of my colleagues. I instantly regretted that I'd said anything, but later I realized that most of my co-workers had no idea what I had been experiencing since my child was two.

After my daughter socially transitioned, I felt more certain of my footing. Our extended family, friends, and small town overwhelmingly embraced and supported us, which made it a whole lot easier to share the news with people outside our immediate circle, like co-workers. With my daughter's permission, I posted the news on Facebook. And because my dad always said you teach people how to treat you, I led with good news about our town's warm embrace at a time of bathroom wars in North Carolina, and the impending Trump administration: "David and I used to be the parents of three boys, but earlier this year we gained a daughter... Gia's smooth transition is my little bit of goodness in the world. That she could find the courage to be her true self at age 12 fills me with awe and pride." The responses from my co-workers were equally gushing. They were sharing in our family's joy.

Your co-workers may not understand what your child and family are going through but if they see that you are clear about your love and support for your child, that's ultimately what they will take away from anything that you tell them. You don't have to be an expert on trans issues or the transgender community, just an expert on your child.

Nathan Glickler: My take on this may differ from others. I say simply "don't." You don't owe them an explanation, and neither does your child. If they ask, your child is the gender with which they identify. If your child is comfortable with you talking about their gender identity and what it means, then it can be helpful to answer honest questions from people who are genuinely trying to understand. If they are not, or are being judgmental, do not engage with them about it. I have found that many people will never understand until it becomes personal for them. And it isn't your job to convince someone else you are a good parent; they don't get a say in how you raise your child.

Clara Lee: I worked at a financial company for more than ten years and we often talked about our own family and exchanged resources. When my son came out as a transgender boy, it took me about a year of struggle to make a decision to support his transition. Meanwhile, I kept things quiet and did not share anything with my co-workers. I was fortunate to live in New York City, a very progressive and liberal location. My company had amazing diversity and inclusion policies and practices, consistently achieving the perfect score in the HRC corporate index for many years. I even got trained on LGBTQ topics, and my boss was a gay man, proudly displaying a photo of himself and his husband in his office.

And yet I was apprehensive and afraid to come out for almost a year at my workplace. At one point, I had to talk to someone at the company for insurance coverage for transgender-related medical care and get the HR records to reflect my son's new name and gender marker. My boss was one of the first people outside my support meeting and therapist that I came out to. I decided to come out to him because instinctively I knew it would be safe and he would be able to advocate for me and my family to deal with HR matters with his influence at work. I remember my voice quivering and heart pumping hard. After I told him that my child was now my son, he looked into my eyes and said, "Clara, when a mother speaks up for her child, people would have to listen." He then connected me to other senior people in the LGBTQ network and allies to build the support system for me and my son within the firm. I eventually joined the LGBTQ network leadership team at the company and co-led the ally program for many years.

Janis Tannehill: You know, a *little* gaslighting never hurt anyone. How well do your co-workers or acquaintance-level friends from the gym or hairdresser really know you? Have they met your kid and would they really remember if they did? Just change the pictures on your desk and causally talk about your family like normal. If and when they say, "I thought you had two girls and a boy," you can respond, "Oh no, you got it wrong, it's the other way around." No one needs to know your business, and you don't need to share any more than you want to.

If you really do want to share, or someone at work really does know your family, the easiest way is to be direct and simple. "My oldest is going by Eric now, so I have a son now." Most people don't know how to react to this kind of thing and are looking to you for how to respond. If you hem or haw it invites unsolicited advice, discomfort, and negative reactions. None of "My kid came out as trans, I don't know what it means or how to feel, it all seems weird." Act bold and, sure, fake it if you have to, but your new reality is a fact and you need to treat it as such. "This is the new name, these are the pronouns, I love and accept my kid and so should you." If they don't, that is their prerogative. Remember, if people choose to act like an ass to you or your kid, talk behind your back, or are outwardly hateful to your face, it says far more about them than it does about you.

The nice thing about HR is that gender variance is under the Health Insurance Portability and Accountability Act (HIPAA) and they have to keep their mouths shut about changing the names or gender markers on benefits forms. If they don't, congratulations on your lawsuit.

If I take away the "girl toys/clothes" will my child behave like a boy? Am I wrong to buy these things?

Darlene Tando (LCSW): Your child already *is* whatever authentic gender they are. You cannot change that; you cannot make a cis-gender child transgender and you cannot make a transgender child cisgender. Behavior is a form of gender expression but often reflects a gender identity. When you buy your child clothes and toys that feel good for them, you are supporting their authenticity and showing them kindness. You are not "encouraging" a specific type of gender or gender expression, but merely reflecting their interests and desires in the things they are gifted. Conversely, if you were to take away the things your child loves, this is not only unkind but sends the message: "You are not okay the way you are."

Luchina Fisher: Long before my daughter transitioned, I knew she was not like other boys. Almost as soon as she could walk, she began putting on my shoes. Walking in Daddy's shoes is a rite of passage for most toddler boys. But our child was only interested in my shoes—the higher the better. Soon, she was turning my shirts into dresses. And before long, she was demanding her own dresses, shoes, dolls, and more. We had some awkward moments giving in to these demands—for example, the time we ran into some family friends at Payless while shopping for shoes in the *girls' section*. Mostly we didn't care, because our child was happy and was clear about the things that made her happy.

She played with girls' toys and clothes all through preschool. But when it came time for kindergarten, she suddenly stopped wearing girls' clothes outside the house. She was still a boy who liked girls' things, but now our child was keeping a "secret" from most people outside our immediate family. And then, around second or third grade, she suddenly decided to give away all of her dolls, little ponies, and princess dresses to a younger cousin. I kept asking, "Are you sure?" In her child's mind, she must have thought that giving away all of her girls' toys and clothes would make her more boyish. Instead, she appeared even more conflicted about her identity, and on top of that, she had none of her favorite things to comfort her. Within a year, she began collecting new girls' toys, but to this day, she still regrets giving away her first ones.

Clothes and toys may not make the person, but in our daughter's case it was a connection to her identity that the world could not see until she socially transitioned. Then, it was no longer a matter of playing dress-up—our daughter could finally be herself. She's now well past the point of playing with Barbies and My Little Ponies, but any suggestions of donating them are off the table.

Jennifer Solomon: As a parent, you are in control of what your child is exposed to, from the food he eats to the clothes he wears. What you aren't in control of is what your child's preferences are. They are born with likes and dislikes. When Cooper was two years old, we went to a toy store, and he made a beeline for the Barbies. The sparkle and colorful display were more inviting to him than the sports section. As his mom, I had a choice—force him to conform with "boys'" toys or let him choose the doll and be happy. Either way, I wasn't going to change the person he was. I only risked being his first bully by not allowing him to express himself. I chose happiness and would do it again over and over! It is never wrong to support your child. He is the confident child he is today partly because he could explore who he was without society's gender roles being an obstacle. Taking his dresses or dolls away would not make him more of a boy.

My child is adopted and is scared he will be abandoned again now that he has come out as trans. How do I reassure him that he will always belong?

Darlene Tando (LCSW): You can reassure him with your words in the beginning, but over time your actions will reassure him the most. Continuing to show him your unconditional love and affirming him with pronouns and access to gender-affirming care is the most concrete way to show your love during this time. You can also assure him that it is his soul, not his gender, that you are most attached to and will never let go.

Marsha Aizumi: My child was adopted, and was scared when he came out that he would be abandoned again now that he is trans. I found multiple ways to reassure him that he will always belong. First, I had to realize that since he saw himself abandoned by his birth mother, there would be an innate fear that this could happen to him again. As a child, I saw that he had separation anxiety over and above what other children felt, and this just increased as he had to face coming out as transgender. I believe reassuring my child will be a lifelong journey.

I have reassured Aiden through my hugs and by telling him how much I love him. I have sent him random texts or called him to share how proud I am of him for specific things that he has done, not only for me, but for others. And when I tell him "I love you," I try to look him in the eyes and hope that he feels at a deep level my love and commitment to be there for him no matter what. His father and I have also written him a "love letter." I hope that when we are gone that this letter will continue to assure him that he always belonged and was deeply loved.

Finally, there have been situations where he has been unsure of whether we would stand by him as our son and as part of the trans community. We have called family meetings to discuss our position and, in the end, we have *always* reassured him that we would support him. After one particular meeting, he told me that he was afraid that after all we had gone through with him, this would be the "straw that breaks the camel's back." He hugged me and his father and thanked us for continually standing by him. I think every challenge that we stand up against, and every time we stand by him, it gives him greater assurance that he will always be part of our family.

I am afraid of my family's reaction to this information and don't know how to protect myself and my child from that.

Cristy Mereles (LCSW): It is hard to not live in fear of what others might say or do in reaction to a child coming out. This is magnified when it comes to family. Ultimately, we cannot control how others react, but we can control how we inform them and how we prepare our child to thrive in their own life. This is just one of the many times that your child, regardless of age, will be watching you to see how you respond, the words you use, and your attitude.

Sharing the news with family members in a way that is positive, with a tone that is also positive, is a must. This will likely have to be faked at first because many parents are not confident in the beginning. They are learning everything brand new themselves. Many of my clients find success in sharing with family members their sense of relief at understanding this part of their child more than they did before. Many are also open with their family, sharing that they too are still learning about all this but are excited to know that their family is there with them as they learn, and for support along the way. When you put the support out there as a given, you leave family members with nothing but support to give. Front loading your family with the appreciation you have for their relationship, and appreciation for previous support in past unrelated situations, provides a basis for a positive and supporting conversation around your child's gender.

Preparing your kid to thrive is the other part of this equation. Despite your best efforts to avoid a negative family reaction, some family members may react negatively. Put simply, some people need more time to learn/unlearn gender. I find it more effective to prepare children to be strong and build their self-esteem, rather than preparing them for all the possible "what ifs" that may happen when people are learning about their gender. Make sure your child knows that understanding gender beyond the cis normative way is a new thing and might take time for some people. This lets them know that it is not about them, but rather about their relative's learning curve. Remind your child of how long it took them to learn something in their life recently. This gives them space to go on being their awesome self while not carrying the weight of another's learning curve.

Noah Berlatsky: We were fairly confident that our family would be supportive, but it's still something you worry about. It's a good idea to ask your child what they're comfortable with, and how they want to handle coming out (or not coming out) to various people. My daughter, for instance, did want to come out to her grandparents, but didn't want to be the one to tell them. So, I did it.

I think it's important to recognize that you don't *owe* anyone information about your child. Your child doesn't have any obligation to come out to anyone in any situation where they'd feel unsafe. Concealing information from family isn't great and can be uncomfortable and painful. But if you or your child really feel telling family members would be unsafe, it's okay not to do so until you feel more confident.

Nathan Glickler: Don't be afraid to cut people out of your life who are toxic to it. "Blood is thicker than water" is rubbish. Your chosen family (which "can" include your birth family) is all you need. Anyone who can't respect you and your children and love you and them for who and what you are isn't worth your time. The most important thing to remember is to remind your child that it isn't their fault. The people you cut out of your life made the choice; they alone are to blame.

Rachel Gonzalez: I was raised to believe that biological family is who you trust. They are supposed to be the people in your life you can always rely on. It's scary to recognize when that is not actually true. To have the unwavering support of our community of friends, those who actually know and love our transgender daughter, but not from biological family who don't have a personal relationship with her, is a sad realization. Recognizing that extremist news sources are more trusted than personal experience is a sharp pain when you have been raised to believe those are the people who are meant to implicitly have your back.

I spent months crafting a letter to family that left enough room for questions and curiosity but was firm enough to relay the message that disputing our daughter's existence and identity would not be tolerated. We left the door open, but most did not take the opportunity to educate themselves. We have a firm boundary: no one has contact with any of our children who is not loving and respectful. My husband and I have role-played various potential encounters prior to obligatory family engagements, and we have enlisted friends to be present and act as physical barriers when needed. The top priority, and bottom line, is always the physical and emotional safety of our children. We have always hoped that our family will support us and our child but if they don't, they lose the privilege of knowing our amazing children—all of them.

Debi Jackson: Ooooh, I feel this question so much! My family is very conservative, military, GOP (Grand Old Party, i.e. Republican)-supporting, and Southern Baptist. They were horrified when they thought my daughter Avery was a "boy wearing pink princess pajamas" at the age of four. I was afraid to tell them that she was actually a girl and would be socially transitioning to live authentically. I knew how the conversation would go. I started by letting them know we had spoken with our pediatrician, a child psychologist, a gender therapist, and a pediatric endocrinologist, and that all of them had explained what gender dysphoria is and that they all agreed Avery was experiencing it. The professionals also all agreed that the best course of action was to affirm her and let her live as a girl.

The announcement to our families didn't go well. They refused to use she/her pronouns, said it was bad parenting (and even sent us religious books that were essentially guides to "do-it-yourself-conversion-therapy-at-home"), and said they would pray for our souls. I tried—really, really tried—to patiently educate them for a few years, sending them regular updates with photos to show them how happy she was. But eventually I had to acknowledge that the relationship was toxic; they would never see her as a girl, or even pretend to. Things came to a head with the 2016 presidential election and the release of the *National Geographic* magazine's "Gender Revolution" issue with Avery on the cover. That was when I had my last conversation with my mother (via Facebook Messenger) where we were essentially disowned.

In hindsight, I wish I hadn't tried so hard. I thought I "had" to give them explanations and teach them. That was a decade ago when information was harder to find. But that takes so much emotional energy, and I could have and should have devoted that time to Avery, her brother, and my husband. I do still believe we can and should offer some resources to family, but I think that as parents, we should set boundaries at the same time because our responsibility is ultimately to our child and not to everyone else. If your family loves you and your child, they will want to do the work to learn. But it's okay for you to let them know that they "must" respect your child's name and pronouns even if they read books, watch documentaries, or go to LGBTQ support group meetings.

Clara Lee: I have a large extended immigrant family, which immigrated from Korea in the 1970s and mostly lived in Southern California. It helped that we lived on the east coast, which gave us ample time and space to get our heads around my son's transgender identity. When it was time to come out to the family about my child, I started with a few members of my family with whom I have a close relationship. I talked to my sisters and my father first when I visited them in person. They were supportive and asked me what they could do to support the family. It took me two years to come out to my mother, who was a devoted Catholic and very conservative. I prepared myself mentally, and then came out to her.

I made it clear to her that we as parents had done our own due diligence and got advice from experts including gender specialists and therapists before making our decision to support our child. My son's high school graduation was coming up and she was to visit NYC along with other family members. I was nervous about how my mother would react when she saw my son for the first time since his transition. I was determined to intervene if necessary and thought through other lodging options for her to stay at, if she were to misbehave toward my son and my family.

In Korean culture, there is the concept of filial piety where children are expected to respect and obey their parents and elders, but I could not just let my mom hurt my child. Fortunately, my mother did wonderfully, embracing my son while calling him "my grandson" and new name when she arrived. I continued to keep an eye on family members and gently reminded them when they used the old name and incorrect pronouns. I think it helped that they were at my home as guests and had to be respectful of the new rules. Also, already having a supportive father and sisters during that time made things easier for me when dealing with my mother throughout their visit.

Wayne Maines: It is fairly easy to protect yourself because you are an adult, and if needed you can just walk away. It is very difficult to tell a child that they are no longer welcome or why. Sooner is better than later, but you need to talk to your family and friends eventually. Some may surprise you though.

Journal entry, 2008:

Just up the road from our house is my dad's deer hunting camp. It is a typical Adirondack hunting camp. For men only, a place to play cards, drink, and tell stories about the big bucks that got away and bigger stories about the bucks that did not get away. Whenever my dad wanted to get away from a family function, he said he needed to check on something at the hunting camp. We all knew he was just trying to get away from the crowd. When he said he needed to go to camp, I jumped at the opportunity to go with him so I could talk to him and my brother. I said, "Dad what have you guys been working on at camp?" Then I said, "Billy do you want to go take a look?" On the ride to camp, I thought about starting the conversation, but we were sitting too close together. I could not bring myself to start the conversation, even though I had rehearsed it over and over in my mind.

While my dad was showing us the new floor in the kitchen, I brought up the subject of Nicole. I cannot remember exactly what I said, but my goal was to tell them that we were doing the right thing. I said that this was not something Kelly or I "made happen." I talked about my new focus to help Nicole become a healthy, confident, happy, and successful little girl. They were both very quiet; they nodded and said they would do whatever I needed them to do. I remember my brother saying that if anyone ever touched her, they would have to go through him. At some point my dad gave me a big hug. He did not say anything, just a big hug. Then Billy said, "Let's go get a beer." That was it, my big discussion.

Should I have said more? Kelly would have wanted me to. Maybe I should have told them my fears and worries and how hard it was to openly discuss our situation. Maybe they needed to know that I was still learning and I needed their help. At the time, I did the best I could; the Maines men do not talk about feelings and problems. Now I realize I needed to know what they were really thinking so we could talk about it.

The stress and worry involved in raising a transgender child are often overwhelming. Family and friends are an essential part of your inner circle. Most often I have found that family is harder to approach than friends. Maybe it is because you know their weaknesses and preconceived opinions. You also may be aware of family values that do not support your current needs. Approaching your friends might be easier because you choose many of your friends after leaving the fold of your family support group. These new friendships are often based on common ground that goes beyond your family's core values. Keep in mind that it is also easier to establish new friendships with people and organizations that will support the needs of a transgender family. In the beginning, it might be difficult to search out new friends who will support your family, but the rewards will be great.

Jennifer Solomon: At around age two, my child Cooper started showing preferences for female clothes. This was around the time my older daughter was having her Bat Mitzvah and I struggled with what Cooper would wear for such an important event. Everyone we loved would be in temple seeing our family "on display." I was scared that I would be judged as a bad parent for allowing my little boy to wear a dress. I had to decide if it was worth risking losing some family members or showing my child that I valued him and respected his gender expression.

I love the analogy of keeping your immediate family on an island as a safe space. This island allows visitors if they respect and support your family. If not, they are not welcome. This way your child will know that the people in their lives are not going to make them feel bad for who they are. Unfortunately, not all extended family will understand, and they may need more time off your island to become educated. Offer resources and opportunities for them to learn but don't forget that protecting yourself and your child is top priority. We've had to distance ourselves from a homophobic family member and it wasn't easy, but I know it was the right decision for our family. Remember, your child is looking to you for guidance. If they see that you are afraid to talk about them to the extended family, they may internalize that. But if you are confident and introduce them in a loving and proud way, these actions will speak volumes to them. I always say my child is the bravest person I know because he lives as his authentic self regardless of anything others may say or do. I feel so lucky that I get to be his mom!

Janis Tannehill: We made the decision to only come out to family in the immediate area, and only then to those who would be sympathetic. We had heard stories of extended family members calling Child Protective Services (CPS) claiming supporting trans kids was abuse. Some families keep "go files" with proof of appropriate medical care and legal prescriptions, affidavits from medical and psychological professionals that their kid is not being abused or coerced, and copies of name change and other legal documentation.

We never fully trusted our ultra-religious and conservative family members many states away not to call CPS. We made the conscious decision not to tell them or see them until said child was 18. This was awkward and probably somewhat painful for my other children, but we made sure that they knew that we were protecting their brother from people who might not treat him nicely anymore. They accepted this, but I really do think secrets hurt kids and I'm sure my choice of their brother's well-being over their relationship with their grandparents will be something they have to carry. I regret if this causes them hurt, but I do not regret the decision.

After his 18th birthday, I wanted to let my kid come out to the grandparents in his own time. He kept putting it off. I told him, "You know we have been screwing up names and pronouns on the phone enough the past few years that this is probably not going to come as a great surprise, right?" He said, "Yeah, I know. But worrying about my grandparents not accepting me and confirming it are two different things. It might go okay, but it might not and that is what scares me more." Things turned out okay; I would say that they don't get it and they keep screwing up pronouns but the cops haven't shown up on the doorstep, so our worst fear did not happen. I feel my kid can handle misnaming and misgendering better because he is an adult and can choose not to interact with people who don't respect him.

Your family needs to understand this, and that includes extended family, unsupportive parents, and nosy family friends who like to continually mention sin in casual conversation: if you do not support your gender-variant family member, someday the child will be an adult. As adults, they will be able to choose which family members they continue to associate with, including you. Family can act like a bunch of asses and feel they can get away with it because a child has no choice but to go where they are told and interact with family who treats them poorly. However, these people will be cut out of the lives of your child when they become adults.

Unsupportive people need to be made responsible for their actions and choices when interacting with gender-variant children in their family. It ultimately comes back to you, the parent, to protect your child's mental health and physical well-being. It is painful to cut family out of your life or have your family members cut you out of theirs. Family needs to understand that they are making the choice to either be supportive or not. Make sure grandma understands that choosing to invite to Christmas dinner family members who have been abusive to your kid means that you will not be there. Make sure your brother understands that you and your family will not be at the family dinner because they refuse to use the correct name for your kid. It is not your responsibility to make other people comfortable around your child. Remember that what is best for your kid is protecting them from people and situations that hurt them.

How can I ensure that my gender non-conforming kid has a good life? Will they ever be successful, loved, or live a "normal" life?

Noah Berlatsky: A good way to find better representation of trans people is to read trans journalists, critics, and writers. Julia Serano, Katelyn Burns, Tre'vell Anderson, Parker Molloy, Daniel Lavery, Grace Lavery, Nico Lang, Kate Sosin and Chase Strangio are some writers whose bylines you can look for. These can give you positive "possibility models" for you and your child.

Wayne Maines: This is a hard question to answer. In general terms, the answer is yes...but a great deal depends on you, and the team you build around you, as your child grows to adulthood and beyond. Our jobs as parents are never really done. As our kids get older and we are a bit wiser, we have more moments of calmness, fewer worries, and a great deal less control in our child's life. But the worrying and coaching will never end.

With our support, they have every opportunity to reach for their dreams. I had mentioned earlier that there were times I thought Nicole would not make it to adulthood. There were definitely times that I asked myself and others whether she'd get to lead a normal life. When the kids were young, we established a common practice called "Secret Time" to encourage the kids to describe what was troubling them. It always started with us telling a secret, and then they would tell us a secret. I had a hard time coming up with secrets, but for the most part it was fun. I made up secrets about my brother. I would tell them that when I was their age Uncle B was afraid of cows or he did not know how to spell spaghetti, they would laugh and then tell me something that happened at school or something they were afraid of. One night, probably around age ten, when it was Nicole's turn, she said, "Daddy, no one will ever love me."

I was crushed. I am getting emotional as I write this. I have never forgotten this event, and it broke my heart that my child could feel this way. It breaks my heart today because I am aware that it is a common thought for many gender non-conforming youth and transgender adults.

It was not long after that our family was targeted by special interest hate groups, and our story became a state and national rallying cry for everyone who feared transgender children. We tried to live in a small bubble. The kids were very aware of the fear and hate that surrounded our story. Kelly and I lived in a war zone, huddled in the only safe space we knew: our home in the woods. We had a sunken living room floor, and while the kids watched television, we sat behind them on the couch trying to demonstrate a sense of normalcy.

One day, the kids were watching a teenage movie where at the end of the movie the geeky girl got the handsome, cool boy. Jonas turned around and said, "See Nicki, there is someone for everybody." Both of us had to fight back our tears. I was so proud of Jonas for recognizing her pain and doing everything he could to help his sister.

There *is* someone for everyone. Life may be complicated, people will be difficult, but there are so many people who love our children and will help protect them. As teenagers and adults, they will find many challenges and safety concerns that need to be addressed, but without a doubt they can and will be successful if we work hard to help them develop a high level of self-esteem and remind them every day that they are loved by many.

Lastly, when Nicole was young, I made sure to point out and surround her with excellent gender non-conforming/transgender role models. The first was Jean Vermette, an electrician from Maine, who was leading the fight for equal rights in the state. There was also Dana Zirker, a senior executive in the IT world; Joanne Herman from Boston, who was instrumental in supporting legal protections for transgender people; and of course leading attorney and dear friend Jennifer Levi, GLAAD's Transgender Rights Project Director.

Today there are many role models for our children, such as:

- Brynn Tannehill, who provided the energy to make this book happen. She graduated from the Naval Academy and flew SH-60B helicopters and P-3C maritime patrol aircraft during three military deployments between 2000 and 2004. She continues to work as a senior defense research scientist in private industry.
- Admiral Rachel L. Levine, who serves as the Secretary for Health for the US Department of Health and Human Services.
- Senator Sarah McBride, who represents the First State Senate District, in Delaware.
- Jazz Jennings and her family, who are dear friends who continue to do a great deal to support transgender youth and educate others.
- Avery Jackson, who started educating others at age seven and is an awesome role model for kids who are struggling to find their way; and her mother Debi is a strong positive force who keeps us all energized.
- Of course, my own daughter Nicole, who is a national and international advocate for transgender rights and was the first transgender Superhero on television.

Janis Tannehill: The thing that terrified me the most when my trans son first came out was prospects for his future. How will he live and thrive in a society that, as I have come to find out more and more, hates him for being trans? With lawmakers that continually act to remove our gender non-conforming children from public life? What kind of stress is it going to put on my kid every time a law is passed denying basic human rights to healthcare and bathrooms?

Join social media message boards. Parents exchange information on a variety of topics including finding affirming and representative books, movies, TV shows, and online content. There is positive, age-appropriate messaging out there; you just need to look for it. Most transgender youth know that they are ambassadors of their communities and know that inappropriate behavior on their part will make the world react negatively to all trans people. Trans youth make excellent spokespersons and their online content is usually good.

Representation matters. When your kid sees people like them and their family in the mainstream, they feel seen and heard.

Transgender people have always had a problem being under-employed and finding adequate housing, unless they are deeply stealth. Will my son be denied entry into the university of his choice? Or dorms? Or the workforce (not just military service)? What about relationships? Will he be able to find someone to love him, especially being a five-foot tall gay trans guy in a community that has a reputation for being superficial? Will he be safe just walking down the street or in a relationship? Will he ever be able to have children and a family of his own?

Knowing people in the transgender community, I have seen how they struggle in society. I have seen adult trans people struggle with their health because of inadequate medical care, both from being denied reputable transition-related care as well as being denied general preventative medicine from unsympathetic doctors. I have seen adult trans people struggle in their relationships, end marriages catastrophically due to transition later in life, and lose custody of their kids...or even the ability to see their children at all. I have known trans people who have lost their jobs, been kicked out of the military, been under-employed or unemployed, and face homelessness, deal with crippling depression, or struggle to handle the fallout of sexual assault, and abandonment and abuse by their families.

I have also seen these same people pick themselves up and find safety and resources in their community. Through each other, transgender people have an underground network of knowledge on healthcare and legal issues, companies with the best reputation for hiring and providing benefits for LGBTQ people, and how to phrase paperwork in just the right way to get needed documentation for work, housing, and ID. I have seen some of these people find love, get married, have children of their own either biologically or by adoption, go to top-tier universities, get their dream jobs in great companies, travel the world, and buy houses and dogs and chickens.

In short: yes, your gender non-conforming kid can have it all. Everything they want in life for themselves, and everything we have ever wanted for them as parents. Do transgender people have a steeper hill to climb? Yes. But the first step, and one of the most important in helping them achieve all that we know they are capable of, is to accept them and love them as they are. Family support has been proven, time and time again, to be the most important factor in our children's success. It is our duty to support our children, and the most sacred vow we made to them when we brought them into this world. Love, always, is the answer.

Chapter 4

Social Transition

At some point after your child has come out to you or indicated their gender identity, they'll likely first experiment with their gender expression at home. Or you may find out they have "tried on" using a different name or pronouns with their circle of friends they trust. Either way, social transition is the process of increasingly presenting publicly in accordance with your identified gender. This period brings about more stressors: from interaction with families, friends, and co-workers, to concerns about safety, to learning to roll with the (inevitable) fashion disasters.

The questions presented here were all taken from online boards for parents of trans youth and were things that our parent panel had to deal with as well during their child's transition. Each had their own approach which worked for them, their child, and their family. Our panel of subject matter experts addressed each as well, having worked with innumerable families negotiating similar terrain as part of their work as counselors, therapists, and psychologists.

My child can't seem to settle on a new name and keeps changing what they want to be called. How can I handle this, while still being supportive?

Darlene Tando (LCSW): This is very common! It can be frustrating for parents, as they feel they are trying to gain footing on shifting ground. However, can you imagine being able to pick your name? What a huge choice! Many trans youth "try on" names several times before they find one that feels like the perfect fit. The name may also evolve a bit as the child does, and there's nothing wrong with that. Thank your child for trusting you enough to share a new name choice, even if they worry they might be inconveniencing you with another change. Reassure them you are willing to adjust to changes to make them feel as affirmed and supported as possible.

Nathan Glickler: Choosing a new name is a big deal. They want something that they are going to be able to see as identifying them. It may be difficult but talk to them about it. Tell them that you will respect their decision, and that when it comes to a legal name change you will need them to understand that it will be very hard to change their name again afterwards, so they need to be sure when they are ready for that step. Tell them, in the meantime, that you will do your best to remember the name they are using. Ask them to be patient and remind you if you forget or use the wrong name.

Clara Lee: I think it's important to show our children that we are supportive of their journey by using their new name even if they change their mind. It might reflect their continuous journey to find themselves, and they may settle on a new name eventually as their legal name on paper. I really appreciated it when my son made the decision to take the name we chose for him if he had been assigned as a boy at birth. It made me feel as if I was finally part of his transition and his new life.

I am still not sure how my son came up with his new boy names in the beginning. As part of his social transition and while we (his parents) were still trying to figure out how to support him with medical and legal transition, my son started using a boy name and a male pronoun in high school and at home. My son had both Korean and English names and we often used both names at home. Since his Korean name is not a typical girl's name, and can be gender neutral, my son was okay with us continuing to use his Korean name. I do not think he was particularly attached to the new English names he chose, other than wanting people to respect his wishes to be called by the new name and pronoun.

When I was having a hard time pronouncing his new name because it contained a character "z," which is really hard for many

Koreans to pronounce correctly, my son did not hesitate to take on the boy's name that his father had prepared at the time of his birth.

My child identifies as a boy, but still is okay with wearing some clothing that is gendered for girls. What does this mean?

Cristy Mereles (LCSW): Gender identity lives in the brain, just like being left- or right-handed lives in the brain. Like handedness, gender is something you know from within, but cannot "prove" to anyone.

Gender expression, on the other hand, is how you "wear" your gender, including clothes. You cannot and should not presume someone's gender identity based on their gender expression. Nor should you presume someone's gender identity based on their choice in activities, favorite color, friends, decision to wear makeup, and so on. There is not a one-on-one relationship between gender identity and gender expression; they exist separate from one another, and are two distinct bits of one's overall identity.

Nathan Glickler: Generally, I see this as your child recognizing that gender norms are an invention. They also change over time. Men used to wear tights, high heels, long shirts that were belted in a way that they looked a lot like dresses, and so on. Fashion changes over time and will continue to do so. Don't get hung up on it. It could also simply mean that your child likes the feel of "girls' clothing" or feels comfortable with an appearance that is perceived as more feminine. Either way, it's not a big deal. Let them be who and what they are.

Janis Tannehill: Boys' clothes suck. They come in black, grey, and blue. To my budding, "Queer Eye" loving, "totes Feroch" gay boy, this was wholly unacceptable.

The push-pull between wanting to be properly gendered as male and yet wanting the perfect skinny jeans in an acceptable array of colors was quite difficult to navigate. In the early days, before testosterone did away with his bubble butt, it was really dysphoria-inducing. He would oscillate between jammie pants and a hoodie no matter the season when he was feeling bad, and then swing to being the most put-together, smartly dressed metrosexual when feeling good.

I was more concerned about his mental health when I could tell he was hiding under multiple layers of clothing to disguise his body shape than I was when some of the old "girl" clothes would work their way out of the closet. Plus, leggings are super comfortable.

My child seems to go back and forth in how they present themselves. Is this common? How should I handle this?

Cristy Mereles (LCSW): Gender identity looks different for everyone. I tell my clients that there is no one right way to do gender. When it comes to gender identity and expression, each person will figure out what is comfortable for them. For some people this looks different day to day, moment to moment.

Support your child and check in with them often about the right pronouns to use, and how you should refer to them with others (child, daughter, son). There are various ways to help identify this. I have heard of kids wearing colored pronoun bracelets on the right wrist to communicate the right pronoun to use. I have heard of pronoun pins being used, with whichever one is visible being the right pronoun.

Really, there are endless ways your child can communicate this to you moving forward. The families who have set up a system (bracelets, pins, or other) have the least number of issues around switching day to day, moment to moment. Supporting your child to be their own best expert about themselves is the important point here. Following their lead is crucial, and as long as they know that you are trying, kids are pretty forgiving of mistakes.

Debi Jackson: If your child goes back and forth in presentation, you might be a bit confused. But don't worry! We all vary our presentation more than we realize.

When Avery socially transitioned at four, she was all about pink, sparkles (sequins, glitter, sequins and glitter together), and swishy, fluffy tulle skirts. But after a few years of that, she was bored. And since her hair had grown longer and she was feeling more confident in herself, strangers automatically gendered her as a girl—something that didn't always happen during those first few months of her transition. She didn't have to work to prove to others that she was a girl.

And with that, she decided that she really wanted to wear blue again because she loved all shades of blue. And she wanted to wear the boxy boy-cut t-shirts with her favorite video game characters on them because she loved the characters.

I mentioned above that we all vary our own presentation, so I'll use myself as an example. I'm not super-feminine, and my wardrobe choices have some masculine details even if they come from the women's section. I mostly wear black and white clothes, pants, and little to no makeup. But sometimes, I feel like wearing a pink top with matching lipstick and a lacy pencil skirt...and my gender doesn't change based on what I wear.

In some ways, you might think that difference in presentation could be akin to someone who is gender fluid; but a lot of us are a bit "fluid" in our presentation if we really step back to look at it objectively. Trans masculine folks can wear nail polish, makeup, and dresses. Trans feminine folks can wear t-shirts, jeans, and Chuck Taylors. (That's my uniform of choice.)

It all works.

Jennifer Solomon: When the movie *Frozen* came out, my son was in preschool. Every day he wore his Elsa dress until it was finally so dirty and torn that I had to buy another one. Often, he would pair a Teenage Ninja Turtle t-shirt with a bright pink tutu. Other gender creative combos would be Woody's cowboy hat from *Toy Story* with a ruffled *My Little Pony* dress.

As a parent, I was so confused! Did he feel like a girl? Was he non-binary? Nope! He was a preschooler who was creative and loved to design outfits that represented all his favorite characters. As he got older, he would slowly leave the masculine clothes behind and shop exclusively in the girls' section of the store. Many children express themselves through hair or style of clothes.

Supporting your child's passion for fashion, or just encouraging them to be themselves, is never wrong. If one day my child decides to cut his hair short and sport a baseball t-shirt, I will follow his lead and know that it's all part of his journey of exploring his style. Always remember that children express themselves differently as they grow and enter new stages of life. Our gender creative kiddos will do the same thing.

Our child came out as trans to us but doesn't seem interested in some/all of the usual things involved with transitioning, including social transition. How should we handle this? What does it mean?

Dr. Matt Goldenberg: Every person has their own pace in a gender journey and has different influences on their behavior or gender expression. One influence is your child's temperament. Each child has unique behaviors and reactions, some noticed even in infancy, that continue to influence them throughout their life. Additionally, your child's personality influences their choices when it comes to highly sensitive decisions.

For example, imagine a child who is typically shy and tends to stay closer to one or two peers rather than being in the middle of a large group. This child may want to take their gender transition more slowly, as they might feel uncomfortable with a lot of attention or questions. Be aware of the influences your child is experiencing, including the climate at school; the level of affirmative support from family members, community members, and peers; the child's access to scientifically accurate information about gender; and the child's use of language.

One thing that helps is increasing the representation of gender-diverse youth in the media you have at home. This can include children's books that show characters of different genders and styles, or television shows, films, and podcasts that feature gender-diverse voices. It is as normal for gender-diverse youth as it is for cisgender youth to try on different styles and trends as they grow. Stay engaged with your child and help them with their challenges. Regardless of how your child expresses their gender, you should talk often about what may be bothering them and what questions they have.

Kelly Storck (LCSW): This likely means you get to sit back and do less. This is sometimes a difficult thing for us parents to embrace, especially when we're feeling anxious! The central tenet to remember here is that there is no one way to understand, embody, or live a gender. Yes, many people who are transgender need us to make some changes to honor them and increase their alignment, comfort, safety, and well-being. Even then, there is no right way to explore or enact any step of a transition, so it's best to follow your child's lead. Your kid may not need such changes now, and they may not need them in the future; that's all okay, as long as it continues to be genuinely true for them.

Do keep in mind that coming out can be very emotionally taxing, and fears of rejection can lead people to keep quiet about what they need or delay their movement towards gender alignment to avoid painful experiences. It is also possible that your child's needs will shift over time, meaning you need to stay open to change. There are so many possibilities for how this unfolds, so how on earth are you supposed to show up?

Fortunately, there is an approach that fits all these scenarios, and still provides the support your child relies on to flourish. This approach centers on *what we know right now*. It focuses on making room for the child to express their truth of the present moment, and to be affirmed in that light.

If you can show up within this framework, over and over, you will be right where you need to be no matter what is going on for your child. I know I've made it sound simple, but it will likely require some frequent reminders and some deep breaths! This approach means letting your child know that you see and love them as they are today, and that you will do whatever is needed to show up as a loving, affirming parent to support their life every day.

You can let them know that you are open to any and all layers of their gender, invite them to continue to share their experiences and needs with you, and let them know you promise to respect their privacy and autonomy as you go. Kids who feel supported in this way often exhibit a softening, like a deep exhale, or a brightening, like a sweet smile. I hope you get a chance to see these things in your kid too. All we really have is this moment, right? Just do your best to show up in it with more love and peace and less pushing and clinging, and then repeat that in the next moment. And the next moment...

Paria Hassouri: I'm not trans, so I can only try to imagine how difficult it must be to come to realize that you are trans in a binary, heteronormative world. Every child has their own timeline of when they come out to themselves, and then slowly to the rest of the world. And I can again only try to imagine how scary it would be to first go out into the world dressed differently than you ever have, worried about getting misgendered or called names. When our daughter first came out to us, she had told a few friends, but she was not ready to come out to her siblings.

She asked us to try using she/her pronouns in private so that she could get a sense of what it would feel like. In my anger and ignorance and denial, I stupidly told her that I couldn't use one set of pronouns when it was just us and another set when her siblings were in the room. I told her I couldn't be expected to look around to see who is in the room before opening my mouth to address her. This was just one of the many mistakes I made. She was trying to rely on me as a safe person with whom to explore her gender, to see what it felt like, before inviting in the rest of the world. I was refusing to be that support she needed.

If your child comes out to you as transgender but isn't interested in doing some or all of what others may do to transition, it doesn't mean that they are not transgender. It just means that they need time. Listen to your child. Ask them what they need and want from you. Check in and revisit every couple of weeks to see if anything has changed. Not every transgender person wants to transition in the same way or at the same rate. Everyone has their own timeline and journey.

How do we tell people our child is socially transitioning?

Kelly Storck (LCSW): When you are deciding how to tell people that your child is socially transitioning you need to consider multiple factors. These include your knowledge of a person's social ideologies, your trust in their ability to protect your child and their privacy, their access to your child, and their connection to others in your life.

For people closer to you or your child, you may choose to have a phone call or meet up to talk directly. It can be helpful to make an outline of the points you want to share so the discussion covers the bases, even when emotions or questions arise. The benefits of direct conversations include a richness that can feel really rewarding, and the ability to alter your disclosure based on real-time assessments of the other person's reactions. But talking to people directly also comes with some risks. These include uninformed or hurtful responses, or a derailment from what you aimed to share at a time that likely feels raw for you.

You probably know too many people to handle every disclosure with a personal conversation. Many families find written communication easier to manage. Writing also allows for the receivers to get curious, do some research, and feel out their responses before responding to you. This slower process can create the space for you to choose every word of your message, and to provide recommendations for folks to further educate themselves. This increases the chances that the people you share with will provide you with a kind of mindful and loving support that is not always readily available in a live conversation.

Keep in mind that writing your disclosure down means this private information exists in hard form and could be shared. Be explicit and unapologetic about how you wish to have your child's privacy protected.

Luchina Fisher: When our 11-year-old daughter slipped a note under our door saying she couldn't be a boy much longer, the biggest question for me, and then my husband David, was "What do we do now? Wow, do we tell other people that our child is socially transitioning?" For us, taking a step-by-step approach, starting with the school she attended and the folks who love us most, turned out to be the best way.

You can't start early enough with the school, which may need to train staff and get things in place. As we sat down with the principal discussing all the preparations, the principal asked our daughter, "Have you told your friends yet?" The answer was no. She was still terrified of how her friends would react. So, we started with family first. Before meeting up with my sisters and their families for a summer vacation, I sent an email letting them know that our child would be appearing as a girl in public for the first time and using a new name and pronouns. Having been on this journey with us since our child was two, they weren't at all surprised, and their warm and loving embrace was just what our daughter needed to gain confidence.

Next up was my husband's family reunion, with his mom and siblings, aunts and uncles, and dozens of cousins. My husband and I decided the best way to tell everyone was to send them a letter ahead of the reunion. After a brief explanation, we listed some ways that they could be supportive: use her new name and pronouns, while adding it's okay to make a mistake (even we still do); avoid asking about the school year ahead, which was still a source of uncertainty and concern; and, most importantly, keep in mind that our daughter is still the same person—just the presentation is different.

The letter and the reunion were a huge success, so much so that when it came time to tell our daughter's friends, we decided to send a letter as a family to the entire middle school community. After stressing that our daughter had the full support of extended family, doctors, and the school, we wrote, "Making this step requires our daughter to be brave and courageous—and she cannot do it alone." It was an invitation to our town to support our daughter on her journey, and it was met with an immediate, overwhelming rush of love and support.

Debi Jackson: A great way to let others know your child is socially transitioning is through a written letter. This can be mailed, emailed, posted on social media (private or friends-only settings), or printed and hand-delivered. A written message allows you to say precisely what you want to say without accidentally forgetting something in conversation because you get nervous, and it allows the other person to read, re-read, and process their thoughts in private away from you.

When Avery was going through transition, I wanted the parents of her friends at preschool to know and understand exactly what that meant. I created a short note to them that acknowledged that they had probably noticed some changes with her (wearing girls' shoes and headbands along with her other otherwise "boy" wardrobe) and that we had realized it wasn't just about clothing and wasn't a phase. I explained about all of the professionals we had visited, offered an explanation of gender dysphoria, and provided a couple of links to LGBTQ organizations where they could get information about being transgender so they could confidently have open conversations with their own children. I also gave them my contact information so they could reach out with questions, and I ended with a hopeful message that we looked forward to future playdates because their friendships were important to us.

Another technique I have used is to tell the person that I was about to disclose very personal and private information to them, but since I knew they loved our family and Avery, I was confident they would honor that information and want to support us. My goal was to set them up for success and have them want to agree with my assessment of our relationship rather than prove me wrong with a negative reaction. It works!

Janis Tannehill: I have found the "pull the band aid off" method to work best: Son A is now daughter A, their name is B now and we are using this/that pronouns. Yes, it is somewhat of a shock, but my kid is my kid and I will do everything in my power to love and support them.

I am also not above the hard sell and will pull out the suicide statistics as a way to say that this is something to take seriously. A suicide attempt rate of over 40 percent is not a chance I am willing to take. I am literally in a battle for my kid's life. It makes my kid being trans real and makes it clear that I am far more afraid of my kid dying than anyone else's opinions on the subject.

People who have never had any experience with gender non-conforming youth or trans people probably have *Ru Paul's Drag Race* in their head as their only frame of reference. To them, gender non-conforming and trans people are a joke, or entertainers, or put on gender as a costume. Making your experience real and your child's journey serious and valid is the first battle. This is your life now and it is not a joke, a fad, a phase, or a passing fancy. Before you socially transition as a family in the world, know your path. Having a plan for your path forward, whether it be legal or medical, will help other people get on board with your new reality. It amazes me how many people turn into concern trolls seeking to sow seeds of doubt, saying that you have suddenly gone stupid and don't know how to take care of your kids. *Yes*, you have medical and psychological specialists involved. *Yes*, you are doing your research on the what, why, and how of treatment. *Yes*, this is the best thing to do for your kid. Do not leave any room for discussion. Otherwise, people will pick up on your doubt and pick at it like a wound.

There are people who get it, people who don't but want to, and people who just won't. You will figure out really quickly who you are talking to and what kind of friends, family, and acquaintances you have. You need to be prepared to distance yourselves from those who will not understand and will not respect you or your child's identity, name, and pronouns. Your kid is your primary concern and making them be around people who are outwardly hostile is damaging. Pick the people and family members who are on board and forget the rest until they get on board.

Schools are a different matter entirely. A lot depends on which state and county you live in, so make sure to look up the policy in your area before you engage with your school. Most public schools will have to look up their own policy since gender non-conforming kids are relatively rare. Coming in armed with knowledge will help greatly. Knowing the policy in advance is also a matter of safety— some private schools will kick you out on the spot, and some school districts will not make any kind of accommodations with regards to bathrooms or non-legal names or pronouns. Some states will not allow trans kids access to sports and some will; some school districts will punish teachers who misname and misgender your kid, and some won't. Know what kind of school you are dealing with before coming out.

Our (pre-pubertal) child wants to socially transition, but people tell me that it's better to make them wait until puberty. Should I let them?

Sebastian M. Barr, PhD: Research suggests that parental support is the best indicator of trans youth's well-being.[1,2] By listening to them, and moving forward with a social transition, you are offering that critical support. We also have research that shows that pre-pubertal youth who can live in their affirmed gender (that is, those who are able to socially transition and are supported by parents) are as mentally healthy as their cisgender peers and siblings.[3]

This is a big deal, because we consistently see mental health disparities between trans youth and cisgender youth. This research suggests that social transition protects against the risk of poor mental health. At the same time, research has consistently found that not having one's gender affirmed (e.g., not being able to socially transition and/or having the wrong name and pronouns used) will probably result in many mental health issues.[4,5,6,7]

In short, the research literature *overwhelmingly* supports letting young people socially transition. Denying this to your child would likely place them at greater risk for significant mental health issues.

1   Travers, R., Bauer, G., & Pyne, J. (2012). *Impacts of Strong Parental Support for Trans Youth: A Report Prepared for Children's Aid Society of Toronto and Delisle Youth Services*. Ontario: Trans PULSE.

2   Fuller, K. A. & Riggs, D. W. (2018). Family support and discrimination and their relationship to psychological distress and resilience amongst transgender people. *International Journal of Transgenderism, 19*(4), 379–388.

3   Olson, K. R., Durwood, L., DeMeules, M., & McLaughlin, K. A. (2016). Mental health of transgender children who are supported in their identities. *Pediatrics, 137*(3), e20153223.

4   Barr, S. M., Snyder, K. E., Adelson, J. L., & Budge, S. L. (2021). Posttraumatic stress in the trans community: The roles of anti-transgender bias, non-affirmation, and internalized transphobia. *Psychology of Sexual Orientation and Gender Diversity.* https://doi.org/10.1037/sgd0000500

5   Puckett, J. A., Aboussouan, A. B., Ralston, A. L., Mustanski, B., & Newcomb, M. E. (2021). Systems of cissexism and the daily production of stress for transgender and gender diverse people. *International Journal of Transgender Health*, 1–14. doi: 10.1080/26895269.2021.1937437

6   McLemore, K. A. (2018). A minority stress perspective on transgender individuals' experiences with misgendering. *Stigma and Health, 3*(1), 53–64.

7   Pollitt, A. M., Ioverno, S., Russell, S. T., Li, G., & Grossman, A. H. (2021). Predictors and mental health benefits of chosen name use among transgender youth. *Youth & Society, 53*(2), 320–341.

Social transition can also be a valuable opportunity to see how your kid does and feels when they are able to be seen by others in this different gender. This often helps families feel more confident in the stability of their child's gender identity, which will be important when puberty begins to bring bodily changes that might need to be addressed. Pre-pubertal social transition doesn't require medical intervention, yet still gives a young person room to figure out what might not fit or feel right about this new gender—in a way that they can't know without trying. Finally, puberty can be acutely distressing and even traumatic for children whose internal gender doesn't match their bodies when they start to change.[8,9] Helping a child understand and affirm their gender before they must go through these bodily changes is very valuable...and can even be lifesaving.

Amy Cannava (NASP): Social transition is completely reversible. It's modifications to hair, clothing, makeup, mannerisms, or the name and pronoun they use socially (not requiring any legal changes). These changes are significant and meaningful to your child in the moment, but they are not life-altering—actually, they can be lifesaving, and should not be feared.

Children under the age of nine who assert they are a different gender than that assigned at birth may not persist in asserting that gender in adolescence and early adulthood. That is perfectly okay! Whether a young person persists in their affirmed gender, or reverts back to that assigned at birth, there is no harm in affirming a young person and supporting them in their growth to self-discovery.

However, a young person will not forget if you deny them who they believe themselves to be.

Children between the ages of one and three years of age begin to recognize and understand gender. In their play, they will assign

---

8   Medico, D., Pullen Sansfaçon, A., Zufferey, A., Galantino, G., Bosom, M., & Suerich-Gulick, F. (2020). Pathways to gender affirmation in trans youth: A qualitative and participative study with youth and their parents. *Clinical Child Psychology and Psychiatry, 25*(4), 1002–1014.

9   Deutsch M. B. (Ed.) (2016). *Guidelines for the Primary and Gender-Affirming Care of Transgender and Gender Nonbinary People; 2nd edition.* San Francisco, CA: UCSF Transgender Care, Department of Family and Community Medicine, University of California. Available at https://transcare.ucsf.edu/guidelines

each other roles based on gender: "You're the girl, so you be the mommy." "You're the boy, so you can be the firefighter!" Gender roles are socially determined and culturally based, but they are all around us. As soon as kids can recognize gender roles and gender itself, they are old enough to begin to feel uncomfortable with the gender they were assigned. It is both acceptable, and advised, to allow a young person of any age to wear clothes socially attributed to their affirmed gender. Whether or not they persist in that gender is irrelevant; on the other hand, by not affirming them in the gender they wish to embody, we can be endangering them today.

Children aged 11 and older who assert a gender different than that assigned at birth overwhelmingly persist in that identity and do so throughout adolescence and adulthood.[10] Therefore, children of age 11 and older can begin medical intervention through hormone blockers. These blockers are a safe and completely reversible way to delay pubertal onset. They allow them to either take the time to figure out which gender's puberty they wish to undergo, or at least, not develop secondary sex characteristics until they are sure of what they desire those to be.

In fact, 80 percent of trans adults knew they were trans before the age of ten, and 96 percent knew before the age of 18.[11]

There is no harm in accepting a child. And if that child detransitions because the world pushes back too much or they realize something else about themselves to be truer than what they initially thought, accepting them in the moment means giving them the gift of time to figure out who they are meant to be.

Delaying a young person's ability to have external control over their body through dress and mannerisms, which is truly all the young person has control of, means taking away what little self-autonomy they have. As the parent, you must seek to understand. To do so means to listen to what our children are trying so desperately

---

10   Steensma, T. D., Biemond, R., de Boer, F., & Cohen-Kettenis, P. T. (2011). Desisting and persisting gender dysphoria after childhood: A qualitative follow-up study. *Clinical Child Psychology and Psychiatry, 16*(4), 499–516. doi: 10.1177/1359104510378303

11   Savage, T. A. & Lagerstrom, L. (2017). *Understanding and Supporting Gender Diversity in Schools.* Accessed 06/07/2022 at https://masp.wildapricot.org/resources/Documents/Gender%20Divesity%20Presentation.pdf

to communicate to us through their words and actions. Allow them to be seen, heard, and valued.

Darlene Tando (LCSW): Making them wait until puberty could have profoundly negative impacts on your child's mental health. If a child is aware of their authentic gender identity and wishes to socially transition, best practices suggest we should follow their lead and affirm them in the gender that feels best. Often going through the puberty that comes with their assigned gender creates a crisis and does not bode well for their mental health or well-being. Dysphoria at the time of puberty can be dangerous. Affirming your child when they tell you who they are and then intervening as necessary to prevent the "wrong" puberty is a compassionate, loving thing to do.

Wayne Maines: My first thought is: what people say they should wait till puberty? Is it the school, your family, your church, or friends? Have any of them been down this path? I might not be so concerned if it is your child's mental health specialist or a medical professional from a gender clinic, or a pediatric endocrinologist who has been trained to care for a gender non-conforming child. They will work with you to develop a plan.

Most of the people who tell you to wait have good intentions...but a few may not. For example, many schools across the nation, even those in states that mandate equal rights, will not want to deal with the special needs required, or the potential storm of protests that may occur in the community. I advise you to proceed with caution, and a team of experts, if possible.

Every child, every family, and every community situation is different. The decision to socially transition may need to change or be different given a number of common situations. Your child may socially transition within your inner circle, or just in the summer, and not at school. My family did so in the third grade but Kelly and the kids had to move to Portland, Maine (leaving me behind to work in Orono) in the sixth grade to return to stealth mode. A return to stealth mode may happen at different ages, or quickly change due to a threat outside your control. In our case, Nicole often made the choice to tell the world, without input from others. She was always open, honest, and sometimes forceful about making sure everyone knew who she was. The only time she was not was when it was critical for her safety.

During that time, we saw a significant negative change in her behavior. I can only imagine how hard it must have been to return to a time where she must live in secrecy, lie to her classmates, and no longer have playdates, sleepovers, or any other activity that might reveal her true self. (Note: Having the opportunity to transition in a totally safe environment socially is a beautiful example of love and caring. When you decide it is a family social transition, everyone will be impacted. Please check-in with your other children to provide them with the tools they need to support their sibling and to reduce their anxieties or concerns.)

I can only tell you what we did, and what Nicole did on her own. When she was old enough, she told her friends she was a girl/boy. She had no other way to describe it: in many ways, she never had to socially transition because she innocently told everyone. As she grew, with the same innocence she provided clarification by stating she was a girl trapped in a boy's body. She did so without emotion or concern, just as a matter-of-fact fact. Her classmates and most of her teachers were very supportive.

The next stage was much more complicated, and sometimes stressful. As she told people she was a girl she still was using her given name and presented mostly as a boy. We had already noticed the stares and whispers that came from older kids and many of the adults, but until this point Nicole appeared to not know or not care. This changed in the third grade when we worked with our school to begin a more formal transition at school and in our community. It all went well, until the fifth grade when bathrooms were no longer single stalls.

Our family, for the most part, is on the other side of our journey. Both kids are doing well, and Kelly and I are still recovering in some way. We all have a few scars; we all made mistakes, but today when we discuss them, we agree we did the best we could do. We were in many ways the first family to tackle many of the things you must consider. I am so proud of the children and parents who have followed us. It provides me with great pleasure to see a large population of transgender children and youth who are being supported by their parents. The questions that have been asked and answered in this book will help us all continue to grow.

What options are there for swimsuits for trans girls, trans boys, and gender non-conforming children of various ages?

Dr. Matt Goldenberg: Swimsuits and intimate wear can be a tricky topic for gender non-conforming youth, as that clothing tends to be highly gendered and may be more likely to accentuate secondary sex characteristics (like breasts). Swimwear can also be difficult for gender-non-conforming youth, because wearing it may involve use of a locker room or a public bathroom. Thus, youth may have additional concerns about where they can be safe when changing in or out of swimwear.

While masculine swimwear has not changed much over recent years (e.g., longer shorts are common for boys) there has been more evolution in feminine clothing (such as board shorts for girls, bikinis, different styles for both one-piece and two-piece suits). Some youth may prefer to add a swim shirt, which can be functional as well as mitigating the water temperature and blocking the sun. Some youth may choose an additional item of clothing like underwear under their swimwear to help conceal middle parts, or breasts.

Tighter underwear that is made to conceal bulges (called a gaff) is also available online, and many products are specifically for swimming. In addition to style, colors and patterns may help your child express their gender in swimwear. It is best to offer at least a couple of options for your child for swimwear. Additionally, to avoid difficult experiences in trying on swimwear, some youth may prefer to shop online where they can have privacy to try on items.

Jennifer Solomon: Living in Florida means we have warm weather 99 percent of the time. We wear swimsuits and flip flops when other folks are bundled up under scarves and mittens, so having swimsuit options for our queer youth is really important. Part of feeling good about yourself is being comfortable in your skin. Swimming in the pool is a great way to get exercise and enjoy time with family and friends. For our trans youth, not having a bathing suit that covers them properly limits these types of activities. For my child, a two-piece bathing suit with a ruffle bottom gives him the confidence to join his peers in the pool. For trans boys, a swim shirt with surf shorts can provide the coverage they need. Some opt for a binder under the swim shirt, but you have to be careful about getting the binder wet, and having it so close to the skin for any length of time. There are more and more companies that are seeing the need for specific swimwear for our trans youth, so I encourage you to research and find the bathing suit that gives your child the confidence to go out there and soak up some Vitamin D in the sunshine!

How do we handle slumber parties or sleepovers? What if our child is being excluded for being trans?

Darlene Tando (LCSW): Slumber parties and sleepovers for transgender children should be treated the same as for cisgender children. As their parent, you decide on the "who" and "where" based on their age, developmental stage, and friendships. You take the safety precautions you need to take to make sure your child is safe spending the night at someone else's house or having someone spend the night at your house. Some parents of transgender children feel nervous about not disclosing their child's trans status to the other parents hosting their child. I think this stems from worry that the other parents will feel "deceived" should they find out after the sleepover that their child is trans. While the feelings of the other parents cannot be controlled, it's important for the parents of the trans youth to remind themselves that they are not deceiving anyone.

They are presenting their child as their authentic gender; the child is going to the sleepover in their true form. What anatomy the child has should not matter at any appropriate slumber party! Some parents opt to only have their children spend the night at homes of people who know them well and know their child is trans, and that's okay too. If a child is being excluded from such things due to being transgender, the parents will respond in the same way as any whose child is being excluded from social gatherings. Validate, comfort, and find fun alternatives. Parents may also want to connect the child with friends they know would be affirming, or get involved with trans family support groups where they may find friends their own age who would like to have some fun slumber parties!

Nathan Glickler: With my child, her friends were always supportive. Generally, their parents were as well. Honestly, I am a little torn on this one. If another parent were to find out your child is transgender after the fact, they may react angrily, and you don't want your child to go through that. Generally, I would say it is safest to let them know, but you should talk to your child first. They can always get a gauge on how supportive their friends' parents are. And you can potentially avoid situations where the other parents react poorly and put your child's friendships at risk.

My wife usually identifies supportive families early on and works out slumber parties and the like with them specifically. We avoid families we know are not supportive. We also have no patience for people who exclude our child for being transgender. They are a toxic influence in our lives, and we do not associate with them.

Janis Tannehill: Sleepovers when kids are young is an all-or-nothing kind of thing. He has a girl's body but doesn't fit in with the girls; he wants to hang out with the boys, but he's gay; some friends are gender non-conforming too, so where do they fit in?

So what's the real question here—are you looking for your kid to be with their gender peer group, or are we policing sexual behavior? Either they have sleepovers with everyone, and we trust them to act right, or they have none at all. Discussions on behavior start at home, when our kids are young and have no idea about sex. Tell them to give people their physical space, everyone changes their clothes alone in privacy, sleep in your own bed/sleeping bag, and don't bother anyone while they are sleeping. Normalizing these kinds of boundaries will help avoid misunderstandings when they are young and make the discussion on consent as teens that much easier.

What are the new dating rules?

Darlene Tando (LCSW): There isn't a parenting manual or a rule-book for life, and the same goes for rules about dating while trans. How an individual decides when and how to disclose to potential or current date mates will depend on a variety of factors, such as their own relationship with being transgender, their geographical location, age, temperament and support system, the ideologies of their family, and the background and temperament of the person they are dating. To make hard and fast rules about disclosure would make it impossible to incorporate all these factors and dynamics. People who believe they "must" disclose their transgender status before dating or having any type of intimacy with others are often buying into external biases, such as an implication that they are somehow being dishonest by not disclosing. In fact, being transgender is a private aspect of self, and many will choose not to share this with someone unless they are very close, or the person is likely to be in their life for some time. To disclose before dating someone or as a very first step may result in them having to come out to many people who are not necessarily in need of that information. A trans person presenting as their authentic self is not misleading or deceiving anyone; they are simply living their truth.

Therefore, based on the factors mentioned above, the individual can decide how and when to disclose. There is a balance between living in fear, expecting the worst and using sound judgment, and caution. Violence against transgender women (particularly trans women of color) is real, and a valid concern when it comes to dating and disclosure. These factors should be considered when the individual is deciding when and how to disclose to a potential or current date mate. Some may choose to disclose right away to prevent dating someone who may be transphobic. Others may choose to have safety back-ups in place during the time of disclosure. No matter when or how the individual chooses to disclose, thoughtfully deciding about this and listening to one's gut instincts tends to result in the best outcome.

Janis Tannehill: Dating in their teens brings in the sexual behavior and personal standard aspect that we didn't need to worry about when they were little. Let's face it, as they are going to date on the sly with or without our say so, it is better to get out in front of it. Start with discussions on consent, to make sure that they know and respect both their own boundaries and those of others. Conversations about safer sex practices become more complicated when bodies on the outside don't necessarily match what's on the inside. Double that if they have a queer partner.

When he was in high school, I told my son to wait for university for sexual exploration, since everyone involved would be more mature and have more tools to better handle the emotional repercussions. He didn't listen to me (teens not listening to their parents' wisdom? Shocking, I know). The heartbreak that was the fallout of moving too far, too fast was twofold. I expected the usual, "I thought he loved me, I thought we were going to be together forever" type of heartbreak that we have all gone through. What I wasn't counting on was what was directly related to being transgender: "How could he treat me like an experiment? It turns out he isn't as gay as he thought he was. I feel so lied to." My son was more self-possessed than a lot of teens in that he knew he was male, even though he had a very female body type at the time, and knew he was gay. Being treated like the gay tour guide by another teen who hadn't figured his own orientation out yet was very hurtful. He hated his body even more, since now not only did looking in the mirror show a body on the outside that didn't match the person on the inside, but he was also attractive to teen boys who saw a shapely girl's body on the outside and either had difficultly reconciling it with the boy on the inside or didn't care to figure out the difference. This soured him on relationships for quite a while, but at least it gave his body time to transition to a more male shape thanks to testosterone and top surgery. This extra time has hopefully allowed his peer group to also come out on their own, and not use my son as an experiment or an excuse to figure out their orientation.

My trans son is away at university now, and I am terrified every day for his safety. I'm not sure if that is because I know too much or just because he is my baby, and I will always worry about him. The unfortunate reality is that it is a dangerous world out there, especially for LGBTQ people. Transgender people face a disproportionately higher rate of physical and sexual violence as well as intimate partner abuse than cisgender people. When picking a university, check what their training is and if anti-sexual violence is mandatory for students and faculty, that should give an indicator as to how seriously the campus takes sexual assault and what the culture regarding consent is. One of the first things we did before he moved on campus was to find resources such as security, safe walk and safe ride programs, and the LGBTQ support center.

Now that he is on his own, I can only hope he remembers the basic safety he was taught. He assures me he knows not to go out alone, especially at night, or to places he doesn't know. He knows not to take an open drink in public. Being an especially social person, he has grouped up with a bunch of people from his dorm and they socialize and keep an eye on each other. While first dates are always in public, I do worry about him when he does get into a relationship—no matter our age, gender, or identity, we all want to be loved, and will sometimes put up with abusive behavior for this. All I can do is to keep telling him that he is worthy of healthy love and to not settle for less. Knowing that he comes from a home that has always accepted and affirmed his identity will, I hope, make him able to avoid toxic people, and to recognize those that prey on LGBTQ people who haven't been accepted or have been starved of love and attention.

When do I correct people who misgender my gender non-conforming child? Is there is a right way to do this?

Darlene Tando (LCSW): First, you need to have a conversation with your child about this. Ask what they would like you to do in this circumstance. Some gender non-conforming kids would prefer nothing be said in situations like this, especially if misgendered by a stranger. Other kids would like a correction to be made in most circumstances. This is a personal preference (often based on temperament), and any choice is valid. If your child is out to you but not to others, you need to make sure of their expectations prior to this happening. Your child may opt to have you not say anything at all, as doing so would "out" them or bring them unwanted attention. If your child has recently transitioned socially, and is enjoying being affirmed with their new name, pronouns, and so on, it is usually a good idea to correct the mistake. A quick and friendly correction does the trick; smiling and nodding as you say the right name or pronoun sends the message, "These are the words to use, and please continue to use them." The word "actually" can be a good lead-in before a correction, which sets you up for success. "Actually, he goes by...now."

Again, it is important to check in with your child and ask how you can help them feel most affirmed and comfortable—and revisit this throughout your child's journey. The responsibility for corrections should not be placed on the child; developmentally it is much easier and more appropriate for you to speak up and make corrections as needed.

Jennifer Solomon: My child's gender expression is having long hair, wearing female clothing, and often sporting the latest makeup trend. Because of this, he is always misgendered in public. It's understandable, because he looks like a girl to anyone who doesn't know him.

I've talked at length to him about how and when he wants me to correct people, and we've come up with these parameters: if the encounter is brief, such as a waiter, or the grocery checkout person, we let it go. It isn't worth the energy to get into a whole conversation about his pronouns.

If, on the other hand, the person who mistakenly misgendered him is a friend or someone who will have a continued presence in his life, we do offer to educate them. An example would be a new neighbor or a relative:

Neighbor: Oh wow! Your daughter's hair is so pretty!
Me: Thank you so much. Actually, Cooper is a boy and uses he/him pronouns, but I agree his hair is gorgeous!
Neighbor: Oh, I'm so sorry! I thought he was a girl.
Me: No need to apologize! Cooper is gender non-conforming, which basically means he's the opposite of a tomboy. He's a boy who likes girl things like long hair, dresses, and so on. We like to say that he is redefining what it means to be a boy! It's easy to assume his gender based on his appearance.

Neighbor: I never thought of that before. Thanks for teaching me something new.

Me: No problem! Welcome to the neighborhood and please know my door is always open and I'm happy to provide resources or answer any questions.

There are very specific ways that someone could be misgendered, and your response should match it. I compare it to when someone asks a question: is it being asked in an innocent way to gain information, or does it have a negative undertone that is meant to be hurtful? Misgendering is the same. Is it an innocent mistake, or is the person using misgendering to show they aren't accepting?

Another way of easily correcting the misgendering is to use your child's proper pronouns. Hopefully the other person will hear it and self-correct. Example:

Waiter: What would our little princess like to order?

Me: HE will have the chicken fingers.

Waiter: (thinking about what was just said) Okay...so would HE like fries with that?

Obviously, not everyone catches on, but you'd be surprised how many do...and nothing has to be said. It just magically works! Bottom line is, I would ask your child what makes them most comfortable. When our child was younger, we had a secret hand signal he used if he wanted us to correct them. If he didn't use it, we knew he didn't want to bring attention to the misgendering. It's not your job to educate everyone. Remember, it's about your family's comfort above all else.

Janis Tannehill: Talking about my kid in the third person while he is standing right there helps fill in the gaps before mistakes are made. "*Eric* is going to university; *he* really likes it." People will almost always go along with whatever direction you give them, especially if they are a new or passing acquaintance. Family, and long-term friends of the family, are usually the problem because they have to undo years of habit. Consistency is the easiest way to form a new habit: "What is *she* doing?", "*He* is doing that." Quick, simple, and to the point is best; it is what is real and valid and doesn't require discussion.

When it comes to misgendering, people usually realize they have made a mistake, genuinely feel bad about it and may not know what to do. Correcting yourself and moving on is the best advice to give them. It doesn't need to be a huge deal. "Sorry, Amanda..." or, "They, that's right..." is all that is needed.

However, people who deliberately misname and misgender your kid are doing so because they do not support you or your kid. You can try to educate them, but they are making their own choice to not be a part of your life by not accepting your kid. Choose your battles.

How do we legally change our child's name? What does that entail?

Clara Lee: Each state and city has slightly different requirements and processes for changing legal names as well as gender markers. Before starting the process, we reached out to a local non-profit organization that supports the legal name-change process for the transgender community. With their advice, we first went through the standard legal name-change process via the NYC court system and obtained several copies of name-change certificates to change other IDs and documents.

The first ID we updated after the legal name change was a passport, as it was not hard to fix the gender marker on it with a note from a doctor. With the passport that showed a new name and male gender marker, and the court-issued name-change certificate, my son was able to then change other IDs, including his social security information and driver's license.

Janis Tannehill: The Transgender Law Center (TLC) is your new best friend for all things legal. Every state and county is different. It keeps regulations regarding name changes, social security information, passports and more up to date by state. There is an order of events that may need to be explored to get all government IDs updated properly. Name changes go by current county of residence, not place of birth.

Name changes in particular may differ by state—start with the TLC and your county government site. Make sure to pick the correct form. There may be different forms depending on age of the child, if both or one parent has custody, and the reason for the change. Some counties require taking out an advertisement in the newspaper, some will allow exceptions for minors, and some don't require it at all. Some counties require a court date with all parents in attendance, some don't. Know your rights. We live in a blue bubble, so I just had to drop off the form and money (less than $100) to the court house. No court date, no newspaper ad, and the forms came in the mail less than a month later. Because it is just a name change, not a gender marker change, we did not require any documentation from a health-care professional. For the reason for the change, I did put "name not consistent with gender presentation." However, if your county is not friendly to trans people you might want to put "personal preference."

After the name change comes through, the next stops are the school, human resources where you or your spouse work, and the social security office. The school is easy, just go to the registrar and show them the name-change form with the seal. They may make a copy. There is no reason to give you any grief on this, since they change names due to remarriage of parents and adoptions all the time. If you do get pushback from the office, go straight to the principal and the district office. Name changes are legal documents, and some low-level bigot has no right to refuse a legal document.

The same is true for human resources and the social security office; name changes are relatively simple, and do not require supporting documentation beyond the name-change form. Human resources needs to change your child's name with insurance and issue new cards. Make sure to follow up with doctors and dentists, since they will need to update insurance cards in their systems so claims don't bounce because they're in the wrong name. If your doctor or dentist isn't affirming, now is a good time to change and start fresh with the new name at a new provider. It is important to change your child's name with the social security office, since this will be their secondary form of identification when applying for a driver's license, passport and job in the future. You don't want your kid being outed accidentally by a social security card that will only be used a few times in their lives.

How do I legally change my kid's gender marker?

Clara Lee: My son was born in NYC, and we wanted to change his birth certificate to reflect his new name and gender marker. In 2014, NYC changed the law to allow removal of the original birth name/gender marker on a birth certificate when a new certificate is requested. My son now has a birth certificate that shows his new name and gender marker, without any reference to his prior name and gender assigned at birth. An important thing to keep in mind is that many people change their legal name due to various life events and circumstances, like marriage, divorce, and adoption. The process is not more complicated for transgender people.

Janis Tannehill: In this political climate, it is important for all future ID to match gender marker with gender presentation and legal gendered name in order to ensure your child doesn't get outed in public accidentally to someone in a position of power who may not be sympathetic. This includes law enforcement, travel authorities, government offices like the DMV (Department of Motor Vehicles), human resource departments, and even banks.

Start with the Transgender Law Center. It has up-to-date laws by state, and sample forms for your healthcare providers to support gender-change requests. Birth certificate changes go by the state that issued them, not by where you live. It is doubly important to know your rights here since some states do not allow gender marker changes at all, some will allow amended certificates only, and some require medical documentation of "gender confirming surgery."

For us, changing the gender marker on our son's passport was our only option, and the key to all other gender marker changes. Passports operate on a different set of regulations from states entirely. Starting with a legal name-change certificate and gender-change form from my son's gender clinic signed by his physician, we applied for a new passport in the correct name and gender marker. Since I had the social security card in his legal name, I had a second form of ID. After the passport came in, I was able to go back to the social security office and get his gender marker changed there. With the correct passport and social security information, we could then go and get legal state ID (walker card or driver's permit). You should circle back to the school to get this gender marker changed too, since their transcripts will be sent to universities in the future and to human resources for jobs.

If you have your trans son's name and gender marker in insurance as male and they are prescribed testosterone, it can be billed as HRT (hormone replacement therapy) and not as transgender-affirming care. This might be important, depending on your state and what your insurance will cover. Gender clinics know all the tricks.

What safety rules must I teach my child in elementary school and preschool?

Darlene Tando (LCSW): There are no hard and fast "rules," as much as that would be nice (and would likely give more of a feeling of control!). The truth of the matter is, many factors come into play when it comes to safety, and this creates some "gray areas" when it comes to knowing how to handle various situations. A part of your journey as a parent is acknowledging the discomfort created by the lack of complete control and the lack of any type of guarantees. This is hard! Ultimately, in life and in safety rules for our children, we use our best judgment with the information we have at the time and teach them to do the same. Various personal aspects of your child and family will come into play, including temperament, geographical location, ideological beliefs of the neighborhood, and school.

While children whose trans identities can be disclosed in certain settings tend to have a healthier relationship with being transgender, parents can help them make thoughtful decisions about who to disclose to, and when. In preschool and elementary school, the grown-ups in the classroom and school oversee their safety. Speak to a trusted adult at the school regarding ways to best support your child. In high school, your child will navigate more personal decisions when it comes to safety. As with most topics, explaining parts of rational decision-making and learning to follow one's gut will be the general rule of thumb.

Jennifer Solomon: Safety is always the number one concern in every parent's mind. Teaching your child from a young age about boundaries and safety is crucial, especially for our queer youth. For me, it was important for my child to respect authority but understand it was okay to say no if he felt uncomfortable in a situation. Learning who was an ally and where to go if he needed help while in school or away from home was vital. I always educated his teachers on things like pronouns but more importantly I explained why it was unsafe for my gender non-conforming child to use any restroom but the single-stall type. Because he is a boy who has a female gender expression, it was a safety issue. While physical safety is important, so is being in a safe environment for their mental health. We all know how high the suicide rate is for our children, so making sure they spend time where they are respected, and protected, helps build up confidence and self-esteem. When the opposite occurs, and they are bullied or physically threatened, they can develop trust issues and be more prone to depression or anxiety. When a child doesn't feel safe, they cannot learn. Dinner time, riding in the car or bedtime are good times to communicate with your child and see how comfortable they feel at school. Simple steps put into place, like offering education to school staff, can give you the peace of mind that your child is in a school environment where they can thrive!

My child wants to go public and testify at the statehouse, but we live in a very conservative state. How should I handle this?

Dr. Matt Goldenberg: Your child may be interested in opportunities to influence the environment and the culture they see around them. It can be incredibly powerful to tell your story, and many times others are moved when they hear the perspective of youth. When your child wants to develop as a leader and they see an avenue for creating change, you may be concerned that they will receive unwanted attention. Even worse is the fear that your child may become the center of political controversy or social media bullying. Teaching your child safety rules for social media and use of electronics is always a valuable lesson.

It can also help to identify a few loved ones in your circle of support who can show up with understanding, encouragement, and kindness when needed. Let those friends or family members know you are worried that things might get intense, and it would be so wonderful if they could call and check in more often during that time. As a family, plan to try and have fun experiences together when you can, offering your child positive feedback and reminding them that you are proud of them. Offering praise and showing kindness helps support their resilience.

You might also want to try and connect more with supportive spaces. In addition to online spaces offered by The Trevor Project, your state may have additional resources. For instance, if you are not aware of a local group, there may be resources or connections at your state college. It can also be helpful to consider adding in a mental health provider if your child doesn't have someone to talk to yet, just so that they have another tool should they become overwhelmed.

Debi Jackson: If you want to do any public advocacy, including testifying at your state legislature, and especially if you are in a conservative state, I recommend picking a pseudonym for all of you, getting a free Google phone number, and purchasing a PO Box for your address. Testifying means that your information becomes part of the public record. In today's incredibly ugly and vitriolic political environment, that means taking steps to protect your privacy and your safety. If you must give your address and phone number, having an option that is in your voting district (which is what legislators care about, because they want to know if you are a constituent), but which does not reveal your address to trolls, allows you to sleep peacefully at night.

Another reason I recommend a pseudonym is because, even if your child wants to be a part of advocacy now, they might change their mind later. Media regret is real. Advocacy regret is real. With the constantly shifting political environment, even places that feel safe today might not feel safe in another couple of years. And even if your child is proudly living as an out transgender person today, once they are public in any way and their name can appear in a Google search associated with trans advocacy, they lose the ability to disclose to new people in their lives at the time of, and in the way of, their choosing. Preserving that sense of control is such a gift to them, and it isn't something you can offer once their name is public.

Chapter 5

Family Matters

After your child comes out, especially if they are socially transitioning, you're going to need to have discussions within your immediate family group in the house, and then with the people in your family who will see those changes. These can be difficult conversations, but the parents in this chapter have found ways to negotiate them. The subject matter experts who work with trans youth and their families have helped countless patients navigate these waters as well. There are also some difficult truths to face: your job as a parent is to protect your child, and sometimes that includes protecting them from family members who refuse to accept them as they are.

How do we tell our other children?

Darlene Tando (LCSW): Tell your other children about their transgender sibling the same way you would tell anyone else: in a positive, assertive way. Your other children will "read" the energy you have when you deliver the information. If they sense this is something that is okay, safe, and accepted by you, they will come to understand and accept it much more easily than you might expect. The developmental age of the siblings comes into play. For younger children who are in the concrete stage of development, visual cues such as clothing and haircuts make it easy for them to understand their sibling's authentic gender. Based on visual cues, the authentic gender often simply makes sense to them. Worksheets created by a gender therapist can help you inform younger children and help them wrap their brains around the change in name and pronouns. Many times, younger siblings are the first to catch on to the change in pronouns and their malleable brains help them to adjust quite rapidly. Parents often find themselves being corrected by the younger siblings when they "slip" with names and pronouns!

For older siblings, gender feels like more of an abstract concept, and they may have some trouble with the abstract understanding of their sibling's authentic gender. In middle school and high school, conformity rules and your other older child may be more concerned with what their friends will think than anything else. This is okay, and a natural part of development. Help them find the language to explain their sibling's transition to their friends and how to answer difficult questions. Additionally, older siblings have had longer to attach to the gender they *thought* their sibling was. This may make it take longer or be harder to adjust to conceptualizing their sibling as a different gender than before. Offer support and understanding, along with basic guidelines you expect from them as they are adjusting.

Lastly, give some extra one-on-one attention to siblings of all ages as their sibling is transitioning. Much of the focus can be centered on the transgender child and your other children need to feel that love and specialized attention from you, too.

Marsha Aizumi: How we decided to tell Aiden's younger brother about his transition was to first ask Aiden what he thought would be the best way to tell his brother. As much as possible, we have tried to let Aiden take the lead while communicating our thoughts in a supportive way. Aiden chose to write a letter to other family members and friends about his transition to male, and he felt that this letter could also be given to Stefen. The letter was placed in Stefen's room to read and process privately.

Stefen says there was never any conversation about or acknowledgement of the letter. Stefen is a very private individual who is very articulate, but also a person of few words. So, his support came in two ways. He immediately began using Aiden's name, and he always used the correct pronouns. Sometimes words are not as important as the actions that we take. In this case, it was true for Stefen and his love for Aiden.

Janis Tannehill: We don't call family meetings often, so when we do, the kids definitely know something serious is up. Treating this as a serious announcement and not a joke will go a long way to making changes in the house more natural and accepted. We sat the younger siblings down and in the most basic of terms told them that their sister did not feel at home in her body and that she should have been born a boy. His name was now Eric, and he will be dressing in boys' clothes and using male pronouns. If your kids are older, you can get into the differences between sex, gender, gender expression, and sexual orientation—these are all different things and don't line up for some people. It's a good opportunity to explain which parts are different for their sibling.

The younger kids were at an age where we could appeal to their sense of fairness: it isn't fair that your now-big-brother has to go to special doctors, and that there may be people who are mean to him because of this. It isn't anyone's fault; we just have to make sure we treat him properly so that other people will. I found it helpful to go back to calling people by name and using pronouns purposefully like when they were toddlers just learning language; "Where is *Eric*? I need to ask *him* a question." Modeling behavior, and not making a huge deal out of mistakes ("he," remember?), seemed to work well.

As they got older, we could help them exercise more compassion and empathy: "It hurts your big brother's feelings when we use the wrong name and pronouns." Examples of this include: "Other kids who go through this need your friendship and understanding," "Accepting that everyone is different and on their own journey is how to be a good ally," "Sex, gender, gender expression, and sexual orientation are all different parts of us and may not look the same for people."

There is also a balancing act that goes along with having any child who "needs" more than another, and this is no different. I can't tell you how much time I spent taking my trans son to doctors and psychologists' appointments, attending meetings at the school to get school bureaucrats in line, standing in line at social security, dealing with passports, going to the courthouse filing paperwork, getting new clothes, and just general attention. This can seem really unfair to your other kids, so it is important to try and balance their big brother's new clothes and needs with things that your other kids want and make sure that everyone is getting the attention they need.

Draw the line of acceptable sibling behavior at deliberately screwing up names and pronouns, since this is actively harmful to trans people. This is important. The chances are they are doing it to get attention, whether negative attention or not. Jumping on this early, with real and negative consequences, will help limit this behavior. Only a few trips to the corner were needed to curtail this for our family.

On the other hand, drawing the line at your trans kid screaming, hitting, or throwing things when their siblings mess up their name—either deliberately or by accident—is also required. Remember, being trans is as natural as breathing to your trans kid, and we don't make a big deal of that. Keeping negative behavior on this as low key as possible will help it fade away in favor of other ways for siblings to irritate each other. For my trans son saying "he, him" in a bored monotone voice, versus completely losing his marbles about his little brother "touching his stuff," made touching his stuff the biggest screaming issue in the house...and made pronouns a non-issue.

How do we deal with unsupportive relatives?

Dr. Matt Goldenberg: Depending on the age, temperament, and maturity level of your child, it may make sense for parents to act as a buffer between them and other relatives. If they want you to do that, there are ways to deal with unsupportive relatives.

First, remember that you are not obligated to listen to feedback, answer questions, or justify any parenting choices you are making. Perhaps the most useful tool you have in dealing with relatives is setting healthy boundaries. Researcher Brene Brown wrote in her 2015 book *Rising Strong*: "Compassionate people ask for what they need. They say no when they need to, and when they say yes, they mean it. They're compassionate because their boundaries keep them out of resentment" (p.115).[1]

---

1   Brown, B. (2015). *Rising Strong*. New York, NY: Random House.

Remember that no matter the age of your child, you are constantly modeling behavior for them. How you deal with your own emotions, and the behaviors you choose when things get hard, creates an example for your child for how they should behave. They will have a hard time ignoring this lesson, even if they don't like the way you do things.

You may encounter relatives who seem malicious in their misgendering, or in how they discuss your child's gender expression. They may say, "I just don't think we should allow children to make all the decisions" or, "I'm sure they know we love them."

If the relative's behavior is different from how they interacted with your child in the past, you can gently remind them by saying something like, "You have been close with (this child) in the past, and I want you to still have a good connection with them. I know they want that too. Are you willing to go on this journey with us by using the name and pronoun that they asked for?"

Reminding people of the values they place on family and relationships can be helpful, as most people value connection to their family. This relationship to family may be more important than a person's political or religious ideology. If that is not the case, give your relatives an opportunity to articulate their strongest values.

Darlene Tando (LCSW): When dealing with unsupportive relatives, picture yourself pulling them towards you rather than pushing them away (which may be your instinctive impulse if you feel they are rejecting your child, or your child's transition).

Let them know that many people have the same concerns they do, and in fact you had similar concerns in the very beginning. You can let them know that through research and connection with your child, you now understand things differently. I liken this to acclimating to swimming in cold water. After a bit, it feels warmer, and you may forget how cold it felt at first. Validating the initial shock and the adjustment it takes is important, without forgetting your own acclimation process. Validate the love and fear that likely comes from their resistance, but also make it clear what you expect from them. They can have some time to naturally adjust. Provide them with some reading materials from trusted, affirming sources. If they still don't come around and can't comply with the basic expectations you have made known are required in order to be in your/your child's life, you may need to create some distance. Your child may opt to not attend family functions when they are there. In solidarity, you may need to miss some functions as well. Sometimes, but not always, this natural consequence to the resistance can help family members realize they need to be more supportive to have a relationship with both of you.

Debi Jackson: Most of our family have been unsupportive, and I have tried a few different approaches over the years. At first, I tried to educate them, spending a lot of time sending them articles, videos, book recommendations, and copies of studies that came out regarding trans youth. But over time, I realized that it isn't my job to fix their personal discomfort with trans people and that there are some people who will never be willing to open their minds.

My advice is to set some boundaries with them up front. Let them know that you are willing to answer some of their questions, but in return they *must* respect your child's name and pronouns. And, because this is your child and you have already done much more research than they ever will, you don't need them to send you any negative articles that reinforce their own opinions about the trans community. Let them know that you understand if they will need some time to learn and adjust their own thoughts about trans kids, but that you will be moving forward so that your child can thrive with the support that you are offering them. If your family comes around, that's wonderful. But if they don't, your child will be safe in your home and that's what matters. Sometimes that means cutting ties eventually because you and your child deserve to have people in your life who love and support you unconditionally.

Lizette Trujillo: There is nothing more difficult than having to deal with unsupportive relatives when you are in the middle of trying to navigate a new situation. The judgment from family can feel unnecessary and overwhelming, considering the discrimination that transgender individuals already face. My spouse and I felt that our child's needs had to be the top priority, and so while we invited family to join us on our new journey of affirming support for our child, we also made it clear that anything less would mean they could no longer be in our lives.

It was a hard decision to make, but a stance that we both felt was best for our small family. We continued to send resources and information to our extended family during the two years that we did not speak to them, and connected to a local community for families of transgender and non-binary youth. We filled our son's weekends with playdates and community events. We created new family traditions when the holidays rolled around and built a stronger connection of trust and love with our child. At the time, the loss of family felt difficult, but as I look back, I can see the gift we were given. We were able to focus on our child's needs, while spending time connecting to community, and growing into the allies we are today.

A friend or relative posted or sent something nasty about trans people. How do I handle it?

Cristy Mereles (LCSW): Remember, most nasty things come from a place of either fear or ignorance. There are many ways to handle this, but the focus is to take care of yourself and your child first. It might be necessary to block or silence this person on your phone (and in your life) for a bit. If your child notices you could say, "Aunt Susie is still learning about gender so we are going to give her some space to work on that." If all they notice is that Aunt Susie hasn't been around, you don't need to highlight the gender piece for them, you could shrug it off as missed connections, something that sometimes happens with family or friends, and comment that you have missed seeing her too.

Whether to address this with the person who sent it to you is another thing entirely. Sometimes you can tell why this behavior is happening, which might help you decide if this is someone who might be open to learning. You do not owe it to anyone to be the gender educator. If educating family and friends is too much energy (and it often is), then freely walk away and know that they are adults capable of learning on their own.

Marsha Aizumi: A few years ago, we had an incident with an acquaintance who had written some Facebook posts that were not supportive of transgender people. We immediately called a family meeting to discuss this and indicated our position in supporting both Aiden and the transgender community. This acquaintance argued that we were trying to stop them from having an opinion. In a gentle but firm way, we responded that any opinion that threatened the safety and respect of Aiden was not acceptable. Shortly afterwards, our son Stefen cut ties with them. Stefen said that he could not be around someone who did not support Aiden. Stefen's love and loyalty to his brother is without question one of the greatest gifts he has given to Aiden and our family.

We have also had a couple of close friends who seemed unsupportive of Aiden's transition. One came from a very religious background and sent Aiden some messages that were upsetting. We know the father is very religiously opinionated, so we are no longer in close contact with that family. Another family had concerns because they had a younger child but were willing to discuss their concerns. We had a couple of meetings, listened to their concerns, and talked to Aiden about what they were comfortable with. In the end, we came up with ways that they were comfortable and ways Aiden still felt supported. Today, we are still good friends with that family.

Debi Jackson: You can respond to friends or family posting or sending you horrible things about trans people in a few different ways. If this is someone you are very close to and someone you have already tried to educate, you can choose to not engage. They are probably trying to push your buttons and are hoping for a reaction. Don't give them that. If it's a public post on social media and filled with dangerous misinformation, you could comment by sharing one informative article in response so that others on the thread can see a counterpoint, but then I'd turn off notifications or mute them so you don't have to see anything further.

If the post is from someone you see less often and haven't had much contact with, possibly someone who is extended family and might not even know you have a trans child, you could send a direct message letting them know why the post has incorrect information

or why the meme or joke is hurtful to those in the trans community, and request they remove the post. Publicly calling them out
or attempting to shame them rarely works and often causes people
to become defensive and double-down to save face. But a private
message explaining why the post is harmful gives them a chance
to ask questions or engage in dialog with you. Just don't let that
conversation turn into them gaslighting you about what they shared.
If you are offended, there's probably a very good reason. Stand your
ground, but don't be afraid to block.

Clara Lee: I understand it's not easy to change someone's mind and
heart, but at the same time I know I have to speak up even if there
is a risk of losing the battle, and also losing the person as a friend or
family member in my life. It does take mental energy and time from
my end, but I believe it's worth it. "One person at a time," has been
my mantra to keep myself going.

Through my advocacy work over the past ten years, I have connected with many LGBTQ individuals and supportive parents in
person and on social media. I have close, personal relationships with
many of them. One day, I noticed a comment made by one Korean
American gay person that made me really upset. He shared an article
on a transgender-related topic on Facebook and made a derogatory
joke about it. It was a hurtful and harmful comment. I was fully
aware that even within the cisgender LGBQ community, we still have
openly, or sometimes slightly disguised, transphobia and misogyny.
But I was furious and angry to see those hurtful comments from a
Korean gay person who was fully aware that I have a trans son, and
I support other trans individuals and their parents.

I had to let him know the impact of his comments on myself
and others. Instead of engaging him on social media, I reached out
to him via private text and told him how his remarks could be very
hurtful and harmful to trans and gender non-conforming people as
well as their families and loved ones. I asked him to remove the post.
Although he said he had freedom to speak whatever is on his mind,
he offered to remove the post per my request. Instead of attacking
him on a personal level, I was focusing on the negative impact of his
post and made my request really clear and actionable.

We are no longer comfortable going to family functions. What should we tell our children?

Kelly Storck (LCSW): I imagine this was a difficult decision you made in the name of protecting your child's safety, happiness, well-being, and brilliance. It can be very painful to realize that other people don't respect or love us in ways that support the continued growth of our relationships. Your kids may be faced with similar decisions in their life—knowing when to cut ties with people who feel unsafe or unhealthy for them—so I recommend telling them the truth about why and how you decided to cut these ties with your family. You can share that some people don't understand how gender works and that sometimes those people say and do things that are unkind and hurtful. Remind them that you believe that all people deserve respect and love and that you, as their parent, are committed to surrounding each one of them with the love, respect, joy, and affirmation that they deserve. Create room for expressions of emotion, including grief and anger, and let your kids know that it's okay to feel sad about the way these family members have chosen to act.

Debi Jackson: If you aren't comfortable going to family gatherings anymore because of how some family members act towards your child or trans people in general, be honest with your child. Of course, the conversation should be age-appropriate, but our kids are very perceptive. After all, they had to process all the gender messages our society was throwing at them to know that their gender was different from what others believed.

You might think that teens would definitely know when family isn't supportive and might tell you on their own that they no longer feel comfortable or even safe around certain family members. But I can assure you that younger kids can also pick up on even subtle signs that they are not accepted. When Avery was seven years old, my parents came to visit on their summer vacation. Avery had socially transitioned three years earlier, but because we live in different states, we only saw my family a couple of times each year. When they were visiting, Avery very quickly noticed when they hesitated to use feminine pronouns and restructured sentences to avoid them.

She went to her brother's bedroom and put one of his t-shirts over her ruffled lilac-colored shirt. Later, my mother commented that she was clearly confused and proved it by wearing both boys' and girls' clothing. I asked Avery about it, and she replied that she could tell Grandma and Grandpa weren't happy with her girls' clothes so she thought they might love her more if she put on a boy's shirt.

After that visit, I told them what happened and said we couldn't meet in person again until they fully accepted her exactly as she was. Fast-forward a few months to Christmas, and they mailed her brother a box full of toys but sent her a card with a $50 check in it. Fifty dollars is a lot to a seven-year-old, but she asked that we send it back because they weren't even trying and were trying "to buy" her love. She took a stand that day without even being asked to. She could see where the relationship was going. (Oh, and her brother asked us to mail back his gifts in solidarity to her. That's allyship in action!)

Janis Tannehill: Our out-of-state relative who didn't know, and we considered unsupportive, was easier to avoid. We were able to hide things on the phone, but in the age of Zoom and Skype we chose the path of avoidance. My trans son was in his teens and able to handle himself carefully on the phone, talking about his life in general terms and putting up with being called by the old name. For my younger children it was more difficult. We told them that Grandpa wouldn't understand and to talk about themselves and not about their trans big brother. It was really difficult for them, and I didn't like the fact that they had to keep secrets. My kids have become more and more estranged from their grandparents as time has gone on. In protecting my trans kid I did a disservice to my other children but I'm not really sure what I could have done differently.

My child doesn't want to come out to some of the family because they're likely to be unsupportive. When should they do so? Should we force the issue?

Darlene Tando (LCSW): It's always a balance to try to decide which is worse: family members not knowing about your child's authentic gender identity and misgendering them (which will likely make their dysphoria worse) or informing them, which may lead to a type of resistance or rejection. You, as the parents, can give input to your child on what you think is best, and they can let you know how this all feels regarding their dysphoria. It should not be put on the child to come out to their extended family members. While the family members may eventually want to hear more about it from the child themselves, it is usually appropriate for the parents to initially inform the other adults in the family about the transition.

Sending a letter to family members is usually a great option. This gives you the opportunity to find the words you want to say and revise them as much as necessary. You can include resources to help them understand without bombarding you (or your child) with a lot of questions. Reading the letter also gives them space to have a reaction and digest the news without you needing to hear every part of it. The letter should be written in a loving, assertive, unapologetic manner. You don't need to defend your position, just simply inform them of the changes and outline your hopes and expectations for how they can support your child. Let your child read the letter and make changes as needed before sending it.

Noah Berlatsky: Don't force your child to come out to people they fear will be unsupportive. Your child is probably dealing with a lot of uncertainty and anxiety; if they don't think they're ready to tell someone, they're probably not ready to tell someone. Your first responsibility is to your child's health, safety, and well-being. You aren't obligated to put that at risk for anyone, not even family members.

Clara Lee: It's important to discuss a coming-out process with the child and devise a plan that the child feels comfortable with, even if it means holding off on coming out. Offering to come out to friends and family on the child's behalf might help change the child's mind.

After making the decision to support my son's transition, his father and I wanted to show the world how proud we were of our son. For those who did not know our son before the transition, he passed as a nice-looking Asian boy. For others who knew our child before the transition, they had to go through the coming-out process. There were a few compelling reasons that gave us courage to come out to those who knew our child as a girl.

The most important reason was our desire for our son to continue to be part of the community of friends and family members who have loved him dearly from his birth. We wanted them to join our journey by accepting, supporting, and loving our son. The other reason was because of the physical changes that our son was beginning to go through due to hormone therapy, which included a deepened voice and facial hair; we wanted to make sure people understood why they would see those changes in our child. The last reason was our desire for them not only to accept our child but also to bring more awareness of the broader LGBTQ community to those who would not know otherwise.

Before coming out to our friends and family, we consulted with our son and drew up the following guidelines on what we wanted to tell others. First, we assured those who knew our child that he was still the same person whom they loved and adored. Two, we clearly described our expectations of them to respect our child's new gender identity and refer to him with his new male name and male pronouns. Third, we offered to help with any questions they might have. We also decided on the method of coming out (email, letter, or in person), timing (in one shot or slowly breaking the news), and who would come out to whom (I talked to my parents in LA, and his father to his family in Korea). We then divided the friends and families into multiple groups: those within a same circle of friends, those whom we felt really close to and trusted, and those who would have difficulty due to their cultural background, religious beliefs, or conservative upbringing. We also tried to set realistic expectations so as not to get too disappointed and be able to move on with our life if the response was not positive or accepting.

Janis Tannehill: We were very selective about who we told what and when as a matter of safety. My brother-in-law's exact words were, "Dad is going to flip, I wouldn't put it past him to call CPS on you." For this reason alone, our out-of-state grandparents didn't know a thing until my son turned 18 and they couldn't touch him. The plan was always for my son to come out to them when he was ready and after he was 18, but it took more cajoling than I thought it would take to make it happen. My son told me that even though he knew they couldn't hurt him legally or physically, it would still hurt him emotionally if his grandparents didn't love him anymore.

Not having a relationship with them, and wondering if they would react badly, was different from the worst-case scenario of knowing for a fact that they didn't love him anymore. It took quite a bit of hand holding, but he did it. I would say the reaction was kind of in the middle, and like most things in life, not great but never as bad as you make it out to be in your mind.

A relative sent me something about trans kids, but how can I tell if it's good information?

Sebastian M. Barr, PhD: Unfortunately, there is a lot of misinformation about gender diversity and trans youth. Some of this comes from good intentions and a misunderstanding of the research, and sadly some of the misinformation comes from deliberate efforts to create barriers to care and life satisfaction for trans people. The latter category is often tied to individuals who call themselves "gender critical" or "GC." Groups espousing a "gender critical" ideology have been known to spread false information distorting research and anecdotal evidence. Because of parents' fears of getting things wrong, their discomfort with non-normative gender experiences, or general bewilderment at the newness of it all, some of the misinformation can be appealing. This is because it often lacks nuance and positions parents as all-knowing and in the driver's seat. When things feel shaky, of course we may feel comforted or drawn to this type of discourse. Thus, it's important to be careful about who we are trusting as experts.

It's valuable for parents to know that there is a lot of high-quality research on trans people and on gender diversity and gender development in youth. There's also a robust body of literature on gender-affirming healthcare. (For example, Dr. Jack Turban put together a list of more than a dozen studies on gender-affirming medical interventions for youth for *Psychology Today*, as of January 2022, with more coming out every month.[2]) First-person accounts from trans people and/or supportive families of trans or gender-exploring youth can be useful, but we don't need to rely solely on anecdotal stories anymore.

If you are reading information that doesn't adequately cite peer-reviewed research sources, or only has a handful of studies, researchers, or clinicians mentioned, that should be a red flag, indicating cherry-picking of the research. Additionally, major medical organizations including the American Medical Association and the American Psychological Association have issued evidence-based position statements, fact sheets, and guidelines related to trans youth. If you come across writing that seems out of step with those positions, be aware that this indicates that what you are reading is out of step with research, experts, and clinical/professional consensus.

Another thing to consider is whether the information you're reading comes from trans people or incorporates trans perspectives. Are trans people quoted in the article? Are the researchers or authors involved part of the trans community? It is a good idea to be somewhat skeptical of outsider perspectives and information, though an author's transness alone should not be considered a green flag—they still need to be in line with the research. A good step is to search the internet for the writer of whatever information has been shared with you. Do they seem to have expertise or direct community experience? What groups are they affiliated with and who supports or challenges their work? When you search for them, are there evidence-based rebuttals of their writing? Don't be afraid to be skeptical—in fact, you *should* be skeptical, particularly when information comes from popular press or other non-peer-reviewed sources.

There are also some general themes to look for that can be red flags indicting that the information is outdated, debunked, or was spread in bad faith. The first is what we in the trans research community call "The Desistance Myth." Many excellent trans people and researchers have thoroughly debunked this mythology,[3] and yet you

---

2   www.psychologytoday.com/us/blog/political-minds/202201/the-evidence-trans-youth-gender-affirming-medical-care
3   www.huffpost.com/entry/the-end-of-the-desistance_b_8903690

will see some groups repeating that a high proportion of youth who identify as trans will not identify as trans in adulthood. This simply is not true and is based on old research that didn't differentiate between young people who didn't conform to gender stereotypes, and young people who actually identified with a gender different from the gender they were assigned.[4]

The second theme you may see included in misinformation is an overemphasis on individuals who were not satisfied with their transition, or experienced turbulence around their identity after taking gender-affirming steps. Although this experience is rare (with studies of both community members and gender-affirming healthcare providers suggesting a prevalence of regret of less than 1 percent),[5,6] some groups looking to inflate the sense of riskiness in gender affirmation will share stories to make the occurrence of regrets and what some call "detransition" appear much more common than it is. Additionally, the limited research on individuals who identify as having detransitioned suggests that a great deal of the regret experienced is related to oppression and challenges with marginalization (e.g., family rejection or difficulty finding jobs because of anti-trans bias).[7] Discussion of the experience of detransitioning or having regrets related to transition is not inherently flawed or indicative of bad research—in fact, there's a need for better research in this area to support the small number of people who experience

---

4   Temple Newhook, J., Pyne, J., Winters, K., Feder, S., *et al.* (2018). A critical commentary on follow-up studies and "desistance" theories about transgender and gender-nonconforming children. *International Journal of Transgenderism, 19*(2), 212–224.

5   Narayan, S. K., Hontscharuk, R., Danker, S., Guerriero, J., *et al.* (2021). Guiding the conversation: Types of regret after gender-affirming surgery and their associated etiologies. *Annals of Translational Medicine, 9*(7), 605. doi: 10.21037/atm-20-6204. PMID: 33987303; PMCID: PMC8105823

6   Bustos, V. P., Bustos, S. S., Mascaro, A., Del Corral, G., *et al.* (2021). Regret after gender-affirmation surgery: A systematic review and meta-analysis of prevalence. *Plastic and Reconstructive Surgery. Global Open, 9*(3), e3477. https://doi.org/10.1097/GOX.0000000000003477

7   McLemore, K. A. (2018). A minority stress perspective on transgender individuals' experiences with misgendering. *Stigma and Health, 3*(1), 53–64.

this[8]—but articles that suggest a higher prevalence of regret than is supported by the research, and articles that use instances of regret or detransition to argue against helping people access gender-affirming care, are often written and promoted in bad faith.

The third red flag theme is a causal relationship between mental health concerns and gender exploration or trans identity. One of the most robust research findings related to mental health and the trans experience is that the overall increased risk for poor mental health that trans people face is tied to our society's stigma against and non-affirmation of trans people, and the unique stressors and traumas that trans people face because of this.[9] There is no research that supports the idea that a trans identity can be born out of psychological distress or mental illness, so articles that suggest this are not speaking from a perspective informed by actual evidence.

The fourth theme to look out for, growing in viral spread but lacking any evidence, is the idea that transness is a social contagion. Some groups are using the term "rapid onset gender dysphoria" or ROGD to describe youth who come out as trans in adolescence or early adulthood without visible signs to their parents of gender dysphoria before coming out. Individuals and groups who promote the existence of ROGD typically argue that it is related to peer/social contagion rather than a true inner identity as trans.[10] Individuals and groups looking to reduce access to gender-affirming care often use ROGD to scare parents and loved ones away from supporting their youth who come out as trans. There is no research basis to support this construct or to support the idea that a young person or adult had to have signs of gender dysphoria at an early age to "really" be trans

---

8   MacKinnon, K. R., Ashley, F., Kia, H., Lam, J. S. H., Krakowsky, Y., & Ross, L. E. (2021). Preventing transition "regret": An institutional ethnography of gender-affirming medical care assessment practices in Canada. *Social Science & Medicine, 291,* 114477.

9   Valentine, S. E. & Shipherd, J. C. (2018). A systematic review of social stress and mental health among transgender and gender non-conforming people in the United States. *Clinical Psychology Review, 66,* 24–38; Barr, S. M., Snyder, K. E., Adelson, J. L., & Budge, S. L. (2021). Posttraumatic stress in the trans community: The roles of anti-transgender bias, non-affirmation, and internalized transphobia. *Psychology of Sexual Orientation and Gender Diversity.* https://doi.org/10.1037/sgd0000500

10 Ashley, F. (2020). A critical commentary on "rapid-onset gender dysphoria." *The Sociological Review, 68*(4), 779–799.

or need to transition. The term came out of a set of interviews with non-supportive parents, sampled from gender-critical groups and forums; this single study has had its methodologies widely criticized and was partially redacted because of this.[11] Conversely, when the ROGD hypothesis was tested in a controlled, clinical environment, it proved to be untrue.[12]

Dozens of major medical, mental health, and research organizations co-signed a statement stating clearly that ROGD is not supported by research. They support "eliminating the use of ROGD and similar concepts for clinical and diagnostic application, given the lack of empirical support for its existence and its likelihood of contributing to harm and mental health burden."[13] Signatories included the American Psychological Association, the American Psychiatric Association, the Society for Research in Child Development, and more. If you read an article that uses the term ROGD, it is out of step with these and many more major organizations and should not be trusted. Further, the only research to critically evaluate the idea of social contagion resolutely debunked it. In this study of trans youth, recency of trans identity was not associated with significant differences in levels of gender dysphoria, connection to other trans youth, or involvement in online trans spaces.[14] So if the information you are reading promotes social contagion as a factor in trans identity development, you can feel confident that it is not grounded in evidence.

Other red flags to consider are if the information refers to "youth who identify as trans" or "gender dysphoric youth" rather than "trans youth," or if the information overemphasizes young people's assigned gender or sex assigned at birth by using terms like "biological males" or "natal females" instead of the gender identities of the young people.

11   Restar, A. J. (2019). Methodological critique of Littman's (2018) parental-respondents accounts of "rapid-onset gender dysphoria". *Archives of Sexual Behavior, 49*(1): 61–66. doi:10.1007/s10508-019-1453-2

12   Bauer, G. R., Lawson, M. L., & Metzger, D. L. (2021). Do clinical data from transgender adolescents support the phenomenon of "rapid onset gender dysphoria"? *The Journal of Pediatrics.* https://doi.org/10.1016/j.jpeds.2021.11.020

13   www.caaps.co/rogd-statement

14   Bauer, G. R., Lawson, M. L., & Metzger, D. L. (2021). Do clinical data from transgender adolescents support the phenomenon of "rapid onset gender dysphoria"? *The Journal of Pediatrics.* https://doi.org/10.1016/j.jpeds.2021.11.020

These errors indicate a lack in being up-to-date with the literature and the trans community, and/or intentional non-affirmation.

Two final tips that came from my trans research colleagues:

- It's helpful to be connected to members of the trans and gender-diverse community, affirming providers who are knowledgeable about the research, and organizations that can help you make sense of what information is and isn't evidence based.
- Ask the person sending you the information where they learned about it and why they are sending it to you. Sometimes you can get a sense of the potential bias and evidence-base for an article by sussing out these motivations.

Amy Cannava (NASP): This is a tricky one. Statistics can be used to twist just about anything, and you can't always believe what you read. The University of Washington has published guidelines to help readers think critically (italics added): [15]

Five W questions—help readers to think critically about the source of the information

1. Who is the author? (Authority) What authority does the author have to write what is written? Where does their knowledge come from?
2. What is the purpose of the content? (Accuracy)
3. Where is the content from? (Publisher) *Content published by the same organization who wrote the material is rarely peer-reviewed.*
4. Why does the source exist? (Purpose and objectivity)
5. How does this source compare to others? (Determining what's what)

---

15 University of Washington (n.d.). "FAQ: How do I know if my sources are credible/reliable?" Accessed 02/05/2022 at https://guides.lib.uw.edu/research/faq/reliable

Source check

1. Source: Who or what is the source? Where did the author get their material from? What is the basis for their views?
2. Motive: Why do they say what they do? Scare tactics and inflammatory language are not used in reputable and empirically sound writing.
3. Authority: Who wrote the story? What is the author of the piece known for?.
4. Review: Is there anything included that jumps out as potentially untrue? Remember that scientifically and statistically, words like "always" and "never" are rare finds.
5. Two-source tests: How does it compare to another source?

CRAAP test

1. Currency: Timeliness of the information
2. Relevance: Importance of the information for your needs
3. Authority: Source of the information
4. Accuracy: Truthfulness and correctness of the information
5. Purpose: Reason the information exists

Sometimes it's easier to figure out what to disregard rather than what is "good." Here are some ideas for how to do this:

- Stay clear of intentionally inciteful words such as "gender confusion," "social contagion," "agenda," "prefer," or "preference."
- Steer away from resources which conflate or confuse sexual orientation and gender identity.
- Be critical of writing by cisgender people who compare their experience to that of a transgender person to downplay the experience of someone else.
- Be mindful of similar-sounding organizations whose viewpoints are quite contrary to one another. For example, the American Academy of Pediatrics is a reputable organization with more than 67,000 members. It is not associated with another smaller organization of religious conservatives

(American College of Pediatricians) which has a similar name designed to confuse readers.

- Remember that recommendations for transgender healthcare should be taken from the World Professional Association for Transgender Health (WPATH) Standards of Care, and the American Academy of Pediatrics.
- Remember that laws and policies which support LGBTQ persons are not passed in secret. That's not how laws work. Laws are proposed and then voted on by those who are entrusted by the populace. Executive orders, on the other hand, are made by one person without requiring a vote.
- Fact check. Think about your own gender-diverse child—have you been more worried about them hurting others or being hurt by others? Transgender people are more likely to be the victim of crimes than the perpetrators of them.

Debi Jackson: If anyone sends you something about trans kids, check the source before you even read it. If it's from a far-right or religious publication (Fox News, One America News, Infowars, the Blaze, The Federalist, Focus on the Family), know that they have an anti-LGBTQ slant and their coverage will not include positive trans stories, voices of happy trans people, or any reference to studies recognized by major medical organizations.[16] Look for more neutral sources with a reputation for fair reporting and fact-checking, like National Public Radio, Time, Reuters, The Hill, or the Associated Press.

If a study is cited, look it up to see if it was published in a peer-reviewed journal or a pay-for-publication journal. Look up the authors or anyone cited as an expert such as a doctor, therapist, endocrinologist, or social worker to see if they actually work with transgender or gender-variant youth. Check any organizations that are referenced or who any of the experts are associated with. For example, the American College of Pediatricians sounds like a legitimate organization, but in reality, it is a very small group of people

---

16 Langlois, S. (2018). "How biased is your news source? You probably won't agree with this chart." MarketWatch, 21 April 2018. Accessed 06/07/2022 at www.marketwatch.com/story/how-biased-is-your-news-source-you-probably-wont-agree-with-this-chart-2018-02-28

who oppose transgender healthcare (and other LGBTQ rights, like the ability for same-sex couples to foster or adopt children).

If you are in doubt, there are many online support groups where you can ask for input from others about the information, authors, or experts quoted in the study. The same few anti-trans people are quoted frequently and often, and the group can flag a poor source for you within minutes.

How do we correct people when they ask how our son/daughter is doing?

Dr. Matt Goldenberg: When a family member begins a gender transition, a key question arises: "Whose story is this to tell?" As a parent, you may have your own articulation of what you are seeing and how you understand your child. Tender tendrils of attachment to your baby—this person in whose well-being you are so invested—take shape, with gender as a critical aspect of who that person will be. Parents experience the significance of gender from the beginning, whether that be in gifts given to welcome the child home, the cultural significance of the child's name, and even the picture of their future. It can be bewildering to realize how much gender has played a role in forming who we are, so the questions of who is in the best position to tell the story becomes an ongoing and challenging question.

Over time, and especially with the proliferation of social media, it is hard to keep track of who knows what information about a person's gender transition. Ask your child what information they would like shared and with whom. Offer to talk to others or answer questions on their behalf. If your child is open to you speaking about their transition, it gives you an opportunity to connect with your friends and family about the amazing experiences you are having. If you and your child have spoken and it seems as if you are in a good position to correct others, try to do so with compassion for your child.

When we imagine the person we are speaking about is present and listening, it can positively influence what we say. For instance, you can respond with, "Oh, thanks for asking! Our child has been talking to us about gender, and we are using a different name and pronoun from now on. Can you use this name and pronoun too when you ask about them?" In this way, you are extending gratitude for the opportunity to talk about your child, and you are inviting the other person to come along with you. If they forget or are having trouble with using the right name and pronouns, simply correct them and move on.

Darlene Tando (LCSW): "Actually" is a great way to interject or lead into the conversation. For example, if they ask you about your "daughter," you could say, "Actually…" It is a great way to pause the conversation and let them know you are going to provide them with correct information. It also can buy you a couple seconds to decide how you want to say it. "Actually, we recently found out he's my son! His pronouns are…and he's going by the name…" If you share this assertively with positive energy, the people in your life will read that from you and absorb it as neutral or positive information.

Marsha Aizumi: Since Aiden transitioned over ten years ago, most people either know about Aiden transitioning or only know Aiden as my son. But in the past, when people have asked, I have just stated that our child transitioned from being our daughter and is now our son, Aiden. At a time when the term transgender was not greatly understood, I had to explain a bit more depending on who was asking. And to be honest, it was a bit awkward and uncomfortable for me and the people who were asking, just because over ten years ago, there were no visible people like Caitlyn Jenner, Laverne Cox, Elliot Page, Jazz Jennings and others. The only person who seemed to be in the news was Chaz Bono.

Even ten years ago, acknowledging my child as my son, even if it was awkward, made me feel proud of being a courageous mother who could tell the truth. However, I did not live in a city or state where I felt unsafe, and in many cases it would be obvious that my child was no longer my daughter, especially after Aiden had been on HRT for some time. I remember at one retirement party for a teacher, Aiden was really nervous to attend, but it was a favorite teacher. It was early on in his transition, so many people did not know. There were a few uncomfortable moments and looks of confusion, but I just carried on as if it was nothing unusual.

Today, if someone asks about Aiden, it would not be awkward or uncomfortable for me. I know that it was the best decision that we could have made to support our son. So I would respond with confidence and pride that Aiden is my son, he is living as his true self, and we are so proud of his courage to be authentic and honest in who he is.

Clara Lee: Even after coming out to family, friends, and co-workers who accept and support us, people sometimes would make mistakes about my son's gender and name. I would simply correct them and move on. Most people would apologize and do their best to not make mistakes again.

I was working for a financial company in NYC for more than ten years when my son came out. Once I came out to my co-workers, I started to use "my child" or "my son" when I spoke about my personal life, and everyone was on board, respecting my son's new name and gender. One time, one of my former co-workers who had moved to a different team joined us for a happy hour gathering after work, greeted me and asked about my daughter. I was a bit taken back and didn't want to get into coming out mode in a big social gathering setting. I quickly responded, "Oh I have a son, not a daughter" and a few people from the current team also chimed in to support me, "Yeah, Clara has a son." He then made a quick apology and we moved on to different topics.

After I became more comfortable about coming out to people without getting emotional about it, I actually set up a time with the former co-worker and came out to him officially since I didn't want him to think he had a memory lapse issue. He totally understood and became an active ally in the firm's LGBTQ network. Another time, I saw a co-worker from a previous team in front of the elevator. She and I used to share tips on childcare and swap school news. When she asked me about my child, I noticed I had extra time before my next meeting. I asked her, "Hey, do you have five minutes?" Then asked if she knew about Caitlyn Jenner, who recently went through transitioning publicly through a TV show. I told her that my son is transgender like Caitlyn Jenner except that it was transitioning to male and that I was so happy my son didn't have to wait until his sixties to transition, unlike Jenner. And that was that. She was grateful that I shared the important news with her.

Janis Tannehill: It depends on how well you know them. Most of the time you can get away with a minor correction and moving on since people usually don't want to call attention to this kind of thing in public. Anything from, "How is your daughter?" "Oh, I have a son, he's doing fine," or if you know them better, "Well, my daughter is now my son and he goes by 'Y' now." If this is someone who knows better, I usually treat them as if they are the forgetful one, "'X' is going by 'Y' now, if you remember" or, "*He* is doing fine." If people are not supportive, they have probably told you so by now and for your own sanity, limit your interaction with them. Remember, if someone pushes you into a corner, always choose your kid. "You know I can't condone that kind of thing" should be met with, "Then we have nothing more to talk about" and walking away from them and your friendship.

My spouse just tries to keep ignoring the fact that our child came out as trans and refuses to engage. What should I do?

Darlene Tando (LCSW): It's quite common for one parent to come around and be supportive first, before the other. This can be for a variety of reasons, but it doesn't mean the other partner loves the child any less. Typically, it is a result of conditioning from childhood, attachment to the gender of the child, potential societal stigma, fears, and assumptions; the list goes on. I always liken this journey to two people having to walk a tightrope together; it can certainly be hard if both are not headed towards the same goal. The affirming parent may feel the urge to push their spouse away in the face of behaviors that do not seem affirming. This may create a rift between the parents, and potentially create more resistance from the other parent. Instead, picture pulling your spouse towards you. "Yes, this is hard. But we can do what we need to do for the good of our child." "Yes, this is scary, but we are in this together." "Yes, I felt that way at first too, but here is what I have learned..."

The most important thing is to stay steadfast in your affirmation of your child while gently trying to help your spouse engage. Eventually, you may need to make some expectations of behaviors clear, particularly in order to avoid damage to your trans youth. Finding other parents to connect with can be incredibly beneficial. If your spouse is not ready for a support group, ask the group or perhaps a therapist to connect you with another set of parents to have coffee with or talk about this often-difficult part of the beginning of the journey.

My spouse/family member reacted badly (e.g., freaked out) when our child came out. How can I get them to calm down and work with us on this?

Dr. Matt Goldenberg: It can often be helpful to engage with a family counselor to have more successful conversations with each other. There may be underlying dynamics that are getting in the way of your family member acting as their better self. A counselor or therapist may be in a better position to increase alignment for the family because they are not invested in being right, being persuasive, or benefitting from the discussions. The therapist or counselor can ask more difficult questions or say things that others have a hard time hearing.

You are not in charge or responsible for other people's emotions, but you can influence how others behave. If you and the other family member have equal authority in your family, then it might feel more comfortable to approach them and attempt to do an assessment of how things are going: "Honey, we need to talk about (child's name). I know it's a lot to adjust to, and we both have a lot of questions and concerns. How do you think we are doing so far?" As observations are made, focus on positive feedback for others and not moving into criticism.

You might also negotiate some family rules regarding how you talk about your transitioning child. For example, consider avoiding conversations that might express anger, worry, or fear around your child. Even if your transitioning family member is an adult, it can be hurtful and unnecessarily raise defenses and contribute to misunderstandings to process all your thoughts and emotions with the transitioning person right there. Consider that your child is already dealing with their own questions and concerns, such as what the future will hold. Asking a transitioning person to also deal with all our reactions, no matter how fleeting or intense they are, is simply unfair.

Many family members will evolve in their own understanding and subsequent reactions to gender transition. When we are guided by our own values, we are less likely to experience distress. It may be helpful to encourage your family member to think about the relationship they want with your child, and what behaviors they can do to help pave the way to connection. Blaming, distancing, minimizing, and rejecting others is not the way to connection, but these reactions can happen when experiencing grief. We move towards our better self with understanding, compassion, and clear boundaries.

As you and your family navigate a gender transition, know that you will have so many new opportunities to build a lasting bond with each other and to re-write stories of how you may have not really known each other before. See this as the beautiful opportunity for transformation it is, and over time it will be clear what gifts each can give to others.

Nathan Glickler: They need information. Tell them that you love your child no matter what, and that being non-supportive dramatically increases the chances of them self-harming. Tell them that being supportive dramatically drops these risks. Tell them this isn't about them, it's about your child and their needs. It is important to note that this won't necessarily change anything. You can't "get them to calm down and work with [you]" because you cannot force their reaction. You can only hope they are mature enough to listen.

Our child is transitioning and doesn't want to visit family members they're not out to. What should we do?

Darlene Tando (LCSW): It can be difficult to balance this during the transition, when not everyone knows. I call this the "limbo stage" and it can be tough for kids and parents alike. Your child may be thrilled about being known and affirmed at home, making it even more difficult to go to other settings where the wrong name and pronouns will be used. Talk with your child about how to best support them in the coming out process. Having parents write a letter to extended family members is often the best strategy. Make the letter a simple explanation of the change in names/pronouns/appearance if applicable. Let family members know what they can do to make you and your child feel supported. Provide resources in the letter. This sets the stage for going to visit when your child is ready. In the meantime, you may need to make visits on your own or forego some of the visits yourself. The good news is that this limbo stage is temporary!

Clara Lee: I think it's important to engage with the child and take cues from them on when to come out to the family members. I waited for my son to feel comfortable interacting with other family members and offered support and tangible help when needed. I have a large extended immigrant family that immigrated from Korea in the 1970s and mostly live in Southern California. After coming out to a handful of close family members successfully in the span of a few years, I started sending annual Christmas cards to the extended family with my son's new name and photo, clearly showing him transitioned into a typical boy with a short haircut and male clothes.

There is a beautiful tradition in Korean culture: family gossiping. I was hoping the family members would get curious and start processing things on their own after seeing the latest photo of my son with his new name. I did not take my son when I visited my parents and other extended family in Southern California, with the good excuse that he was busy with schoolwork. After a few more years, many of my relatives knew about my son, mostly the younger generation. Some quietly talked about it and decided not to make a big deal of it, but some were still guessing. A few years ago, my niece was graduating from college and invited me to the graduation ceremony on the west coast. I asked my son to join me, and he got to meet some of his distant cousins, aunts, uncles, great-aunts, and great-uncles during the trip, for the first time since his transition. He was treated as a young man and hung out with his cousins. Only one person, my uncle who was in his seventies, did not know or maybe forgot and was asking about my daughter. I pulled him aside and quickly corrected him. Fortunately, other elderly relatives including my mom stayed with him and skillfully changed the subject to keep him busy. The trip itself was a big step for me and my son, to know he is loved for who he is by this large extended family.

Janis Tannehill: Right before my son came out to the rest of the immediate family, I insisted on visiting the out-of-state relatives for the holidays in case this was the last time he would be able to see them. If things went badly when he came out, I wanted him to have that memory of things being "normal." It sucked. It was extremely stressful for him to be taken shopping for the wrong clothes and to be called the wrong name, to be told they were a beautiful young lady—all the things you do and say when family comes to visit. The depressive episode this triggered made it very apparent that I couldn't put him through that again. It also galvanized his desire to come out since living as his true self had to be better that being locked in a pink closet. Respect your child's wishes: if they don't want to visit family they are not out to they shouldn't have to, since they are the ones who will have to pay the emotional price for being made to do so.

Relatives keep using the wrong name and pronouns with our child. It's really hurting their feelings. What should I do?

Dr. Matt Goldenberg: If your child has decided to be out and will be using different pronouns or a different name, you can provide the repetition needed for the relatives to learn to also use new pronouns or a new name. For instance, a statement like, "They are using different pronouns and a new name from now on, so when you hear me talk about them either in the present or past tense, you will hear the new name and pronoun. Please try to use the new name and pronoun too, and if you make a mistake, I will let you know so you can try again. This will take some getting used to, but I think if we help each other out, we can get it down." Sometimes there are cues that can help, such as creating a new email address or screen name for your child, so that when relatives are in touch, they have a reminder of the correct name. Given that you can use a different name in most digital spaces, this is often a useful place to start before any legal changes occur.

You can also decide when to correct people who misgender your child or use the wrong name. For instance, you may decide that *after* a conversation in which misgendering occurs is a better time for a discussion. Often people are worried about being rude or interrupting others, or they avoid saying something because drawing attention to a problem can feel as if you are causing conflict. However, remember that you are speaking for your child and on behalf of their integrity. It may never feel like the right time for a hard conversation, and correcting our relatives and others who misgender our children is a hard conversation. Keep your objectives in mind, though: what you are aiming for is that your relatives can get to know these integral parts of your child, so they can maintain and progress in their connections to you and to your family.

Janis Tannehill: Relatives, especially those you see often, really do need to get with the program. I like the anecdote where every time a family member misgendered a person at Thanksgiving dinner, someone hit an airhorn, thereby solving the problem in two minutes.

The soft sell is that, in using your trans kid's correct name and pronouns, they are supporting your kid—and not using them hurts your kid's feelings. Often family members don't take each other seriously; we gossip about how this family member or that is a flake, or weird, or a screw up, and say, "Oh, that's just them, I wonder what caper they will be up to tomorrow." Explaining that this isn't a joke or a phase, but something serious that you and your kid are struggling with may get the point across. Most people want to support you and your family but are just honestly forgetful. Calm, gentle reminders like, "X is going by Y now" or, "He, not she" are a good place to start.

The hard sell is that you are in a fight for your child's survival. With an attempted suicide rate of over 40 percent for transgender people, these are not odds you want to mess around with. Lack of support by family is the number one predictor of suicide, so acceptance and support from extended family is doubly important. If you have read this far, the chances are these family members are not as accepting as you had originally hoped. You need to explain to family that if they can't accept your kid, you will cut them out of your kid's life, and it will be their choice and their own fault. If grown adults can't accept that a kid needs a correct name and pronouns to feel safe, it says more about them than you. Just as parents need to own that we are responsible for our child's safety, extended family needs to understand when they are not.

Our child came out as trans. How do we explain this to older family members (e.g., Grandma) who have never met a trans person, or even thought about it before?

Dr. Matt Goldenberg: Concern that your family members may have little understanding of gender diversity is common, as is the worry that a family member's views on gender diversity are problematic. When coming out or sharing the news that your child has come out, it may be helpful to think ahead of time about what you are willing to share and what questions you prefer not to answer. For instance, you may want to share resources you have found helpful, but may not want to share medical information. It can be helpful to consider ahead of time what the structure of the conversation can be. A recommendation is to start by sharing why you want the family member to know about your child's gender. Something like "I want to talk to you about my child, because you are so important to all of us and we want you to be involved with our lives as much as possible. If you have questions about what we are going to discuss, here are some websites/books/articles to check out. It's okay if you aren't sure what to say or if you have strong reactions. I just ask you to keep in mind that we can talk more about this later."

If you discover that your family member indeed does not have any experience with the trans community, you might offer them media with positive representations of LGBTQ lives. Sometimes it can make conversations easier when there is a point of reference somewhat removed from the family. It also can reduce any pressure on your child as the center of attention, which can be burdensome for youth.

Nathan Glickler: Explain what being transgender is—that it just happens and is beyond anyone's control. Tell them about the statistics on suicide, and that you love your child no matter what. Sometimes older people aren't very understanding; other times you may learn something about them you didn't know. Remember, they grew up in a different time and may have had to suppress parts of themselves. Seeing your support for your child might help them as well.

Paria Hassouri: When my daughter came out, I was very worried about telling my parents, particularly my mom. I was expecting her to have a negative reaction, but her immediate response was to hear the worry in my voice and say that everything was going to be okay. I questioned whether she had even understood me, so I repeated it, saying that this wasn't about being gay but about gender, and explaining the difference. Again, whether she fully understood or not, she repeated that everything would be okay. Now, obviously, not every elderly relative's reaction is going to be a positive one, but in our support group of families with trans youth, I've heard more unexpected positive and supportive reactions from grandparents than negative ones. So first, I would say be honest, genuine, and firm in what you have to tell an elderly loved one—but also give them the chance and the benefit of the doubt. They may just surprise you when it comes to someone they love.

If they have a negative reaction, then you must remember that your priority is to protect your child over the feelings of an older relative, even your own mother's feelings. You simply explain to anyone who doesn't support you that you welcome their questions, and they should take some time, but that until they are ready to support your child, they are going to have to be away from your family. Protect and prioritize your child over anyone else's feelings or beliefs. It really is that simple.

Clara Lee: It's important to remind the older family members that your child is still the same person and to provide a simple explanation of what it means to be a trans person. Showing family members you are 100 percent supportive of your child as parents creates a positive impression. Some people value what other people think, so having some facts and resources handy will help answer their questions.

I have a large extended immigrant family, that immigrated from Korea in the 1970s and mostly live in Southern California. With my parents and siblings who live in Los Angeles, I took an approach of talking to them individually whenever I visited. Because I live far from my parents and extended family, I really didn't have to tell them right away while my son was transitioning. Since my son was busy with school, it was a good excuse not to take him to family functions until he felt comfortable. The first set of people I came out to was my two younger sisters and my dad. I always had a really good relationship with them, so it was more of a brief heart-to-heart talk with them when I visited for a family gathering.

The biggest challenge was my mother, who was 72 years old at that time and a devout Catholic. My mom was supposed to come to my son's high school graduation the following year, and I wanted to make sure she knew before she came. This is what I did: about a year before the graduation, I planted a bug in my mom's ear. I told her a white lie that my son recently came out as a lesbian and was still trying to figure things out just like any other teenagers in America. I highlighted the fact that LGBTQ was not something bad and that I wanted to give her a heads up just in case. She took it well, and I think she saw it as a sign that I needed support from her as my mother. And six months later, I told her the truth in a very straightforward, simple way. I asked if she knew a famous Korean transgender actress Harisu and I told her that same thing was happening to my son but just in reverse. I gave her a brief explanation and told her that we had decided to support my son's transition.

I think she was taken aback, and she stayed quiet for some time.

Then she recommended that I went to talk to the priest at church. I told her that currently most churches did not accept LGBTQ people, so talking to the priest could actually harm my family. I told her we had already gone to the medical and mental health specialists. I reminded her that my son was still the same person inside and we as parents would support him no matter what. My mom asked if the in-laws knew about this. I told her that they already knew and were very supportive, which was true.

She replied, "Well, as long as you've made your decision, what can I say?" My sisters, who lived close to my mom, were very helpful answering some of the questions my mom would later ask, such as, "Will Aiden get AIDS?" or ,"Your sister's family is like this because they don't go to church." I was getting nervous and did not know what to expect from my mother. My parents and my sister's family came to my son's high school graduation. And surprisingly, my mom was absolutely wonderful. Later, I found out she had seen the interview of Lana Wachowski, the transgender director of the movie *Cloud Atlas,* on a Korean talk show. She finally understood what it means to be a transgender person, and that transgender people need support from the family to live a happy and healthy life. I saw the power of positive images in the media.

Janis Tannehill: You'd be surprised about what Grandma knows, or Great-Grandma for that matter. You just might find out more about your family tree than you ever thought possible, like that cousin who went on vacation as Lucy and came back as Luke when Great-Grandma was a kid. There have always been transgender people, but no one talked about it. People were either quietly disowned, died in a fiery car crash to be born again somewhere else, or the new reality was the truth and the past ignored.

The difference now is that we, as a society, talk about it more, make laws for and against LGBTQ people, and work to fight injustice as a result. When senior citizens are asked what they would change about their lives they almost universally say they wish they had worried less about what people thought and lived more the way they wanted to.

How do I even begin to tell my Christian family about my child's name and pronouns?

Darlene Tando (LCSW): It can be scary to disclose to family members who may not be accepting. It's important for the parent to ground themselves in their truth and the truth of their child before having such conversations. Remind yourself that you, and your child, are doing nothing wrong. If others feel that is the case, that cannot be controlled.

Parents can deliver the news of their child's new name and pronouns with a positive, assertive energy. This communicates they are not sharing "bad news" and are also not looking for feedback. If negative feedback is given, parents do not need to respond as if in battle. You can say, "I'm sorry you feel that way" or, "Yes, many people feel the way you do. However, we feel...." Let them know that they can have some time to adjust but ultimately the expectation is that they use the accurate name and pronouns for the child.

Nathan Glickler: You do need to prepare your family so they know, but they won't always be supportive. In my book, that's a "get on board or get out" situation. I will cut anyone out of my life who can't support my children. I would love to say that I remind them that Jesus never said anything about transgender people and only had negative things to say about people based on their wealth or how they behaved. "Love thy neighbor" and "Whatever you do to the least of you, you do to me" and all that. Unfortunately, people tend to bristle when you point out how they are failing to behave in accordance with their own faith's guidelines.

I would say, as long as you don't live in a state where they can take your child away if you are supportive, just be straightforward and matter of fact. Tell them this is how it is, and if they start objecting, tell them you are telling them, not asking them. If they have a problem with it, they have no business being part of your child's life.

Chapter 6

Mental Health and Medical Care

For most trans youth, therapy is part of the process. Parents looking for a therapist for the first time often have questions, including where to find one who has expertise in the field. Many trans youth go on to medically transition later. These treatments can involve puberty blockers at first, hormone replacement therapy, and potentially surgery later. Finding appropriate, experienced healthcare providers is a big part of many parents' worries, as are questions about whether this is the right thing to do. The subject matter experts in this chapter provide the theory and practice behind transition-related medical and mental health care for trans youth. Parents who have gone through every facet of transition with their kids help give context, and practical advice for how they approached a phase in transition that can often be daunting.

What questions do you wish you had asked, or had suggested asking, while looking for a therapist/ counselor/doctor for your trans child?

Dr. Matt Goldenberg: There is basic information that you may want to ask when choosing a therapist. Here is a (non-comprehensive) list of potential considerations:

- Does the provider take my insurance and what are my costs?

- What does a typical therapy session look like with this provider?
- What specific training has the provider had in working with clients who have similar demographics?
- Where are the services offered (such as by telehealth or in person) and is the location of the therapist accessible for me?
- What are my child's goals for therapy and what can the therapist tell me about their ability to work with those treatment goals?
- How will the therapist be available to my child in case of an emergency?
- Does the therapist practice a specific type of therapy, and if so, what do they find is helpful about that type of therapy?
- If your child has ever had therapy before, ask them what was beneficial and what was not beneficial. Share with the provider what their past experiences were and ask them to articulate how they may work differently or in a similar fashion as past therapists.
- Ask how the family will be incorporated into therapy. Though the provider should have a clear understanding of confidentiality, they should also show an ability to discern when they will recommend that family members are included in treatment.
- Most therapists will have a website or work for an agency or group that has a website. That is a good place to start as it will often answer basic questions.

I have experienced potential clients who share with me they only want to see a psychologist or psychiatrist (meaning someone with a doctorate or a medical degree) but would not agree to see a clinician with a master's degree. However, the majority of the field in mental health have master's degrees in areas such as counseling, psychology, marriage and family therapy, social work, and school psychology.

I encourage potential clients to consider providers with various credentials, because the connection that a provider may be able to build with your child is not defined solely by their degree status. Creating a list of what the most important characteristics of the counselor are, and what qualities are important for therapy, would be a good conversation to have with your child before reaching out to providers.

Cristy Mereles (LCSW): You may hear from the trans community which local providers are capable and which are not. If there is not a thriving community of trans kids and families where you are, then this is a different question. The difference between having worked with trans youth and being well versed when it comes to trans care can be huge. Sometimes you may have to settle for a doctor who is willing to learn or has worked with one other trans youth. This can be a situation that feels odd, as you then find yourself in the role of educating a professional whom you are paying for services. There is value in creating more trans-knowledgeable doctors, but it can be burdensome to do so.

Alternatively, I have known families to drive many hours to see an experienced doctor when it comes to trans-related care. If there is not a trans-knowledgeable doctor near you then ultimately you must decide which is the most logical way for you to get care.

Marsha Aizumi: Knowing if a doctor is really experienced and skilled working with trans youth is like choosing any doctor for any procedure, in my opinion. When I needed a urologist for kidney stones, I received a recommendation from my primary care physician. After I met with the recommended specialist, I decided whether the doctor was skilled and competent. My son found his doctor for top surgery through recommendations and research. Before we met with the doctor, I listened to what my son found out in his research and found another family that I trusted who had been to him. I talked to the mother to get a sense of what she thought about her son's experience and the skill of the surgeon. Later on, when my child and I met with the doctor, I was going in with some sense of what others thought about him.

Janis Tannehill: Be direct and to the point. My kid came out as transgender, and we were looking for affirming care. What experience do you have with gender non-conforming youth? We may need you to write letters confirming their gender identity for legal name-change purposes or surgery requirements; are you comfortable with that? There are custody issues and/or non-affirming family involved; will you testify to the necessity of gender-affirming care or confirm we are not abusing our kid in court? Trust is the long pole in the therapy tent. If you or your kid isn't sure they are affirming, get a new practitioner.

What is a therapist allowed to tell us about our child's therapy sessions with them?

Dr. Matt Goldenberg: Each state has different confidentiality laws, which include not just what the provider can share with family members, but also what types of communication can be received by individuals other than the primary client. Communications with providers may include invoices, explanations of benefits, treatment plans, receipts, emails, voicemails, and clinical records. One way to learn about what confidentiality rules apply is to ensure that you thoroughly read the on-boarding paperwork that the therapist you select will provide prior to the first appointment.

In some therapies, family are involved in treatment to improve outcomes. Other therapists work in a more individualistic way, but might rely on contact with family members or other contacts to gather useful background information.

You may also look up confidentiality laws through your State Department of Health website. You can help your child become an informed consumer by making sure they also understand the limits of confidentiality. I encourage parents to also ask their child about how the therapy is going, whether they feel it is helpful, and how comfortable they feel talking to the therapist. While the child may not want to share much about what goes on in therapy, it is important that they know they can share their experiences with others.

In some communities, there may be either a peer support group or a therapeutic group that your child can attend. These groups will also have a set of confidentiality agreements (e.g., group members are asked not to share what they hear from others). Allowing your child to trust the confidentiality agreements, and not pushing them for information, will help them fully participate in treatment.

Janis Tannehill: If your kid is underage, you will start out in the session with them. As trust and comfort is gained by both the parent and child, the therapist will ask to talk to your kid alone. Let them. It is important for your kid to feel that they can truly say anything to their therapist and be honest. As much as we try as parents to put on a good front, our kids know us and can sense our anxiety, fear, or hypervigilance with the whole situation. Kids need to be able to talk to an expert without self-censoring, to spare our feelings and get to the heart of their own issues and needs.

Therapists will share what is relevant, especially when asked point blank, "Is this kid trans, non-binary, or just confused? What can I do to help them?" Ours told us straight out that "Yes, this is happening, and stalling is hurtful to them." Any therapist, teacher, or health professional is duty-bound to report plans or threats your kid has to harm themselves, or others. I've been in the waiting room more than once when an ambulance arrived to take a client to inpatient care (feeling simultaneous relief that it wasn't my kid, and guilt for feeling that way about someone else's kid).

After our child came out, they said they didn't want to see a therapist. Should we get one?

Cristy Mereles (LCSW): For many people, working with a therapist after coming out is very helpful. This is a time where many thoughts, feelings and social experiences arise surrounding gender. Once a kid has finally said out loud that they are not cisgender, this can bring a flood of gendered thoughts, feelings, and dysphoria which was previously stuffed down or misunderstood by your child. Having a therapist is not necessary, but can be helpful, especially if it is a therapist who specializes in gender. Working with such a therapist can help your child more efficiently sort through gendered thoughts, feelings, and dysphoria.

Clara Lee: When a child refuses to see a therapist, there must be some underlying reason. It is important that parents understand the barrier and try to remove it for the child. I also want to highlight the importance of having a therapist, if you can afford it, for parents and family members.

For many Asian families, there is stigma in seeking mental health care. Parents often avoid seeking therapy sessions. I think parents should also seek therapists themselves, to work through their own personal issues and care for their own mental health while supporting their children.

Right after my son came out, his father and I frantically looked for a gender therapist. We had a few initial sessions with different therapists before settling on one person. The therapist wanted to see my son for quite some time, to confirm the insistency, consistency, and persistence of his gender dysphoria, before giving him a go-ahead for medical transition.

However, after only a few sessions, my son decided to stop seeing the therapist. Later I found out that the only reason my son agreed to see the therapist was because he'd heard he would need a letter from the therapist to be able to start medical transition.

On the other hand, I wanted to see a therapist who specialized in gender issues in the hope that they would confirm this was just a phase. I hoped that there was some type of treatment for gender dysphoria. The therapist we chose was not going to give us what we were seeking, so we stopped.

Fortunately, my son found us the Gender Identity Program at the local LGBT Center, and we started attending the monthly support meetings. We met other parents and their trans children. The support meeting allowed us as a family to understand that we were not alone in this journey and helped us feel more comfortable with my son's transition. Once we made the decision to support my son's transition several months later, we found a wonderful therapist in NYC who was a transgender man himself. Under his care, my son went through social, medical, and legal transition in high school. When my son went to college, he looked for other therapists because his needs from a therapist had changed.

Janis Tannehill: Absolutely. They might think they don't need to talk to anyone now. They might be afraid that a therapist will try to "cure" them. But affirming mental health professionals are essential. The world is a terrifying, hateful place for gender non-conforming people. They might not be feeling that kind of stress now, but they will. Having a trusted mental health professional available will come in handy.

Many medical professionals and insurance providers require sign-off from a mental health professional before medical treatments and surgery. Therapists also work as marvelous gatekeepers to medical intervention to make sure your kid is ready ("Needles will be a part of your life now; we really need to work on your son's needle phobia if he wants hormones"). They are support both for when bodies change from hormone therapy, and when they don't change fast enough, causing frustration. They are great at aligning expectations about the outcomes of hormones and recovery from surgery. My son knew exactly what to expect mentally, emotionally, and physically every step of the way, because he had the support of therapists.

Our child is experiencing mental health issues after coming out as trans. What should we do?

Dr. Matt Goldenberg: It can be scary and concerning when your child starts to show mental health issues. If you have not dealt with the mental health system before, it can be complicated. It can be difficult to get the care that you need. Parents often report they have had to make many calls before getting in touch with someone who can potentially help. The time between noticing your child is struggling, and finding appropriate resources, can be stressful for all parties involved.

Sometimes your child's school will have ideas about what resources are available, or things you can try at home. Reaching out to the school counselor may be an option. Contacting your child's doctor is also a possibility. If mental health symptoms seem intense or sudden, it can be useful to consult with a medical doctor to review any other symptoms and ensure that your child's psychological or behavioral issues may not be better explained by another medical diagnosis.

Creating opportunities for connection and conversation is especially important when your child is showing signs of distress. It helps to set aside a regular time for conversations, such as checking in over dinner, or in the morning before the day gets too busy. You may want to encourage your child to keep a journal or use a drawing pad as a way to communicate and let out what they are going through.

Most parents will need to have frequent and consistent conversations about social media use as well. Online bullying has increased tremendously, and researchers have found links between social media use and mental health issues in youth. Check in with your child about any social media use they may have, and ensure that you are aware of what sites they are visiting and how much time they are spending online. It may help to institute family screen time breaks, especially overnight and during meals.

Noah Berlatsky: A lot of therapists are not used to working with trans people; many are actively transphobic. Ideally, you should look for a mental health provider who has experience with trans clients. Being trans is not a mental health condition, but many trans people experience dysphoria which can exacerbate depression and anxiety. Hormones don't help everyone to the same extent, but they help a lot of trans people. And it can be slow to get access while waiting; this can cause additional harm.

One thing you should avoid, unless it becomes an emergency situation, is having your child committed to a psychiatric facility. Mental health wards are often divided by gender, and do not allow for much privacy. Your child will have little say in which therapists see them, and a lot of therapists are poorly trained. Some are outright hostile to trans identities and may push some form of harmful conversion therapy. Most mental health wards are just not safe for trans people, unfortunately.

Debi Jackson: If your child has mental health issues, before or after coming out as trans, please get them in with a good therapist. Being trans is not a mental disorder, but it also doesn't make a person immune from other mental health struggles. Millions of cisgender people have anxiety, seek therapy, and take medications for it. The same is true for depression, obsessive-compulsive disorder, attention deficit hyperactivity disorder (ADHD), and so on. There is no reason to believe a trans person can't have separate mental health issues unrelated to being trans. Don't try to blame being trans on any of those struggles they may face.

We knew Avery was transgender at four years, because she told us very directly. But we didn't realize that she has ADHD, because we had a preconceived idea of what that was supposed to look like. When she was six or seven and we were struggling with her mood swings and some behavioral issues, we made an appointment with her gender therapist. After 20 minutes or so, she said, "Have you had her evaluated for ADHD, because she seems pretty textbook."

WHAT?? I was trying to ascribe all of her behaviors to anger or resentment over not being able to control how others perceived her gender, but that wasn't connected at all to these particular problems.

A few years later, she started experiencing some depression and anxiety. I wanted to find her a therapist who regularly supported teens through those issues. But I also needed that therapist to be trans-affirming, should any discussion of gender come up during sessions. That was a nightmare. Because trans identities weren't their specialty, the first three "affirming" therapists wanted to question Avery's gender even though she had been firm in who she was for almost a decade at that point. Finding someone who was willing and able to focus on helping her develop tools and techniques to deal with anxiety attacks or the negative self-talk associated with depression was a bigger challenge than it should have been.

My advice is to carefully screen any mental health professional you want to work with your child before sending them in alone. Some will be adept at helping your child come out and transition, and ideally, they could see your child for other issues. But if not, finding someone who won't start questioning your child again and forcing them to prove who they are repeatedly is important, too.

Jennifer See: Find a local therapist who has experience with transgender and gender-fluid clients. Some towns may have a gender-specialist clinic or a non-profit organization that supports gender questioning or LGBTQ youth. They may have programs to help you and may be able to help you contact the most knowledgeable people in your community. Make sure the school is supportive, and identify toxic parents of their peers who might be another source of strife. Give family members specific things that help you support your child, no matter how resistant they are to the idea.

Locally, we were lucky to have a youth organization and a parent support group. We both attended regularly for a while, and it really helped us realize that our daughter's difficulties were not unique. Both groups had a good resource list that helped us find a good therapist and an experienced endocrinologist, whereas our pediatrician was unable to give us a reference.

Janis Tannehill: For us, it was like a floodgate opening. I think my kid might have been spending so much effort keeping feelings about their gender under wraps and struggling to control previously missed ADHD that when one thing was addressed, much more than we ever expected (depression, anxiety and post-traumatic stress disorder (PTSD)) came streaming out in rapid succession.

Originally, our son started seeing a therapist for ADHD. Then he came out as trans. To this day, I honestly think if things had progressed along at a normal pace, he would have been able to deal with what was happening mental health wise in a controlled fashion.

But as it was, the concussion/low grade traumatic brain injury that he suffered at school took away any emotional control he had to mentally deal with being trans. As a result, he couldn't keep any of his anxiety at bay. Everything, both past and present, hit him all at once—and it was beyond the ability of any 15-year-old to cope.

He ultimately ended up in inpatient care in a youth mental health ward, for suicidal ideation. The best thing that came out of it was psychiatric care and medications that thankfully worked for him. Later, when we asked him which things were causing him depression and anxiety, he told me that it was maybe 5–10 percent being trans. The majority of it was fallout from the concussion, and PTSD from bullying and sexual harassment.

Being trans doesn't spawn other mental health issues. Do some people have issues with depression or anxiety because of the hateful world around them, lack of family, school, or medical support or dysphoria? Of course. However, none of these things are caused by being trans in itself. Rather, they are caused by the burden of being transgender in an intolerant society. This is why being trans is no longer considered a mental illness. My son could have handled being trans in a vacuum quite nicely, but that is not the way the world works. We did what we could about the hateful world and gave him all the support he needed and addressed his dysphoria with as much medical intervention as he needed. Now he is doing very well at university.

My child wants blockers or hormones. Should I let them have access before they're 18, when they can do what they want with their body?

Sebastian M. Barr, PhD: There are multiple things to consider with this question, but two primary ones are:

- the distress your child is experiencing and the level of urgency in addressing it
- the importance of your support of your child's well-being, and the strength and health of your relationship with them.

Most of what I share here is based on robust research and clinical experience. First, we must consider the distress your child might be experiencing. A young person who feels a need to pause their endogenous puberty or to introduce exogenous sex hormones (i.e., testosterone or estrogen) is likely struggling with an incongruence between their internal sense of self and their body, between their internal sense of self and how others gender them because of their body, or both.[1]

This is not to be taken lightly or treated as something easy to put

---

[1] Cooper, K., Russell, A., Mandy, W., & Butler, C. (2020). The phenomenology of gender dysphoria in adults: A systematic review and meta-synthesis. *Clinical Psychology Review, 80*, 101875.

off dealing with. The distress related to this incongruence, which the trans community and health professionals call *gender dysphoria*, can be devastatingly painful and disorienting.[2,3,4] It is associated with symptoms of depression and anxiety,[5] and can contribute to suicidal feelings and behavior, especially when paired with hopelessness and the conviction that their body is going to irrevocably change.

Gender dysphoria can also lead young people to use harmful coping techniques like self-harm, substance abuse, and social withdrawal. Youth with gender dysphoria are also at increased risk for engaging in disordered eating or unhealthy fitness behavior to try to control their body's appearance.[6,7] Even in less acute situations, gender dysphoria can become a preoccupation that interrupts healthy development.

Affirming psychotherapy and community-based interventions (like connection to other trans or LGBQ+ youth, affirmation of body diversity, and disruption of gendered norms) can protect young people from the worst psychological outcomes. I recommend this for anyone struggling with gender dysphoria.

Still, gender dysphoria is ultimately only relieved by helping the person live more in accordance with their understanding of their gender. This can involve access to blockers or hormones. If a part of your child's gender dysphoria is associated with features of their

---

2   Austin, A., Holzworth, J., & Papciak, R. (2022). Beyond diagnosis: "Gender dysphoria feels like a living hell, a nightmare one cannot ever wake up from." *Psychology of Sexual Orientation and Gender Diversity, 9*(1), 12–20.

3   Galupo, M. P., Pulice-Farrow, L., & Lindley, L. (2020). "Every time I get gendered male, I feel a pain in my chest": Understanding the social context for gender dysphoria. *Stigma and Health, 5*(2), 199.

4   Pulice-Farrow, L., Cusack, C. E., & Galupo, M. P. (2020). "Certain parts of my body don't belong to me": Trans individuals' descriptions of body-specific gender dysphoria. *Sexuality Research and Social Policy, 17*(4), 654–667.

5   Lindley, L. & Galupo, M. P. (2020). Gender dysphoria and minority stress: Support for inclusion of gender dysphoria as a proximal stressor. *Psychology of Sexual Orientation and Gender Diversity, 7*(3), 265.

6   Cusack, C. E., Iampieri, A. O., & Galupo, M. P. (2022). "I'm still not sure if the eating disorder is a result of gender dysphoria": Trans and nonbinary individuals' descriptions of their eating and body concerns in relation to their gender. *Psychology of Sexual Orientation and Gender Diversity*. Advance online publication. https://doi.org/10.1037/sgd0000515

7   Coelho, J.S., Suen, J., Clark, B.A., *et al.* (2019). Eating disorder diagnoses and symptom presentation in transgender youth: A scoping review. *Current Psychiatry Reports, 21*, 107. https://doi.org/10.1007/s11920-019-1097-x

body, a delay in getting them medical interventions can have devastating, lifelong consequences. Retrospective studies have consistently shown that adults who wanted puberty blockers or hormones in their youth, but were denied them, had worse mental health outcomes (including greater suicidality) than peers who got access to gender-affirming medical care.[8,9]

There are also numerous long-term studies that show improvements in well-being when youth who express a desire or need for medical interventions are able to get them.[10,11] Health professionals and parenting experts would never advise delaying care that could reduce suffering and improve well-being in other cases (e.g., a child with anxiety wanting or needing a therapist, or a teen with ADHD needing a behavioral coach, or a young person with diabetes needing insulin), and that frame should be applied here.

It is also important to note that puberty blockers and hormones can be reversed in most ways simply by stopping the treatment.[12] Furthermore, the physical effects of testosterone, estrogen, and androgen-suppressants take many months to begin taking effect, and in most cases years to reach full impact.[13] As with all medical and mental health care, clinicians experienced in this care will start at an appropriate dose, and check in over time to see how the youth is responding both physically and emotionally/psychologically. Many

8   Turban, J. L., King, D., Carswell, J. M., & Keuroghlian, A. S. (2020). Pubertal suppression for transgender youth and risk of suicidal ideation. *Pediatrics*, 145(2), e20191725.

9   Green, A. E., DeChants, J. P., Price, M. N., & Davis, C. K. (2021). Association of gender-affirming hormone therapy with depression, thoughts of suicide, and attempted suicide among transgender and nonbinary youth. *Journal of Adolescent Health*, 70(4), 643–649.

10 Achille, C., Taggart, T., Eaton, N. R., Osipoff, J., *et al.* (2020). Longitudinal impact of gender-affirming endocrine intervention on the mental health and well-being of transgender youths: Preliminary results. *International Journal of Pediatric Endocrinology*. doi: 10.1186/s13633-020-00078-2.

11 Kaltiala, R., Heino, E., Työläjärvi, M., & Suomalainen, L. (2020). Adolescent development and psychosocial functioning after starting cross-sex hormones for gender dysphoria. *Nordic Journal of Psychiatry*, 74(3), 213–219.

12 Olson-Kennedy, J., Rosenthal, S. M., Hastings, J., & Wesp, L. (2016). *Health Considerations for Gender Non-Conforming Children and Transgender Adolescents*. San Francisco, CA: Center of Excellence for Transgender Health.

13 Deutsch M. B. (Ed.) (2016). *Guidelines for the Primary and Gender-Affirming Care of Transgender and Gender Nonbinary People; 2nd edition*. San Francisco, CA: UCSF Transgender Care, Department of Family and Community Medicine, University of California. Available at https://transcare.ucsf.edu/guidelines

parents are relieved to understand that medical intervention is nothing like a switch that is flipped, but instead is a slow journey with lots of opportunities and freedom for the young person to assess their needs and change direction if necessary.

The slow impact of these steps should also be considered when you think about the distress your young person may be experiencing, as it often takes months or years of medical affirmation to experience the full relief of gender dysphoria that medication can bring.

Let's get to the second piece of this response, which is also incredibly important: your relationship with your child. We know that parental support is a critical part of healthy development for young people. For trans and gender-diverse youth, parental support is one of the most significant factors in their well-being.[14,15] Studies show that the majority of trans youth who report very supportive parents have very good mental health. On the other hand, the vast majority of trans youth who describe their parents as only somewhat or not at all supportive do struggle.[16]

Beyond that, supporting and affirming your child creates the opportunity to build your relationship.[17] Youth will not hear "wait until you are 18 and this can be your decision" as support or affirmation. They will interpret this delay for needed gender affirmation as a sentence to more years of preventable suffering, as I described above. Additionally, young people will often also hear your resistance as a rejection of them and their needs. They will be concerned that you do not care about them. Empathetic and mentally sophisticated youths will hear in your response a level of ignorance, which, even

14 Ceatha, N., Koay, A., Buggy, C., James, O., et al. (2021). Protective factors for LGBTI+ youth wellbeing: A scoping review underpinned by recognition theory. *International Journal of Environmental Research and Public Health, 18*(21), 11682. https://doi.org/10.3390/ijerph182111682

15 Simons, L., Schrager, S. M., Clark, L. F., Belzer, M., & Olson, J. (2013). Parental support and mental health among transgender adolescents. *Journal of Adolescent Health, 53*(6), 791–793.

16 Travers, R., Bauer, G., & Pyne, J. (2012). *Impacts of Strong Parental Support for Trans Youth: A Report Prepared for Children's Aid Society of Toronto and Delisle Youth Services*. Ontario: Trans PULSE.

17 Pullen Sansfaçon, A., Medico, D., Gelly, M., Kirichenko, V., et al. (2021). Blossoming child, mourning parent: A qualitative study of trans children and their parents navigating transition. *Journal of Child and Family Studies*. https://doi.org/10.1007/s10826-021-02178-w

if benevolent in origin, will lose you their trust. They will no longer turn to you as a guide in their development, and they won't consider you a source of refuge in their distress.

I have witnessed this phenomenon as the beginning of a preventable rift in families. Making gender-affirming care something your child must wait until they are old enough to do on their own also means you don't get to be a part of a really wonderful and important part of your child's life. I frequently sit with young people who began hormones and started pursuing surgery as soon as they turned 18 and/or moved out from their parents' home. They are supported in their endeavors by friends, community members, and providers; but the separation between this major piece of their life and their parents or family creates a distance that I fear will never fully be healed.

On the other hand, in my work with PFLAG parents, I get to know families who have maintained a closeness—or grown even closer—by facing these decisions and processes together.

Janna Barkin: Every transgender person has a unique journey. There is no one answer to this question. This is a decision that is best made after consulting with medical experts and educating yourself about the benefits of hormone therapy for transgender youth.

When my child went through his transition ten years ago it was not common for people under 18 to have access to gender-affirming medical care. I didn't even hear the word "blockers" until well after my child hit puberty. When he did talk to me about taking testosterone, I was scared about the long-term effects and permanent changes. I was also uninformed about how they could be beneficial. I knew my child was suffering, but I didn't have the information or resources to help him, yet.

We gathered information by attending Gender Spectrum conferences and learning from medical and mental health experts in the field. Still, it was only after speaking to a mom who had gone down the path before me that I was able to take the necessary steps for my son's health and well-being. She pointed out that by doing it *now*, before he went off to college, I would be able to be involved, to help prepare him for the process beforehand, and take care of him both physically and emotionally as he transitioned. "You are preparing to launch your transgender child," she said. "What could be more important than helping him realize his true self?"

Yes, I thought, I was preparing to do just that, and knew what we needed to do to get in gear. We found gender-affirming doctors who could help us make these important decisions. The more we learned, the more we knew that the risk of *not* allowing our child to start hormonal treatment would likely be worse than any possible side effects. If we *didn't* try the hormones, our child would most likely continue to suffer from gender dysphoria.

Is this the right decision for every transgender youth? I can't say. What I do know is this: about a month into his hormone treatments, it was as if a fog had lifted in my child's inner being. The light that had been missing from my child's eyes was back and brighter than ever! Looking back, I am glad we didn't wait longer, and wish we had acted sooner.

Janis Tannehill: Consistent, insistent, and persistent. Blockers and hormone therapy are part of affirming support of your gender non-conforming child. If they are consistent, insistent, and persistent about their gender identity then don't wait for an imaginary age of responsibility for medical intervention.

The point of hormones is so that your kid goes through the puberty of their gender identity rather than their biological sex. Blockers are only useful before puberty, and act as a completely reversible pause button—18 is too late. After puberty, hormones are just damage control. Surgery will be needed to get rid of breast tissue on a trans boy and correct the facial bone structure of a trans girl. The earlier your kid can start blockers, and eventually gender-correcting hormones, the more successful their physical outcome will be and the less pain they will go through both emotionally and physically.

Putting off medical intervention until they are 18 is putting your parenting responsibility onto them. You are the parent, and you are responsible. Gender non-conforming kids who are denied affirming support from their family and lack access to medical care have a much higher risk of suicide. Blockers and hormones are part of affirming support.

Our child is going on blockers. What should I know? How do I pay for it?

Dr. Danielle O'Banion: This is a valuable time for your child and family. Doctors generally do not recommend that young people suppress puberty for more than one to three years, depending on the provider and individual young person. After this, the youth can either begin gender-affirming sex hormone therapy, which will lead to pubertal development like cisgender peers of their affirmed gender, or they can enter into their endogenous puberty (the body's natural course without intervention). This is a time to be open to hearing your child's experience and future desires and needs related to gender, so you can work with your provider to make a plan for the transition to whichever puberty path they take.

For most young people, being on blockers (gonadotropin-releasing hormone (GnRH) agonists) can be an anticlimactic experience, because it essentially places their body and its development in a holding pattern. Some children and families welcome this pause of sorts, but in our experience, many trans youth are impatient to begin puberty and develop the secondary sex characteristics associated with their affirmed gender. They can feel frustrated and even dysphoric, especially after some time on blockers, as their peers go through puberty and start to look more masculine or feminine than them.

Medically, puberty blockers have few if any side effects.[18] In the first month, youth can experience fatigue, headaches, mild dizziness, and mood swings. These side effects should resolve. There may be a surge in GnRH at initiation of the blockers, which can cause a temporary surge in sex hormones. This can cause a temporary intensification of pubertal symptoms like growth spurts and erections, which can be emotionally difficult for young people, but typically resolves within four weeks. Everybody responds differently, and not all young people will experience this temporary sex hormone surge or pubertal symptoms.

---

18 Deutsch M. B. (Ed.) (2016). *Guidelines for the Primary and Gender-Affirming Care of Transgender and Gender Nonbinary People; 2nd edition.* San Francisco, CA: UCSF Transgender Care, Department of Family and Community Medicine, University of California. Available at https://transcare.ucsf.edu/guidelines

After the initial month on blockers, youth with testes often experience reduced erections, which can be a relief if they experience dysphoria related to their bottom parts. Otherwise, there are typically no noticeable ongoing signs or side effects for young people with testes, besides the fact that they aren't advancing in pubertal development.

After the initial month, youth with ovaries enter a temporary menopausal state and can experience symptoms like fatigue, night sweats, irritability, vaginal dryness, and sleep disruption. This typically resolves within one to three months (though we have seen it last up to six months) and is generally well tolerated. There are medications that can suppress menstrual cycles but do not block puberty for youth with ovaries, which may be an alternative to puberty blockers, but will not stop breast tissue development or other pubertal changes.

Young people on puberty blockers often benefit from facilitated affirming spaces, like therapy, to process and cope with the multitude of feelings related to being in this limbo of sorts. Family therapy may be useful, particularly when the young person is exploring their gender and the family is working on decisions related to future hormone therapy.

Debi Jackson: If your child socially transitions at an early age, knowing that they are approaching puberty and might soon be ready for blockers can cause a lot of anxiety. We suspected our insurance plan would not cover blockers, and, at the very least, we would have to fight for coverage, so we opened a savings account to specifically put money aside for them. As anticipated, our insurance denied everything over and over again even with the expert staff at our children's hospital sending them multiple letters explaining their necessity. While all of this was happening, our endocrinologist started Avery on spironolactone, which a lot of adult trans women use. It's a pill and very affordable. Because it's a diuretic and can cause fluctuations in blood pressure, we had to monitor her water and salt intake, but it was worth doing for three or four months for her peace of mind while we continued to find a way to access a blocker implant.

Our children's hospital eventually received a grant that covered the cost of the implant, so we only had to pay for the procedure itself. As most children's hospitals are non-profits, we were allowed to set up a payment plan for that. I've had some friends who were able to get coverage from similar grants where they live, others who were able to work with the pharmaceutical companies to get a free or greatly discounted blocker prescription, and some who had really good luck with their insurance carriers. My advice is to ask your doctor for their help in pursuing all possible channels (they often have some creative ideas) and start that process a few months before you think your child will enter Tanner Stage 2.

Wayne Maines: If you are just starting this journey with your child at a young age or have been notified by an older child that they have decided to transition, you are in for a life-changing experience. At every stage, there will be many stressors and rewards. It all depends on your patience and communication skills. First, I want you and those around you to always remember; for many trans children, gender non-conformance is a medical condition. A number of years ago I was at the University of Maine at Fort Kent. This small college is fairly isolated, and it sits on the Saint John River that borders Canada. This small community had never heard anyone openly discuss raising a transgender child or talking about hormone blocking as a successful treatment for a 12-year-old child.

At the end of my lecture, a gentleman from the community asked me if I was playing God by allowing my "son" to take hormone blockers. As he asked that question, I could see the anger in the students' eyes who sat behind him. I paused and said, "This is my daughter, my baby, who I will protect and support until I breathe my last breath." Near tears, I said, "If your child had a rare disease and needed this type of treatment to save their life, I know you would approve the treatment. Nicole's medical condition is very treatable. Hormone blockers provide her with the time to grow safely, and with the help of trained medical and mental health professionals and her parents, decide her future. I need you to understand that if we do not allow these children to receive this care, they might not make it to adulthood."

The man sat down, and I could still see the anger in the eyes of the students behind him. I answered a few more questions, and at the end, students and community members came up to the front of the lecture hall to say thank you. I received a few hugs, and one student said, "I wish you were my father." As I tried to respond and comfort that young person, I saw the older man right behind her. He heard what she said and as he approached, I could see he was troubled by it. I thought this might not end well. Then he stepped forward meekly and reached out his hand. He said, "Young man, you are a good father, and God loves you. I will pray for you and your family and thank you for your courage." Then he just turned and walked away before I could thank him for having the courage to speak his mind, knowing there was a hostile crowd behind him.

We, as parents of a new generation that has never openly lived in society, must have the courage to demand they have access to the care they need, the same education as their classmates, and the same rights as every other citizen, no matter where they live. We must have the courage to not delay making the decision to use hormone blockers at the right time in our child's life. If we do hesitate, our hesitation may result in our child having unwanted physical characteristics, performing self-harm, or, worse, suicide. I cannot tell you how many times I had to talk to Nicole when she was younger about friends that we have lost.

Hormone blockers provide our children—and you, their parents—with more time to develop a long-term plan for success. There are options today that did not exist at the beginning of my family's journey. Our only option was a monthly Lupron injection that required a $1600 out-of-pocket expense. It was so new and controversial that we had to pick up the prescription and take it to our doctor who could then administer the drug. It was all hush hush. I still remember Nicole's first shot. She came home with a huge smile, and she seemed more at peace, now knowing that she had a chance to be normal, to not look like her brother who would soon be revealing the signs of male puberty.

There were stressors. Were we doing the right thing? Where were we going to find the $1600 every month, and what were we going to do if others protested? We were often questioned by friends and family about whether we were doing the right thing. We knew many were wondering this but did not have the courage to ask us. I hoped that they might ask so we could have a frank discussion to hopefully explain it to them.

As time went on, we learned that there was an implant that had an up-front cost of $6000 that may last a year or more. The implant lasted almost two years, saving us a great deal of money. Currently, the cost for monthly injections is approximately $1200 and the implant can range from $4500 to $18,000. The good news is that some physicians may code the treatment as being for "precocious puberty," which is typically covered by insurance with no questions asked. Precocious puberty is when a child's body begins changing into that of an adult (puberty) too soon. When puberty begins before age eight in girls and before age nine in boys, it is considered precocious puberty. Therefore, a hormone blocker is used to delay puberty. This treatment plan can provide coverage for the first year or two depending on your child's growth.

It should also be noted that some of the larger healthcare providers now cover hormone therapy as standard treatment. You need to read the fine print in your insurance plan and gather your facts. Talk to your child's pediatric endocrinologist and be prepared to educate your insurance provider. If you can find a gender clinic in a state near home, they may be able to help you find other options for reduced costs or, in some cases, no-cost treatment.

Our journey started around 2001. We spent a significant amount of our income providing treatment and, unfortunately, paying for legal fees and moving home to protect our children and provide them with a safe place to go to school. We never looked back, and it turned out to be the right thing to do. Do not hesitate to reach out for help if you are not sure what to do. Look at your child. Watch how they look when they are at school, in the community. Look for signs of trouble every day. Ask your child, *really* ask them, how is school, do you have friends, what are their names, are you being bullied, what are you afraid of, what do you think about when the doctors say they can help, do you understand what hormone blockers are and do? Watch for changes in their behavior, find out why they are quiet, and look for non-verbal clues that they are troubled. Tell them every day that you love them.

Jennifer See: Blockers come in three types, depending on the age of your child and where they are relative to puberty. A child won't be given any blockers until they start puberty and reach what an endocrinologist calls Tanner Stage 2. Once that point is reached, the blockers are there to stop puberty and give your child time to age up without physical changes.

Since our daughter was just starting puberty when she let us know her needs, we only had limited time to find support. At her age, the options were either an injected hormone every couple of months, or a surgical implant that lasted about 18 months. Later, once she was around 16, we switched from these medications that stop puberty through intercepting brain hormones to pills that stop male development by blocking just testosterone production.

Things have changed since we went through this. Insurance didn't cover any medications for us, and the injections and the implant were ridiculously expensive. At the time, the injections were $14,000 each or the implant was $25,000 a year. Fortunately, when we had to replace her implant, insurance rules had changed to it being a covered item, which brought the cost down significantly.

Our trans son is starting testosterone. What should I be ready for?

Sebastian M. Barr, PhD & Dr. Danielle O'Banion: The biggest thing to remember when a person is starting gender-affirming testosterone is that everyone's course is different. Some people experience noticeable changes pretty quickly, while for others, changes can take longer or happen in a different sequence—much like the course of puberty differs between kids. For adolescents in particular, this can be hard to internalize, and they may feel frustrated that their experience of starting testosterone is different from someone else's.

That said, while the sequence and timing of changes are person-dependent (and largely related to genetics), we generally know what the testosterone will ultimately do. Some of the early outward changes will be increases in body hair and changes in oil and sweat production. Much like in any testosterone-dominant puberty, this can cause the development of acne. Testosterone will also cause the thickening of the vocal chords, which will lead to the voice cracking and an eventual deepening. Slower or more gradual changes will include shifts in fat distribution and increased building of muscle mass. Your son's provider will likely share information with him regarding all the changes. Another good resource is the overview of masculinizing hormone therapy written by Dr. Maddie Deutsch and the Transgender Care team at UCSF.[19]

Over time, your son will look and sound different. This may seem obvious—and indeed is likely what your son is hoping for—and it is why testosterone is associated with reduced gender dysphoria in trans boys.[20] But it's important to know, because in many ways the largest changes related to testosterone initiation are social and emotional/psychological. On testosterone, a young person's transition becomes much more outwardly apparent to family, friends, and community, and they will be increasingly likely to be recognized as a boy or man by strangers. This can be both welcome and disorienting, and will likely take some adjusting to as they might be treated differently from what they are used to. Their involvement in extra-curricular activities, especially gendered athletics or performance-based activities (e.g., choir, theater), may be affected.

There are also changes to the reproductive system—namely that for the vast majority of people, testosterone will suppress the menstrual cycle. If your son had his puberty suppressed and never began menstruating, he likely will not unless he stops testosterone at some point in the future. If he was not on puberty blockers and has already started having his period, this will probably stop. His menstrual cycles may be irregular before they cease altogether. Importantly, testosterone does not eliminate a person's ability to get pregnant. Testosterone alone is not a contraceptive. To avoid unwanted pregnancies, people with ovaries on gender-affirming testosterone should use birth control methods if they are having vaginal sex with someone capable of producing sperm. You or your

---

19 https://transcare.ucsf.edu/article/information-testosterone-hormone-therapy
20 Grannis, C., Leibowitz, S. F., Gahn, S., Nahata, L., *et al.* (2021). Testosterone treatment, internalizing symptoms, and body image dissatisfaction in transgender boys. *Psychoneuroendocrinology*, *132*, 105358.

son should speak with his medical provider about contraception. Note that if your son ever wants to become pregnant or use his eggs to create a pregnancy, he would need to stop testosterone for this purpose. It is important to discuss fertility considerations early in the process with his medical provider, as it is uncertain what long-term impacts testosterone might have on a person's eventual ability to have viable eggs. Most reproductive endocrinology programs at major hospitals have ever-evolving technology allowing transgender people to preserve their sperm and eggs, and the options available are advancing rapidly. However, if your son were to become pregnant accidentally, and the pregnancy were desired, he would need to stop testosterone as it can have damaging effects to a developing pregnancy.

On the subject of sex and sexuality, testosterone often causes an increase in sex drive. This is reported by people starting testosterone at any age, but may be particularly noticeable and new to a teen, especially one who has previously been on puberty blockers. The increase in sex drive is typical in adolescence and can be a welcomed and valuable part of your child's development. For some youth with a lot of dysphoria related to their genitalia, the increased awareness of these parts of their body might be distressing. Additionally, this aspect of development may increase their interest in sex and dating, which brings both opportunities and challenges related to transness. Having an open, sex-positive frame of mind for discussions with your son is important, while avoiding communities or spaces that shame sexual desire will improve your son's ability to navigate his evolving sexuality. This can also be an area in which an experienced therapist or connection to trans peers can be helpful.

We also know that because many of the changes on testosterone can take longer than expected, people—perhaps especially teens—can feel impatient and even dysphoric in the initial months after starting testosterone, particularly as their cisgender peers may be further along in their pubertal development. Starting testosterone usually comes after a lengthy period of family discussion and clinical assessment, so it is often a very exciting time for a young person. However, as the newness of starting wears off, it can be frustrating if the changes lag behind expectations, particularly as young people can continue to be misgendered by other family members and peers. Additionally, there are some limitations as to what exogenous testosterone can do—even in youth who have successfully suppressed puberty, the most effective course of testosterone therapy will not be a perfect analog to a cisgender male's puberty. Trans men and other people with ovaries who take testosterone are on average shorter than cisgender men; we don't have the data on what these differences look like in youth who have been on blockers, but it's important to help youth set realistic height expectations. Testosterone also cannot alter bone structure, so if a person has undergone some pubertal development, which can include the widening of hips, testosterone will not change this. None of this is inherently bad, but it does create a risk of gender dysphoria and disappointment if youth have internalized masculine cis body ideals and/or have expectations of testosterone therapy that don't match their physical capabilities. It is particularly important to adopt a body-positive, weight-neutral approach in caring for transgender teens, as this incongruence between body expectation and body experience can trigger disordered eating.

Perhaps the most important thing to know, however, is that gender-affirming testosterone is safe and well tolerated in the typical young person or adult. Most gender-affirming care can be managed in a primary care context,[21] unless there are complicated medical conditions or issues, in which case a general endocrinologist or pediatric endocrinologist will likely be involved in care.[22] Unfortunately, many providers have not received adequate training and may also hold some biases that prevent high-quality care,[23] and trans people are at risk of facing what community members have dubbed "trans broken arm syndrome." This is when a medical

---

21   Feldman, J. & Deutsch, M. B. (2021). Primary Care of Transgender Individuals. In J. G. Elmore & K. A. Martin (Eds). *UpToDate*. Accessed 02/14/2022 at www.uptodate. com/contents/primary-care-of-transgender-individuals

22   Wylie, K., Knudson, G., Khan, S. I., Bonierbale, M., Watanyusakul, S., & Baral, S. (2016). Serving transgender people: Clinical care considerations and service delivery models in transgender health. *The Lancet, 388*(10042), 401–411.

23   Nolan, I. T., Blasdel, G., Dubin, S. N., Goetz, T. G., Greene, R. E., & Morrison, S. D. (2020). Current state of transgender medical education in the United States and Canada: Update to a scoping review. *Journal of Medical Education and Curricular Development, 7*, 2382120520934813.

provider misidentifies the cause of a totally unrelated condition (e.g., a broken arm) as related to transness or gender-affirming healthcare. We have witnessed patients be counseled inappropriately to stop gender-affirming hormones when the hormones were not yet determined to be the source of a symptom, nor were they likely to be. If testosterone is a critical component of your son's well-being, you may be called to advocate for him in such situations. This doesn't happen to everyone but is common enough to mention. That said, this could be prevented by working on the front end to make sure his primary care provider and healthcare teams are knowledgeable, experienced, and affirming when it comes to trans health and gender diversity. There are many free, comprehensive sources available online.

Dr. Matt Goldenberg: You should have a good relationship with the prescriber for medical information. A list of side effects and expected changes should be given to you in writing, even before a prescription is issued, so that the patient and their family have time to review and understand what gender-affirming hormone treatment will offer. Many families will review gender transition stories that are available online, particularly on social media like YouTube or TikTok. While hearing other people's stories may bring insight, it is essential to have regular conversations with the young person about media literacy and teach youth the distinctions between anecdote and peer reviewed/science-based information.

Starting gender-affirming hormone treatment is often an exciting time for gender non-conforming people, no matter how old they are. Essentially, use of hormones will mirror the changes that occur during organic puberty, such as developing secondary sex characteristics (e.g., breasts, facial hair, deeper voice). Genetics, dosage prescribed, and adherence to the medication protocol are some of the factors that will influence what changes occur and when, as well as how noticeable those changes are. There are also a variety of ways to administer testosterone, such as intramuscular injection, subcutaneous injection, topical gel, and dermal patches. Talk with your child's provider so that they can be aware of all their options and what your insurance covers. Out-of-pocket cost is an important consideration when starting gender-affirming hormone treatment.

Changes in your child's body can cause a lot of emotions for your child, as well as for those who are close to them. Notice your own feelings as your child grows and develops more masculine or feminine features. You may feel happy and relieved; you may feel sad, confused, or overwhelmed. Ensure that you have medically accurate information and a resource to go to for your own support as you watch your child emerge.

Amy Cannava (NASP): I think the first thing to remember, and sometimes to remind your child of, is that pubertal changes happen gradually. Taking testosterone allows a trans masculine person to enter second puberty (if they underwent the first already) and the expected changes are similar to that of an assigned male at birth person.

Testosterone is prescribed by a doctor and is either taken by injection (intramuscular or subcutaneous), applied externally as a gel, as a slow-release patch, or through pellets placed under the skin which gradually release. According to the Mayo Clinic, changes begin happening within weeks to months and will vary from person to person.

One of the first changes that happens is voice deepening—the Mayo Clinic (2021) indicates that this happens between 3 and 12 months after starting treatment, with the maximum effect occurring between one and two years.[24] In my experience, if you're observant, changes in voice can be seen earlier. During this time, the voice may "crack." Facial and body hair can be seen between three and six months after treatment, with the maximum effect apparent within two to five years. Within the first 6–12 months after starting testosterone, there will be increased muscle mass and strength which will continue for the first two to five years. During this same time, body fat, particularly around the mid-section, thighs, and buttocks, will redistribute. As early as two months after starting treatment, and normally within the first six months, menstrual periods will stop. Finally, although your child is unlikely to want to share or discuss

---

24 Mayo Foundation for Medical Education and Research. (2021, July 21). *Masculinizing hormone therapy*. Mayo Clinic. Accessed 01/17/2022 at www.mayoclinic.org/tests-procedures/masculinizing-hormone-therapy/about/pac-20385099

such with you, there will be clitoral enlargement and vaginal atrophy beginning after between three months and a year, with maximum effect taking place within one to two years.

When we made the initial appointment for testosterone for my son, knowing that he was not going to wait any longer than need be, we called ahead and asked what lab tests would be needed before starting testosterone. We got the orders and completed the required tests before the first appointment.

His gender dysphoria improved, his suicidality decreased, and his mental health improved, but we also maintained mental health appointments while starting HRT. I think that all too often, people expect everything to be better immediately after HRT or surgery, and while many things may be, perfection only exists in the movies. He was hungrier, moodier, his acne and eczema increased, and he smelled all of the time (showering more often became a thing). He wasn't thrilled with hair growing on his back initially, breaking out when shaving, and increased perspiration, but he loved the deeper voice, facial whisps of hair, and increased metabolism.

Janis Tannehill: In my experience, trans people are not patient people. Hormone therapy is a gradual process that rarely moves fast enough. That said, testosterone is almost a magic bullet and the transformation of trans guys is astounding...over the course of years. Kids want a deeper voice in a week and a beard in a month; this isn't realistic, so aligning expectations is important. Cis guys don't go from a boy to a man in a matter of months and neither will your trans guy. The effects of testosterone on hair growth, bone growth, and voice are permanent. We had to sign release forms that we understood what he was getting into.

For my son, testosterone made his already crappy skin far worse, but acne is to be expected in a cis guy. His acne required him going on Accutane, but this was consistent with the men in his family so not a great surprise. Emotionally, he said that he was quicker to anger and had to figure out how to control that, but he saw the same struggle in cis guys his age. I honestly think trans guys are the best of both worlds: all the perks of being a man in this society, but with the strong ethic to care for others that comes from being socialized as a girl.

Our trans daughter is starting HRT.
What should I be ready for?

Dr. Danielle O'Banion & Sebastian M. Barr, PhD: Hormone therapy for transgender girls and non-binary AMAB youth can vary depending on provider, location, and embodiment goals. There are a few different options for therapy that focus on the dual goals of blocking testosterone and inducing estrogen-influenced physical changes. The specific therapies available should be discussed with your provider as the modes of delivery are nuanced. The average response to hormone therapy is gradual and can take months to years for noticeable physical changes to occur. This can feel particularly long for adolescents and young adults, who are often less able to endure lengthy responses to desired interventions. So, while it is often exciting to begin hormones, your child can suffer some disappointment, frustration, and even worsening dysphoria once the novelty fades and more substantial changes take time to develop. It's helpful to set expectations in an affirming and compassionate way around this and work on supporting them through it in the short term. It's also important to remember that the sequence and timing of changes is affected by genetics and other person- and body-dependent factors, so your child's experience won't look the same as anyone else's and may not line up with the expectations they have set in their head.

One of the first physical changes most people on estrogen therapy (and testosterone blockade) notice is the beginning of chest or breast development. Breast growth is unpredictable in terms of rate of development and size. At some point during hormone therapy, providers may add progesterone, which can help with further breast development in some individuals. The chest tissue can be very sensitive and tender during this period, which usually takes years. Try to avoid household comparisons between your child and cisgender female family members who have breasts. It is common for well-intentioned parents to encourage their transgender child by saying they will probably "look just like" that person in terms of breast size. Though genetics are a significant contributor to breast development in transgender youth, on average, those on exogenous estrogen will have smaller chest sizes than their cisgender female family members and this can be another source of distress. It is common for trans and non-binary youth to need breast augmentation surgery to achieve their more desired breast size.

Other physical changes that you and your daughter will notice: body fat may redistribute to the hips and buttocks (person-dependent) to various extents, skin appearance may soften and become less oily and acne-prone, and body hair may thin and decline. If your daughter has been on puberty blockers, she will likely experience more ease in this transition as her body hair will be less present than someone who has moved through some or most of their natal testosterone-influenced puberty. If your daughter has developed body hair that causes distress, she will likely need permanent hair removal (electrolysis or laser) in order to achieve desired results.

An important side effect of suppressing testosterone is a reduction in muscle mass from baseline, as well as some fatigue. These side effects are temporary as her body adjusts to being on hormone therapy. It is important for young people to stay active, so some gentle modifications to her usual routine may be necessary as she is adjusting to her medications. If she is especially active in sports or dance, expect that she will have a temporary reduction in her endurance for weeks to months and may need additional recovery time. In general, these side effects pass as the body adjusts.

It's important to understand possible limitations to the physical impacts of gender-affirming hormone therapy. Hormone therapy cannot significantly change a voice that has already deepened, and indeed some young people can experience breakthrough voice changes on puberty suppression and even HRT. Voice deepening will not be as significant as it would be for someone who is not on puberty suppression or HRT. Unwanted vocal changes can be reduced for trans youth by working with a vocal coach or speech therapist to move their voice into a pitch that causes less dysphoria.

Furthermore, HRT cannot modify a young person's bone structure. While puberty suppression can block some skeletal changes during puberty, it may not block all skeletal changes, particularly regarding height. Many youths find that they continue to grow despite puberty suppression and, as you might guess, HRT does not reverse height accrual. We are writing all of the above to prepare young people and their loved ones for these possibilities, not because we believe that there is one right way to express one's gender. We understand that adolescents are very aware of norms and will encounter those norms with various levels of desire or rejection.

HRT will almost certainly alter your daughter's experience of libido and sexual arousal. It is a myth that being on estrogen-dominant hormone therapy will "lower" an adolescent's sex drive in the long term; rather, most youth report feeling a difference in how they experience it. However, at least initially, youth feel a drop in both libido and energy if puberty blockers are not on board. Furthermore, being on puberty blockers and HRT will almost certainly reduce the presence and intensity of erectile function. If a young person has distress and dysphoria around erections, this will be a relief. If instead she is sexually active and wants to use her genitals for sexual activity, this may be frustrating and she may need to discuss options with her doctor for how to overcome that.

There will likely be some side effects as her body is adjusting to the new hormones and the suppression of her endogenous testosterone. Typically, we see some fatigue, moodiness, and nausea with each successive increase in dose, but these effects are temporary. Sex hormones are actually involved in multiple organ systems in the body, so there can also be other mild and temporary side effects, like stomach upset and intestinal discomfort with stool changes. Initial drops in testosterone can make someone a bit dizzy or lightheaded. Discuss your daughter's individual medical conditions with her provider and ask questions about how HRT might impact them. In general, HRT is safe and very well tolerated, and side effects are mild.

It is difficult to discuss family building with preteens and adolescents, but it is important to do so. It is not clear how permanent fertility is impacted by estrogen, but sperm counts do reduce significantly while on hormone therapy and in many cases do not improve. That said, some people maintain the ability to produce sperm and your daughter should understand that penile-vaginal sex without birth control could result in pregnancy. Your daughter should talk to her provider about contraception to avoid unwanted pregnancies and seek trans-informed fertility counseling if she is hoping to contribute to a viable pregnancy. Also, trans youth have the right to know their options with regard to having biological children of their own in the future. Fertility preservation technology is advancing very quickly, and young people on puberty blockers have more options to harvest their sperm/eggs than ever before. All youth should be informed of their risks of fertility reduction in the future and be offered an opportunity to preserve their gametes for future use. In the current climate, this opportunity may be limited by cost and financial ability, as most commercial insurance providers do not cover this service for transgender youth.

Although moodiness is to be expected for many during HRT initiation and adjustment, the overall impact of hormone therapy on moods and emotions is unclear. Most commonly, patients report increased emotional lability (mood swings, quickness to crying) and a different experience of their emotions. In our experience, however, it is impossible to disentangle potential direct impacts of hormones from the complex psychosocial impacts of transition (e.g., being socialized as a young woman, feeling excitement and relief from gender alignment), stressors and sources of joy/resilience from sociopolitical contexts (e.g., the impacts of bullying, anti-trans policy debates, community acceptance), adolescent/young adult brain development, and the psychosocial factors that affect all teens and emerging adults. As your daughter's physical appearance develops, her transition will be more apparent to people who've known her previously. At the same time, her appearance (e.g., height) may be different from her average cis girl peers. While some people on hormone therapy feel most affirmed by being gender non-conforming, others can experience dysphoria.

In the initial period of their transition, girls and young women can be more identifiable by strangers as trans, which can put them at risk for experiencing bias and non-affirmation. As such, for a young person experiencing gender dysphoria, hormone therapy can be a key part of their embodiment and alignment process and help to reduce the distress of gender dysphoria significantly. However, most trans young people's complete alignment will lag behind their expectations, which can make their experience a bit mixed in the initial weeks to months of starting HRT. Adding external factors as your child initiates a "second puberty" can also make this time challenging. Connection to an affirming community, celebration of body and gender diversity, engagement in meaningful activities both related and unrelated to transness, and mental health support can all be critical in healthy emotional development during this time.

Cristy Mereles (LCSW): Just as when puberty starts with cis girls, changes on HRT are slow and gradual. Over time, you might see more fat distribution to the hips and chest area, softening of facial features, pimples, breast buds, and mood swings. Beyond that there are mental health changes as well, which can include:

- Ability to access more fully her feelings (as described to me by many clients).
- Daily dysphoria showing up in a new way, as she is reminded each time she takes her pills that she is not cis (an experience that for some is mirrored in parents through their awareness of this as well).
- Excitement over having access to the puberty she has always envisioned for herself.
- Well-meaning (and sometimes just plain nosey) family and friends noticing and commenting on physical changes such as breast buds, and extended unsolicited discussions with them as they understand that medical affirmation was started.

Debi Jackson: I was one of those people who feared having a teen go through puberty because I remember what my own was like. I wasn't looking forward to wild mood swings and the like. But the great thing about HRT is that it's very slow and measured! Avery chose to use patches for their ease of use, and since it's an application of a precisely dosed amount of estrogen on each patch, and you simply change it out in the middle of the week, there are no highs and lows from swinging hormone levels.

You'll work with your teen's doctor to monitor how your daughter is doing, if she's having any hot flashes, acne, or other negative effects. Your doctor will check levels with regular blood work and check bone age every few months to ensure she isn't progressing through puberty too quickly (estrogen causes the growth plates on the ends of bones to close, so the slower the progression of estrogen, the taller she can get). Avery felt such a relief to be able to start puberty at an age close to her peers and said, "I finally feel like my life is moving forward." It's been the easiest and most mentally beneficial part of her journey to date.

Our assigned female at birth (AFAB) child wants to bind their chest. Is this safe? What do I need to know?

Dr. Danielle O'Banion: Binding is, in general, safe and well tolerated. However, plenty of people have negative effects from binding their chests that are important to be aware of. (We like to use the term "chest," as "breasts" is often coded feminine or female and can trigger dysphoria in a young person, while "chest" is a more neutral term.)

There are many different ways to bind one's chest. The best method is dependent on an individual's chest size, concurrent medical conditions (e.g., asthma, anxiety), tolerance of discomfort, and how much they want or need to compress (i.e., how flat they want or need their chest to appear). Binding techniques can range from wearing tight sports bras to specially made products like trans tape and compression binders. Many people prefer the specially made binders as they are more effective and are designed to maximize comfort. Trans tape is quite effective as well but can cause skin irritation, which can be quite severe for anyone with sensitive skin or skin conditions like eczema. If your child or family cannot afford a binder, there are numerous micro-grants and mutual aid opportunities to make these more accessible. Many of the larger brands of binders also have special programs to offer reduced cost or free binders.

Compression of the chest will restrict breathing capacity to some degree. For people who are minimally binding and/or have smaller chests, this restriction will be mild and may not be particularly noticeable. At the other end of the spectrum, for people who are trying to compress large chests to a very flat appearance, the restriction can be more severe. Anyone who has other conditions that already restrict breathing capacity (particularly asthma) will need to be cautious about the intensity of their compression methods. Similarly, if a youth is active (e.g., sports, dance), they should be prepared that binding can limit aerobic capacity. They may want to adjust to less restrictive methods during the activity.

Some negative effects of binding include: chest, neck, and back pain; heartburn/reflux and increased irritable bowel symptoms; shortness of breath or chest tightness; and pelvic pain. These effects are generally not permanent and will be relieved when the person stops binding. However, if a person binds over the course of years, their body may develop physical compensations that can cause lingering effects for some time afterwards. Sometimes a course of physical therapy may be required to recover from the negative effects of binding. Importantly, young people may be hesitant to report their discomfort to their parents for fear of not being allowed to use the binder, so you may need to proactively check in and be open to a harm-reduction approach. Your child may prefer the side effects of binding over the emotional distress of gender dysphoria that binding can alleviate. Their provider team should be made aware of any impacts of binding so they can help address them. If the binding causes mild to moderate symptoms, you can help your child find an optimal balance of physical and psychological comfort and well-being. If symptoms are severe, strategizing with your child's doctor around the risks and benefits of binding is a good idea. Sometimes it is recommended for young people to take intermittent breaks from binding, for example on the weekends or after school, to minimize its negative health effects.

Amy Cannava (NASP): It is neither atypical nor uncommon for AFAB persons who are transgender, non-binary, agender, gender queer, and so on to want to compress their chest area so as to diminish what is generally regarded as a "feminine" physique. Binding does have some physical health risks, but also likely has mental health benefits. There are ways to bind "safely," but any time you are compressing your body for an extended period, there will be consequences. Wearing a binder can result in the breakdown of fatty tissue, restriction in lung expansion, and so on. It can also relieve dysphoria.

While I recognize professionally that I was "gatekeeping" with my own trans child, I used a "Binder Contract" in my own home. This made me feel better in knowing that the young person in my care had made knowledgeable and informed decisions *and* that they were binding as safely as possible.

Sometimes parents will ask "Why can't he/they just wear a sports bra?" Well, sports bras are intended to minimize movement of breast tissue, which sometimes also compresses it slightly, but the intent is not to conceal it. The tightest part of a sports bra is the elastic band which lies *underneath* the breast tissue rather than on top of it, thus compressing the rib cage. In contrast, a binder has spandex throughout which allows for chest compression. Sometimes youth will try wearing multiple sports bras backwards, which is not safe, because this results in the straps being over the breast tissue. Similarly, ACE bandages can cause asphyxiation and should never be used. Binders must be sized appropriately, using the manufacture's sizing guidelines, and people should wear what is recommended for their dimensions and not attempt to downsize to look "flatter." Binders should also be worn for less than 12 hours at a time and not during physical activity.[25]

That said, in listening to transgender physical therapists and massage therapists, I've learned to modify my expectations as a cisgender person and recognize that sometimes we have to consider "less risk" because there is no such thing as "no risk." For example, we may not want a young person to sleep in a binder, but there may be times when wearing a binder (such as overnight at a sleepover, school trip, nights of high dysphoria) is *less* risky than the risk in not wearing one which can "out" our young people or create dysphoria which leads to self-injurious behaviors or suicidal ideation. We also must realize that while binders do cause breakdown of tissue, it's likely to be breakdown of tissue that they desire to be ultimately removed. Trans-affirming physical therapists and bodywork specialists can be instrumental in working with people who bind to discuss safer binding, how to work muscles and posture to relearn bad habits from hunching to conceal chest size, and so on. In general, it's important to find trans-affirming medical and mental health professionals so that young people feel confident and competent in discussing their experiences.

---

25 Peitzmeier, S., Gardner, I., Weinand, J., Corbet, A., & Acevedo, K. (2017). Health impact of chest binding among transgender adults: A community-engaged, cross-sectional study. *Culture, Health & Sexuality, 19*(1), 64–75. doi: 10.1080/13691058.2016.1191675

Janis Tannehill: Binding is a stopgap measure to help your AFAB pubescent-to-post-pubescent child deal with breasts. From their perspective, they are seeking to minimize a body part that doesn't fit with their self-perception of male or non-binary. Breasts to them might be anything from an inconvenience to a source of anguish and betrayal of their body that outs them and reminds them constantly that they are in the wrong body. My son felt better when his "boy" shirts fitted properly as a result of compressing his breasts. Binding is good for mental health for these reasons.

Binding can be done safely if the proper precautions are followed. It is easy to get a proper fitting binder if you follow the sizing instructions correctly (our preferred vendor is gc2b). A binder should be snug enough to compress breast tissue but not so tight that it is difficult to breathe. My son could safely bind for 8–12 hours a day but was careful not to bind while exercising and never while sleeping. My son was short and buxom, so he found the long binders that went down to the waist far more useful than the half-length ones that would roll up. ACE bandages or sticky binding tape should be avoided since they can carry severe health risks.

Binding is a good way to help your child through a difficult patch. Some people may find binding a temporary or perfectly acceptable long-term solution, especially those gender fluid or non-binary people who come to find that they enjoy some flexibility in their look. Some people do not, and binding is an intermediary to top surgery. Binding galvanized my son to work towards getting top surgery as quickly as possible and made him very, very sure that surgery was what he wanted.

What if I agree to let my child (under 18) have top surgery and then my child regrets it? I worry my child will blame me for not being the adult and setting the boundary.

Darlene Tando (LCSW): It is so hard as parents to feel that we're in the position of making decisions for our youth, and it can feel heavy, especially when there are no guarantees. Rest assured that while no outcome is guaranteed, the rate of regret from top surgery is extremely low, and top surgery can have a profoundly positive impact on dysphoria. Another thing to keep in mind is that if your child has gone through an estrogen-driven puberty and has a male/trans masculine gender identity, getting top surgery is more of a compassionate intervention than a decision.

Cristy Mereles (LCSW): Investing in your child's ability to know themselves is more powerful than trying to protect them from themselves in this situation. It is such a boost to their self-esteem when their parent(s) trusts them to be their own best expert on who they are. Research shows that affirmed children are as secure in their gender identities as their cisgender peers.[26] Other studies have shown that trans youth can have mental health outcomes not statistically different from the general population.[27] Other studies looking at top surgery have found that trans masculine youth who have had top surgery have significantly better mental health and less dysphoria than their peers who have not had access to it.[28]

Janis Tannehill: Top surgery was the best thing I could have ever done for my kid, and I only wish I had done it sooner. My son's breasts caused him so much self-hate and emotional torture. So much of his life was spent hiding his body—poor posture, giant hoodies no matter the season, showering in the dark or only showering when he could watch YouTube videos to distract himself from being naked. He hated how he looked, hated that boys' clothes were not designed to fit double Ds and never looked right on him, hated that binding was a constant reminder of being trapped in the wrong body, making it hard to breathe and be active. Sparing your child this kind of pain is not something that you will regret. They won't either.

---

26 Gülgöz, S., Glazier, J. J., Enright, E. A., Alonso, D. J., *et al.* (2019). Similarity in transgender and cisgender children's gender development. *Proceedings of the National Academy of Sciences, 116*(49), 24480–24485. doi: 10.1073/pnas.1909367116

27 Olson, K. R., Durwood, L., & McLaughlin, K. A. (2016). Mental health of transgender children who are supported in their identities. *Pediatrics. 137*(3), e20153223

28 Olson-Kennedy, J., Warus, J., Okonta, V., Belzer, M., & Clark, L. F. (2018). Chest reconstruction and chest dysphoria in transmasculine minors and young adults: Comparisons of nonsurgical and postsurgical cohorts. *JAMA Pediatrics, 172*(5), 431–436. doi:10.1001/jamapediatrics.2017.5440

Transgender people changing their mind later is exceedingly rare. I told my kid while we were waiting to go into surgery that if he changed his mind in the future that he could get a really nice, tiny, perky rack. He scoffed and told me that wasn't going to happen (his exact words were probably closer to "I'd rather eat fucking broken glass"). He was sure. I needed to be as well.

I am serious, it is the best thing I have ever done for him. After the initial recovery and spending a week in the easy chair on pain-killers and watching Bob Ross paint happy trees, the change in him was astounding. It was as if his body opened up. He stood taller, his shoulders went back, his chin rose, he looked people in the eye and smiled more. The baggy clothes went away and a shopping trip for shirts that actually fitted him was in order. He dressed better, took care of his body more, went out and chose to spend more time socializing with his peers.

Your kid is going to blame you for a lot of things in their lives; it is a part of growing up, understanding that your parents did the best they could with the information they had at the time. If they blame you for giving them something that they desperately wanted and needed as a child that they later regret, then they know that you did what looked to be best for them at the time. But, based on the evidence out there, the odds of them regretting it are very low, and the odds of causing metal harm to them by creating an artificial delay are high.

Our trans son is having top surgery. What do I need to do to prepare?

Dr. Danielle O'Banion & Sebastian M. Barr, PhD: The first thing we would stress is to make good use of your consultation and pre-op appointments with the surgeon. Even if your son is not a minor, if you are going to be helping him during recovery, you should attend those appointments, ask questions, and take notes. The surgical team will have guidance on medical preparation and on recovery specific to both the particular procedure and to your son's individual needs. It is important that the surgical team and surgical center are affirming of your son's gender, and it is appropriate for you and/or him to advocate for that and incorporate it into decisions about where to go for surgery.

Generally, you and he should anticipate that he won't be able to lift his arms for up to a month after surgery. Everyone heals a little differently and on a slightly different timeline, but plan for four weeks of reduced mobility, which means letting school and work know about those limitations. Make sure he has all his routine medications refilled and with him, especially if he is traveling for surgery. Plan ahead for sedentary and low-movement activities that can be engaging and comforting during the acute recovery phase (movies, video games, puzzles). Help him set up his recovery space so that he can comfortably recline and have access to these activities. You may also want to plan what foods and beverages he will need in the days following surgery. His surgical team will have guidance on post-operative diet and the timeline for gradually transitioning from clear liquids back to a full diet.

This is an outpatient procedure but does require general anesthesia, so be prepared for the after-effects of anesthesia—namely that immediately after surgery he will be quite out of it and will need a lot of hands-on care from you, and he may experience nausea (which can also be brought on or worsened by the pain medications he takes). Anesthesia can also impact mood negatively and sometimes we see the emergence of depressive symptoms in the days and weeks after surgery, which can be worsened by lack of mobility, as physical movement is often an important part of our mental health. Reduced independence can also have negative impacts on some people's moods. Of course, the psychological impact of top surgery is complex because generally people report a great deal of excitement and relief after the surgery. Helping your son lean into those feelings and celebrate or reflect on what he's accomplished and gained can offset the potential mood impacts of the anesthesia and recovery limitations.

Other good ideas for managing mood: prepare in advance to have fun social activities (e.g., video calls with or visits from supportive friends); follow the surgeon's guidance on gradually reintroducing movement (e.g., short walks) as soon as possible; try to find ways to incorporate brief time outdoors; have your son think through in advance what is good for his mental health generally, and incorporate accessible versions of those things into recovery plans.

It is good preparation to have a clear sense of what to expect medically from recovery. Again, his surgeon will be able to get into specifics regarding his case, but generally, expect acute recovery to be confined to one to two weeks. During this phase, most surgeons use drains to help the body remove fluid that might otherwise build up and get in the way of inner tissue healing. Your son will need help emptying the drains—and ideally, the person helping him with this aspect of the care shouldn't be very squeamish as they'll be dealing with blood and bodily fluids. This will also be the phase when there is the most soreness and tenderness. Most folks only need non-steroidal anti-inflammatory drugs (like ibuprofen or Celebrex), but his surgeon may prescribe a short course of low-level narcotics (e.g., tramadol, hydrocodone).

Although the acute recovery phase is over by about two weeks, it typically takes four to six weeks for the healing process to complete—though again, this is different for everyone and dependent on a lot of factors, so the surgical team can give him a more specific picture of this. Aesthetically, you and he should also anticipate that his chest is going to look as if he has just had surgery during this period. Additionally, for the first six months or so the scars at his incision sites will be discolored (darker colored or bright pink, depending on skin tone); this will become less noticeable after time. There is nothing he should be doing during the healing process for scar management. After that four- to six-week period, there are differing opinions on scar management. There's not great evidence that advertised scar reduction techniques work, though some people like to try these. If he has a known history of keloid scarring, you should be in good communication with the surgeon about whether there are ways of minimizing this, though this may be an unavoidable way his body heals. Many trans guys and non-binary folks who have top surgery embrace their scars; others use tattoos to celebrate their surgery or to make the scars less apparent; others still have scars that fade over time naturally.

We'll end with underlining the importance of being in good

communication with the surgical team. You should closely follow the surgeon's advice on aftercare, as this will be critical for the best outcomes. Additionally, although quite rare, surgeries can have complications or aesthetic imperfections, which surgeons can address through revision.

Amy Cannava (NASP): There really isn't that much you need to do to prepare! I was incredibly surprised at how easy the entire process was. We drove to the provider's office for a consult, scheduled the surgery, did the pre-op lab work and medical/mental health clearances locally, and then drove back down for the surgery. Different providers may be different, but there were few appointments. The day after the procedure we had a post-op appointment, then another a week later to remove the drains, and then I believe two more after that. I say "we," but it was really his appointments; I was merely the chauffer and the funding source!

Before surgery, I wish we'd done more research on providers—we ended up finding one who "everyone" went to and that was who we stuck with because this doctor was the first person to tell him that he could have the surgery. The doctor became instantly revered in my son's eyes. She recommended pineapple beforehand and he ate lots of it, which helped to keep swelling down.

After surgery, what we weren't told is that we needed to stay in the area for a post-op the following morning. I'll never forget him turning to me when coming off the anesthesia, worried that they hadn't removed his breast tissue because he woke up in a packed compression vest. The first time he tried to sit up in bed I wanted to help him sit up because he was in pain, and it broke my heart, but the nurse stopped me. She told me he had to do it on his own. That was among the hardest things, not helping too much. I was most cautious in putting his seatbelt on and taking it off in the car so as not to add extra pressure.

After surgery, in the hotel, he mostly slept so he didn't need much help. He was hungry the first night and wanted Panera soup but needed some help to eat it because of the "T-Rex" arms (doctors recommend that you do not extend beyond the range of a T-Rex's arms). He was a little nauseous but had medication to prevent it. He was a little sore when the meds ran out, but the pain diminished quickly and by the middle of the week following surgery he was telling me to go back to work. When I did so I left things for him near his bed on a tray table, and the stuff on the counter I left close to the edge so he could reach it. We put a stepladder near the microwave that was over the stove so he could reach it without over-stretching. I put a folding chair in my shower and had him sit in it with a poncho over it so I could wash his hair. Prior to the surgery, I'd done research on what to have on hand. He really liked the "elephant pillow" which allowed him to sit up as straight as he could and feel supported, as well as the lap desk which allowed him to easily eat in bed.

Once we had approval to use them, he loved the silicone strips and Vitamin E cream to prevent/reduce scarring. A cursory look on Amazon revealed how much easier it is to find silcone strips now! They also make silicone gel but he didn't like it as much. We covered the incision with Tegaderm when he was allowed to shower, and that helped to keep water off of the incisions. I am very squeamish around blood and was worried about having to drain the drains, but it was really easier than expected! The hardest thing was the daily bribes for him to keep the compression vest on post-surgery as directed, which is honestly the most important part, and I believe what saved him from having to have a revision.

Lessons learned: if we could go back and do it again, I would have interviewed multiple surgeons so that *I* felt more comfortable with the one chosen. I also wouldn't have reluctantly agreed to have his girlfriend to stay with us during the surgery (I'm sure partners are often desired and vary from person to person but in my case it resulted in me having two "kids" to take care of as opposed to a second set of hands). I would also have motivated him to further develop his core muscles before surgery—that is what actually caused him the most pain, because your core muscles go into overdrive when you're not allowed to reach with your arms or support yourself in sitting/standing up.

Another concept for you and your child to be familiar with is post-operative depression. There can be an over-reliance or over-dependence on medical transitions, with the expectation that they will completely eliminate gender dysphoria and other mental health concerns. While medical transitions often have positive benefits for mental health, they are not magic cures. The Gender Confirmation Center's article, *Being Ready for the Ups and Downs of Recovery*, is quite useful to help prepare parents and children for distinct possibilities.[29]

Janis Tannehill: Top surgery is the best thing I could have done for my son; it made the largest and most immediate positive impact on his life. By supporting them in this surgery, you are absolutely doing the right thing for your trans son.

The best source of information and advice I found was a Facebook group for top surgery and breast reduction. You will realize that there are many kinds of people going through this: trans men, non-binary people, cis men with medical issues, women recovering from cancer, the list goes on. They will compare results, issues, surgeons, costs, packing lists, you name it. They are also a great source of support and validation.

Money is a huge consideration. Depending on your state, your insurance and your kid's age, there is a wide range of what insurance will cover and when. One of our insurance providers would not cover anyone under 18, and the other had a huge deductible and was specific as to what kind of procedures it would and would not allow. Waiting was not an option for my son, so we ended up paying out of pocket then turning around and claiming it as additional medical expenses on income tax.

Age turns out to be a huge consideration in picking a surgeon. In our area of over six million people, there were only two plastic surgeons recommended to us by our gender clinic who were willing to work on transgender youth. Finding a surgeon can be difficult, but worth the research into their track record with results. People online will dish the dirt and share pictures, so don't necessarily take the glossy pictures in the waiting room as the only story. How respectful the office staff are of pronouns and chosen names is very telling, since they will see all the legal documentation. Our surgeon also required both medical and psychological clearance from our gender clinic.

---

29 Gender Confirmation Center (2020, June 10). *Being Ready for the Ups and Down During Recovery*. Accessed 01/11/2022 at www.genderconfirmation.com/emotional-physical-reactions

My son was at the surgical center for half a day, then we took him home. He slept in a lounge chair for about a week before going back to sleeping in his bed. The first ten days he had drains coming from his armpits, which is universally the most hated and uncomfortable part of the experience. Once those were out, he recovered quickly. He was off school for two weeks, and when he went back, he used a rolling backpack until he was cleared to lift more than 10 pounds. He couldn't lift his arms and it took him months to get the full range of motion back. He was also puffy and swollen for months, so it was a gradual process to get to the final result.

Our adult trans daughter is having vaginoplasty ("bottom surgery"). The surgery and aftercare really scare me. What should I know?

Dr. Danielle O'Banion: The great news is that the modern patient has a wealth of options and there are many surgeons with an abundance of experience with vaginoplasty and similar gender-affirming bottom surgeries. Many patients and families are comforted to learn that vaginoplasty is far from a recent development. This surgery has been performed for over a century, and in the past few decades has been further and further refined so that the technique is quite elegant.

It's also comforting to know that you should be far from alone in managing pre-operative and post-operative care. A great deal of work has gone on to build infrastructure to fully support vaginoplasty patients and lead to the best outcomes possible. Most of the hospitals in which these surgeries take place have multi-disciplinary teams that facilitate preparation and aftercare. Your daughter will receive education about aftercare over time, starting in the consultations before surgery and continuing to bedside post-operatively and in follow-up appointments and communication. Most surgical teams provide direct dial phone numbers or other direct call lines for questions and concerns in the post-operative period.

This is one reason why I encourage patients to be intentional in choosing their surgeon and surgical team. As with any other medical journey—particularly one with this level of pre-operative and post-operative care—the fit of the team cannot be understated. And as I mentioned above, there are now many experienced surgeons and surgical centers offering vaginoplasty and other gender-affirming bottom surgeries. If it is accessible to her and/or your family, I encourage having consultations with multiple surgical teams before selecting.

Another reason to be intentional in the surgeon selection process is that skilled and experienced surgeons have very low complication rates with vaginoplasty. When learning about surgeons and in consultations, don't be shy about pressing the team regarding outcomes and complications. Surgeons can offer photographs of healed surgeries (that previous patients have consented to be shared in this way) so your daughter can make an informed choice about a surgeon's aesthetic results. Additionally, she can ask surgical teams directly about the number of patients who have needed revisions and other corrective follow-up procedures. Because of the historical difficulty of accessing care, trans folks and their families can feel grateful for any affirming care that feels decent, but these days there are too many excellent surgeons and teams to not be a selective patient. She and/or your family should feel confident when going into surgery that she is in the hands of an experienced and skilled provider.

In terms of the surgery itself, there are different specific techniques, but broadly speaking, vaginoplasty is a reorganization of the genitalia. When we consider that everyone's genitalia initially develop from the same tissue—that is, there is no distinction between the tissue that will go on to become a penis or clitoris, for example, until about 11 weeks of pregnancy—it's easy to understand how a reorganization of genitalia can be (and is) quite successful in vaginoplasty. Although serious surgery, vaginoplasty is no more complex than the common cardiac and orthopedic surgeries that are frequently performed in hospitals.

To prepare for surgery, the surgeon will likely have your daughter complete hair removal prior to the surgery, which helps scrotal skin be more effectively used as vaginal skin. I tend to see best outcomes for people who undergo prescribed pre-operative electrolysis, though there are other options her surgeon may recommend. The reason intensive hair removal, which can be quite painful in this region, is important is to reduce the likelihood of post-operative hair regrowth in the vagina.

If possible, I also recommend that patients engage in pelvic floor physical therapy before surgery, though it's particularly imperative *after* surgery. This is because the operation does include some pelvic floor work and without physical therapy, patients may experience discomfort or pelvic floor dysfunction. Most major cities have trans-affirming pelvic floor physical therapists, and your daughter's surgical team should be able to refer her to an appropriate provider.

Here is a list of things you should know about the recovery process:

- As with any surgery, the initial weeks are challenging, because the patient has healing surgical sites. As with any surgery, there is wound care, drains to help heal, and sutures. A catheter is in place for a day or so while the urethra heals but this is removed before discharge. The surgical site itself is swollen in the immediate days and weeks after surgery and does not heal fully until six months after surgery, but patients are often surprised that it quickly looks fine.
- Having a primary care team (or someone) that is comfortable with post-operative vaginoplasty is important, mainly to assuage patient anxiety.
- Although there is a lot of swelling, the healing surgical wounds are intact, and are no different from any healing. Vaginoplasty and penile inversion techniques have been around since at least the early 1900s and have been refined since then—techniques these days are quite elegant.
- Patients will be in active recovery and managing pain and side effects from pain medication and anesthesia, but anesthesia can make you depressed.
- Different surgeons have different demands about whether or not to stop and when to restart HRT. There is no right answer because theoretically HRT can increase clot risk, but research is showing that the actual risk increase is negligible.
- It can be disorienting to have a once quite sensitive part of the body become a less sensitive post-operative site.

- Dilation: patients can experience discomfort, because the operation includes some pelvic floor work, so most providers recommend pelvic floor physical therapy before (and definitely after) surgery. Most major cities have trans-affirming pelvic floor physical therapy.
- The biggest post-operative complication is granulation/healing tissue. Probably the most common reason people have to follow up is because there can be slow-healing tissue, particularly around the opening of the vagina—this is a natural part of healing but the site can be tender, especially with dilation, and there may be discharge. This can linger for months so it's important to maintain good follow-up with the surgical team or primary care physician. It can be easily remedied with treatment options.
- If it is painful to dilate, that could indicate slow-healing tissue this should be followed up with the surgical team.
- Vaginal dilation is a technique that has been used for cis women for decades to help with pelvic pain and pelvic floor dysfunction and painful sex. It is not new and it need not be unpleasant. Dilation is an important maintenance modality to preserve vaginal patency—it's a thing you routinely have to do to keep the vagina healthy and flexible.

Dr. Matt Goldenberg: Medical treatments are a part of gender-affirming care, although others will choose not to take advantage of them or will lack the resources for them. As the parent of a person who will be undergoing gender-affirming surgery as an adult, I know it is common to experience many emotions. You may be unsure of what to expect after the procedure, and sometimes there may be logistics which still need management.

Gender-affirming surgery is often described as a peak moment in a person's transition. There is typically a long wait for the procedure, and a person must go through many obstacles to become eligible. It is important to understand that, as certain as your child may be that surgery is the right decision, they may also feel anxious and overwhelmed throughout the process. Worrying about complications, reaching a pain threshold, and taking the time needed to recover are common concerns. For parents and loved ones, it can be especially difficult to accept and understand that surgery is the next step in their child's gender transition.

Ask your child if they would be open to sharing with you the specifics of what to expect during surgery, or if they know of credible sources for more about the procedure. Many surgeons will provide information through their website and will send patients a packet of information about how to prepare, and what supplies will be needed for aftercare. Sometimes, having concrete information about what to expect can help to relax a worried imagination.

A way to deal with the anxiety or worry that your child is having surgery is to decide with your child what your role will be. There are ways that friends and family can be involved with the surgical process, should the person receiving care be welcoming of that. The initial days following surgery can be frightening for patients; they are often discombobulated from the interruption to their schedules and usual surroundings. Your support may be welcomed to coordinate contact with other friends and family, perhaps keeping tabs with concerned community members or providing updates on recovery. Or perhaps your support can be expressed by cooking meals for your child as they recover, given that immediately after surgery they will have limited mobility. Taking care of pets, cleaning their space, changing bedsheets, or managing mail or other household chores can also be helpful.

Reaching out to other parents who are raising transgender kids is important. You may not know what to ask or how to start a conversation. While in-person parent support groups are becoming more popular, if you do not have a supportive space in the physical community that you can turn to, there are virtual parent support groups as well.

At what point should I start exploring/ thinking about my child's future fertility and the impact of gender-affirming care?

Kelly Storck (LCSW): Exploring the future fertility of a young child can feel tricky, difficult to navigate, and loaded with feelings. Family building for trans people has a long history of being a misunderstood and underserved part of transgender healthcare. The good news is that the body of practice and data about fertility preservation in trans youth is growing, and there are effective options available to trans kids who desire, or may desire, to have biological children. Long-term use of hormone therapy may increase the risk of infertility, so steps toward fertility preservation are best explored between hormone blocking treatments and HRT or before starting HRT.[30] Conversely, there are studies showing that fertility for trans men, who went through endogenous puberty, comes back quickly after discontinuing HRT to a level comparable with cisgender peers.[31]

Currently, the most accessible treatment is the retrieval and freezing of reproductive material (i.e., sperm and egg banking). Sperm banking is less invasive, and more affordable, but the retrieval process can create significant dysphoria. Being unable to carry a pregnancy can be very painful for trans-feminine people, so be mindful of the grief that may occur in that realm. Egg banking is a significantly more invasive and expensive process but, if successful, allows trans men to have eggs available for their own pregnancy, a partner's pregnancy, or surrogacy. Your child's gender care professionals should be able to point you toward qualified and affirming providers for consultation. If fertility preservation does not occur in these early years, be aware that trans people have long been able to have biological children after HRT, often aided by a temporary pause in hormone therapy.[32] It's also very important that young people know that HRT alone will not protect them from pregnancy, so birth control methods should be used.

Janis Tannehill: Be prepared for the possibility that your gender non-conforming kid may not want children. Gender non-conforming

---

30 Cheng, P. J., Pastuszak, A. W., Myers, J. B., Goodwin, I. A., & Hotaling, J. M. (2019). Fertility concerns of the transgender patient. *Translational Andrology and Urology, 8*(3), 209–218. https://doi.org/10.21037/tau.2019.05.09

31 Leung, A., Sakkas, D., Pang, S., Thornton, K., & Resetkova, N. (2019). Assisted reproductive technology outcomes in female-to-male transgender patients compared with cisgender patients: A new frontier in reproductive medicine. *Fertility and Sterility, 112*(5), 858–865. doi: 10.1016/j.fertnstert.2019.07.014

32 Ibid.

does pop up in family groups so there is a real possibility that there is a biological genetic component to being trans. My son put it as, "Why would I want to pass on this genetic shitshow?"

Out of respect for his wishes, I haven't brought up the possibility of egg harvesting. However, as I sent him off to college, I did remind him that trans dudes can get pregnant without having to go off testosterone, and that going on birth control pills is on the table depending on his relationship status. I think his response was, "Eww!"

Chapter 7

Schools

The subject of schools and trans youth is one of the hardest for parents, and is a near universal topic of concern. Schools are a place where we struggle to protect our child, whether from bullies, hostile teachers, intransigent administrators, or hostile laws being passed at the state level. In this chapter, we are lucky to have a school psychologist and parent of a trans son join us as a subject matter expert who knows the ins and outs of laws and policies protecting children in schools. It also contains advice from parents from all over the country whose children transitioned any time between the ages of 4 and 17 and who share how they coped with these challenges.

My child is being bullied for being trans. What rights do I have and how can I make sure the school engages?

Amy Cannava (NASP): There are several laws and executive orders that protect LGBTQ youth from discrimination and harassment. However, I always say that the law protects you retroactively but it does not protect you in the moment. What that means is that the law is on your side when you want to speak out against the bullying behavior, but that hasn't prevented your child from being bullied in the first place. Some legal protections include:

- The US Constitution (and State Constitutions) guarantees all persons equal protection under the law. This means that LGBTQ youth cannot be singled out for discipline, nor can bullying be ignored.

- The 14th Amendment guarantees that no state will "deny to any person within its jurisdiction the equal protection of the laws." This means that schools must take equal efforts to thwart reports of bullying of LGBTQ youth and non-LGBTQ youth.
- The Patsy Mink Equal Opportunity in Education Act of 2002, also known as Title IX, states that a person cannot be excluded on the basis of "sex" (which has been interpreted to mean gender), or be denied the benefits of, or be subjected to discrimination under, any education program or activity that receives federal funds. In 2014, the Department of Education issued guidance on Title IX indicating that it protects gender identity expression as well and that such is retroactive.

On June 16, 2021, the US Department of Education's (DOE) Office for Civil Rights (OCR) issued a Letter of Interpretation reiterating that it would enforce Title IX regulations to protect students on the basis of sexual orientation and gender identity.[1] Acting Secretary for Civil Rights, Suzanne B. Goldberg, stated that "The Department of Education strives to provide schools with the support they need to create learning environments that enable all students to succeed, regardless of their gender identity or sexual orientation."

Equity in education means that all students have access to schools that allow them to learn and thrive in all aspects of their educational experience. As part of the mission to protect all students' civil rights, it is essential that OCR acts to eliminate discrimination that targets LGBTQ students. *Confronting Anti-LGBTQI+ Harassment in Schools: A Resource for Students and Families* was created by the DOE in partnership with the Department of Justice (DOJ) to provide helpful guidance for families.[2]

Many states have laws which prohibit bullying, harassment, and

---

1   www.ed.gov/news/press-releases/us-department-education-confirms-title-ix-protects-students-discrimination-based-sexual-orientation-and-gender-identity
2   US Department of Justice and US Department of Education. (2021). *Confronting Anti-LGBTQI+ Harassment in Schools: A Resource for Students and Families*. Washington, DC: US Department of Justice and US Department of Education. Accessed 18/07/2022 at www2.ed.gov/about/offices/list/ocr/docs/ocr-factsheet-tix-202106.pdf

discrimination. Many delineate LGBTQ youth as part of this law. The Movement Advancement Project maintains an up-to-date map called Safe School Laws, noting anti-bullying and non-discrimination laws by state, as well as whether or not the laws delineate sexual orientation and/or gender identity.[3] Executive Order 14021 of March 8, 2021, by President Joe Biden, guarantees an educational environment free from discrimination on the basis of sex, including sexual orientation and gender identity.[4]

Every child has a right to feel safe at school. Talk to your child. Do they desire your intervention? If your child does not feel safe, the school must intervene. That said, administrative attempts to stop bullying often backfire and make the bullying worse. Before going to the administration, try talking to your child's school counselor, who may be able to address the underlying issue with the bully rather than resorting to zero-tolerance regulations that often fail. If this is not successful or you receive pushback, then go to administration.

Simultaneously, keep the lines of communication open with your child and be vigilant in observing their behavior *and* physical appearance to ensure that your attempts to protect them are not endangering them more and resulting in subsequent or greater bullying or assault. You can also file a complaint with the OCR if the school has not resolved the concern. The OCR will review the complaint, and if they decide to investigate, will notify the school/district that a complaint has been filed, and the case is investigated. The school must then prove that the targeted bullying did not occur, or that they handled it appropriately when first notified.

OCR complaints are not anonymous; but while you have to include your name or the name of the person involved, you can opt to keep your name and contact information confidential during the investigation by indicating such on the OCR contact form. The OCR also publishes monthly lists of the elementary and secondary schools under investigation, which do not contain the names of the petitioners. Additionally, if your child has either a Section 504 Plan or an Individualized Education Program (IEP) and the bullying prevents

---

3   www.lgbtmap.org/equality-maps/safe_school_laws
4   Exec. Order No. 14021, 86, Fed. Reg. 46 (March 11, 2021). Accessed 18/07/2022 at www.govinfo.gov/content/pkg/FR-2021-03-11/pdf/2021-05200.pdf

your child from attending school or accessing instruction, this may constitute a denial of FAPE (free access to public education), which can result in compensatory services. This can be addressed at the school/district level or through the OCR.

Another consideration is recognition of the unfortunate reality of potential harassment and discrimination. While no child should ever face abuse, we must prepare our youth for the world we all currently live in. At some point, everyone will face negativity. Therefore, our job (as parent and professional) requires us to build youth up, by helping them to find resiliency and capitalize on strengths, so that when they are pushed down by external forces, they either remain standing or have the willpower to get back up again. We remind them that they are loved and valued even when they might not feel as if they are. And we remind them that we will always stand behind them or in front of them, as they desire us to.

Janis Tannehill: Bullying is an unfortunate part of the school experience. Kids who are different have always been a target for harassment and bullying, and LGBTQ youth experience greater than their share. Gender non-conforming kids tend to flock together and find safety in numbers that way. Despite the multitude of anti-bullying campaigns, the reality is that schools are unprepared, understaffed, and sometimes just unwilling to handle bullying of LGBTQ youth. It is up to us as parents to go through official channels and document everything if we want to see anything change, but even then, it is a battle that we are often not equipped to win.

Physical bullying that causes injury and leaves marks is in some ways the easiest to deal with since there is evidence of wrongdoing. It is hard for the school to ignore the nurse's report of a bloody nose or bruising. In my opinion, if the bullying is physical the school has exactly one chance to respond to complaints and do something about it. The second time, I'm calling the police and filing an assault charge, and the school can deal with the consequences of their inaction. Kids are smarter than that and will skirt the line of legality knowing that the victim carries the burden of proof; most know better than to leave evidence.

Psychological bullying and exclusion are more likely to happen.

Since it is difficult to enforce behavior based on the lack of some-thing, resolution on bullying like leaving your kid out of a group is almost impossible. In the younger grades, some schools will use restorative tactics and try to talk kids into being one big happy group. Going this route will at least put your kid on the administration's radar and make it easier to get in to see the counselor later. Kids have other plans, though—they put up with intervention as long as they are in the principal's office but will go right back to leaving out the "weirdos" as soon as they leave.

For girls, I think it comes down to the way they socialize each other. To be integrated into the group there are certain societal expectations we are supposed to uphold, and girls seem especially invested in this. If someone they perceive to be a girl is not acting in the socially approved way, the group will work extra hard to make them do so by rewarding "feminine" behaviors with attention and punishing "masculine" ones with harsh words and exclusion. Some of us are just socially awkward and never really figure out how to play this game.

My trans son was doubly thick about it, since his brain worked in a different, more direct, and more stereotypically male way. Of course, he didn't know this when he was young; he just knew girls were mean to him no matter how hard he tried to be the type of girl they expected, and act in the way his peers wanted. They didn't know he was a boy and neither did he. He looked like a girl, had a girl's name and said he was a girl, so why wasn't he toeing the party line and acting like it?

Elementary school was especially lonely for him. Middle school was better when he found other gender non-conforming youth and theater kids. High school only became bearable after transition, when he was seen as one of the guys and got to socialize as one of them. It wasn't perfect but at least he spoke their language.

Cyberbullying can harm just as easily as a fist. For all their bluster, schools will not do a damn thing about kids hounding some queer kid online until they want to commit suicide. Unless it can be proven that the harmful words, embarrassing pictures, or video came from a school computer, were sent using school accounts, and happened in school time, the administration is largely incapable of doing anything about it.

Once the school made it apparent that they were powerless I locked down all social media and started collecting school directories. If the school wasn't willing to let parents know what their kid was up to online, I was.

Sometimes the best way to win the game is to not play at all. As a parent, being involved in my kid's extra-curricular activities and driving him to school helped me act as a physical buffer by minimizing the time he was on his own without a witness. Privacy settings and the block feature are essential. My kids didn't have any kind of social media presence for a very long time and what they did have was severely locked down to people and classmates I knew. Teasing them without their knowledge is no fun. Now that my oldest is off to university and is an adult in the eyes of the law, he is on his own. Maturity counts for a lot, and now that he is dealing with adults as an adult, the bullying element has fallen away. It really does get better; just get through high school.

Our school is not supportive, what should we do?

Amy Cannava (NASP): To answer this question cohesively it would be important to know *what* specifically is occurring that is not supportive of your child. Are you receiving pushback about the school requiring "official" documentation? Is the school protesting about your child playing sports? Is it setting up hurdles? Is the curriculum not trans-inclusive? Are teachers not honoring names and pronouns? That said, contrary to what many schools will try to tell you (and students), students' rights do not end at the school door. Know Your Rights (ACLU)[5] is a phenomenal resource, as are other parents who have forged the trail before you. It's becoming increasingly less likely that you are the first parent of a transgender kid in your district, but that doesn't always mean that children before yours have had the same gender identity or same experience. The waters are likely charted, but they're ever-changing.

5   www.aclu.org/know-your-rights

Before you do anything, however, speak with your child. How much do they want your assistance in intervening? Be ready to listen if they ask you to stop. This will help them feel control and empowerment at a time when they might not feel any, but also ensure that you are supporting what they want rather than proceeding with what you feel they need.

First, consider the difference between levels of ignorance—is the school simply ignorant in that it doesn't know, or is it willfully ignorant in spite of access to and opportunities for information? I'd treat these differently depending on whether the school is naive or hostile. Second, know your allies and know state law. Is the school following the law? If so, your battle might be with local legislators. If your school is not, the local ACLU or other transgender-affirming non-profits might rally for you. Is the school following the district policy? Is the policy inadequate? If it's inadequate, find your allies and start speaking at school board meetings. If it's not being followed, your complaint lies with district administration and/or your school board representative.

In 2020, the Human Rights Campaign (HRC) Foundation published a pamphlet on *Advocating for LGBTQ Students with Disabilities* in partnership with the National Association of School Psychologists' (NASP) LGBTQI2-S Committee and a few other organizations.[6] We all know that being LGBTQ is *not* a disability, but that there are LGBTQ youth who also happen to have disabilities. The pamphlet reviews some relevant laws and how to help students from a best practices standpoint. That said, there's a huge distinction between *accommodations* and *allowances*. Most often, schools push back on transgender rights because they think these students are seeking to be *treated differently* and *accommodated*. This is incorrect; more often than not, students are just asking to be *allowed* to do what every other student does—go by a "nickname," use the restroom they feel comfortable using, play on sports teams corresponding to their gender identity. Taken from this standpoint, the courts have already

---

6   www.hrc.org/press-releases/hrc-partners-release-guide-to-help-educators-and-parents-advocate-for-lgbtq-students-with-disabilities

ruled that "separate but equal is inherently unequal" and there are many laws which recognize this (including the US Constitution).

There is nothing in federal law that states that schools require legal documentation to honor a student's name or gender identity. However, most state laws do allow for them to do so, and some states do require it (or make it very difficult to do so without). Consider working with allied school-based mental health professionals (school counselors, psychologists, and social workers) who can assist in advocating for your child. Also, consider meeting with a school nurse who can advocate from a medical perspective. Your students' rights don't cease to exist because another student is feeling uncomfortable.

Schools cannot show favoritism or punish a small group of students to avoid backlash. Offer to educate the school administration and/or staff, or suggest they bring in someone who can. Always start at the bottom of the hierarchy ladder and only work your way up as needed.

We must remember, though, that at the end of the day, it's still your child and not you entering the building. There's a fine line between advocating on behalf of your child and unintentionally making them a target. Also, realize that because you want what's best for your child and will remain their greatest advocate and ally, you will likely want and expect things at a faster pace than the school can keep up with. Every modicum of positive change toward being a supportive environment will make a difference. When the school experiences hurdles, ask, "How can I help?" This doesn't mean you're solely responsible for doing the work that the school needs to do, but if you make the offer, the school would look foolish to not be doing the work too.

Excellent resources are available which can be shared with schools, including Gender Spectrum's *Gender Inclusive Schools Toolkit*[7] and *Framework for Gender Inclusive Schools*,[8] and HRC's *Welcoming Schools*,[9] which provide excellent elementary school level resources. At the secondary level, much inclusion comes via the curriculum, not just the school climate. The Gay, Lesbian, & Straight Education

---

7   www.gatewaypublicschools.org/sites/default/files/inline-files/gender_inclusive_schools_toolkit.pdf
8   www.genderspectrum.org/articles/framework-for-gender-inclusive-schools
9   https://welcomingschools.org

Network (GLSEN) has resources on *Developing Inclusive Classroom Resources*.[10] Additional resources across grade levels include: *Supporting Transgender and Gender Diverse Students in Schools: Key Recommendations for School Administrators*,[11] *Let's Talk!* (part three of the four-part webinar created by Learning for Justice and Gender Spectrum to think beyond gender binaries in the classroom),[12] *Creating an LGBT-Inclusive Curriculum: A Guide for Secondary Schools*,[13] and *Gender Inclusive Curriculum*.[14] In fact, Learning for Justice (formerly "Teaching Tolerance") has helped to develop many lesson plans that discuss sexuality and gender with youth.

Debi Jackson: If your child's school is not supportive, find a Know Your Rights guide from a trusted resource. Many are available from organizations, including the Human Rights Campaign, ACLU, National Center for Transgender Equality, and National Center for Lesbian Rights. Additionally, these organizations have guides that will explain your child's rights under Title IX and the Equal Protections Clause, offer guidance to schools for creating inclusive policies, and help in creating a transition plan with the school. See the *Schools in Transition* guide as one of the most comprehensive options.[15]

School administrators might assume that you don't know what rights your child has and will position themselves as the authority to deny your requests to affirm your child. Arm yourself with information and speak with confidence. Send copies of the documents explaining those rights to them in an email. Make requests for meetings and follow-up communications in an email. Having a written "paper trail" of those conversations is critical. If you can, have meetings in person, and ask someone from a local LGBTQ organization like PFLAG or GLSEN to attend with you. Odds are the school will have multiple people in attendance and it's a good idea to have some sort of advocate with you, even if it is just to act as a witness in case there is a disagreement about what was said or agreed to later.

---

10 www.glsen.org/activity/inclusive-curriculum-guide
11 www.apa.org/pi/lgbt/programs/safe-supportive/lgbt/school-administrators.pdf
12 www.learningforjustice.org/professional-development/webinars/lets-talk-gender
13 http://the-classroom.org.uk/wp-content/uploads/2018/02/Inclusive-Curriculum-Guide-for-web.pdf
14 www.genderinclassrooms.com/inclusive-curriculum-1
15 www.aclu.org/sites/default/files/field_document/schools.in_.transition.2015.pdf

Regardless of how you communicate (emails, meetings, one-on-one conversations with one teacher or counselor), try to approach them with the attitude that you want to work with them towards the shared goal of supporting students so they can reach their highest potential. Going in with a teamwork attitude rather than a confrontational one can be a game-changer. If that gets you nowhere and your child is still not being affirmed and supported, a sternly worded message about getting an attorney to legally represent you can do wonders.

Wayne Maines: Keep records of the following:

1. All correspondence, no matter how seemingly trivial (include after-school activities).
2. Photos and videos of holiday events, demonstrating your child's displeasure with gender norms.
3. School lesson plans, health class, sports rules, and minutes of parent-teacher association (PTA) meetings.
4. All conversations with school officials, including date, time, who and topic. Whenever possible, follow up via email, "as per our conversation", and cc a friend or trusted community leader. Try to never attend a school administration meeting alone; bring a friend.
5. 504 plans, grades, comments on artwork, written work, and so on.
6. Any time your child complains about being sick or sad. (Tell their doctor; if the doctor says it is nothing, explain why it might not be true, and if they do not understand, find a new doctor.)
7. Your child's friendships, and whether these increase or decline.

My child never wants to go back to school due to taunting and bullying. What should I do?

Amy Cannava (NASP): Communicate. Seek help. Advocate. Do these three things simultaneously. I'll break them down:

1. *Communicate.* Keep the lines of communication open with your child; being bullied can result in people shutting down and withdrawing, which is counterproductive to their mental health. It is important that they feel loved and valued by you, and that they know they can talk to you about anything. You also want to make sure they're on board with you seeking help and advocating on their behalf. In fact, for older kids, asking *how you can help* is a good start. If they feel you can't, which is not uncommon because victims often feel hopeless and helpless, reassure them that you might not have all the answers, but you'll find them.

2. *Seek help.* Professional help. Being bullied has short-term and long-term consequences for mental health. Mental health professionals can help young people to understand that the bullying is more about the bully than the one being bullied, rebuild resiliency, build self-empowerment, reduce anxiety, address depressed moods, and teach coping skills. Unfortunately, past victimization leads to greater likelihood of subsequent victimization. Therefore, it is imperative to break the cycle. Ofer Zur, PhD, of the Zur Institute, which studies the psychology of victimization, postulates that, "Without blaming, the therapist's goal is to move the victim from blame to responsibility, from helplessness to accountability, and from hopelessness to empowerment."[16]

3. *Advocate.* As mentioned previously and by other parents, the school not only *should* do something, they *must* do something. The 14th Amendment guarantees that no state will "deny to any person within its jurisdiction the equal protection of the laws." This means that schools must take equal efforts to deal with reports of bullying of LGBTQ youth and non-LGBTQ youth.

If a student has a disability and the bullying has resulted in them not going to school, this constitutes a denial of FAPE, which is illegal.

---

16 Zur, O. (2008). Rethinking "Don't blame the victim": The psychology of victimhood. *Journal of Couple Therapy, 4,* 15–36.

Additionally, Title II of the Americans with Disabilities Act of 1990 applies if the bullying/harassment prevents attendance. Laws aside, the longer a student is out of school, the harder it is to get them back into school. Friendships continue and the curriculum is taught during the student's absence, making it hard for a student to keep up socially and academically. The school should work with you and the student to do a Return-to-School or Attendance Improvement Plan. Either should include interventions the school will take to help make the student feel safe, and a plan for who the student feels comfortable talking to when feeling unsafe or simply overwhelmed.

For example, who can the student report the bullying to? Who can they talk to? Is there a place in the building they can go to take a break and de-escalate? Who is providing counseling at the school level to help with reintegration into the school setting? All parents want to protect their kids but protecting them doesn't always mean removing them from the stressful environment. All students in America have a right to a public education and there are compulsory attendance laws requiring students to attend school. Work your way up the administrative bureaucracy chain reminding everyone you talk to of this, including school level administration, central office administration, school board members, and the State Department of Education. Additionally, filing a complaint with the Office for Civil Rights for students with disabilities can also light a needed fire. Students need to feel psychologically and physically safe to learn. When they don't, it's time for parents and educators to act.

Marsha Aizumi: My child did not want to go back to school after two years of being taunted and bullied. It was right after winter break of his senior year. I was devastated. I couldn't believe that I, a Director of Educational Programs for a drop-out recovery charter school, could not prevent my own child from wanting to drop out six months before graduation. I did not know at the time that my child was being bullied and harassed almost every day. He didn't want to tell me. He knew I would go down to the school to fight for him. Aiden said that on top of being bullied, he did not want to be a target for more humiliation by being a "mommy's boy." So my child told me that his panic attacks were getting so severe that he could not be in school. He was eventually diagnosed as agoraphobic.

Since Aiden only had six more months to graduate, I still met with the school. A plan was agreed, where he would get assignments from his teachers and work remotely. I wanted him to get a diploma from the high school and not the continuation program. Fortunately, the principal agreed with me. We also encouraged Aiden to go to school once a day to work in the administrative offices, since one of his electives was office aide. Aiden agreed, because he felt he would be protected from student taunts and bullying in the school office. I was grateful that he was able to get out, otherwise he would have spent the next six months isolated in his room.

For me, it was important to meet with the school to find options, while advocating for what I believed was best for my child.

Debi Jackson: If your child feels bullied to the point that they no longer want to go to school, escalate, escalate, escalate! Too many schools don't take bullying of LGBTQ students seriously, especially if they don't have enumerated policies about the bullying of, or discrimination against, those students. Sadly, in many states, not having those enumerated policies is the norm. All communications about the bullying should be in writing with a specified date by which you want to have a resolution. You have probably started with a teacher or counselor. If that doesn't get a result, move up to the principal and a Title IX coordinator. Above that, go to the superintendent and school board. All students have a right to a safe learning environment, no matter what any of those adults/authority figures personally believe about trans people. If you still get nowhere, consider getting an attorney, reaching out to a local LGBTQ equality organization, or approaching the media (only with your child's permission).

If all else fails, consider a transfer or homeschooling. We had to opt for homeschooling. When Avery socially transitioned at four, she was in a preschool and we had plans for her to attend a private school with most of those same classmates. When the classmates' parents ended up not being supportive, and we spoke to the school about affirming her as a girl and they said they wouldn't, we felt that we had very few options left. This was a decade ago and the first few cases fighting for the rights of trans students were just making their way through the courts. We couldn't imagine forcing her to go to school in a boy's uniform and being pushed into a boy's bathroom. It was a huge financial hit for me to leave my career behind and we struggled financially for years.

I know that homeschooling isn't an option for a lot of people. But depending on the age of your child (some middle school or high school age kids could stay home alone), it's something to consider. Many homeschooling communities are secular and filled with LGBTQ students. And after online schooling through the COVID pandemic, a lot of kids learned to adapt to that kind of learning environment. It might be an easier option now than it was when we started.

My child has a teacher who refuses to call him/ her by the correct pronoun. What should I do?

Amy Cannava (NCSP): Always talk to your child first. Depending on their age, they may or may not want your involvement and if they do, they may want it under certain terms. While you likely want to go in all Mama/Papa Bear with "guns blazing," I recommend saving the bravado until you need it. I would suggest going in to talk to the teacher, after setting up a time, or emailing them. Start from a place of confusion/fact-checking; keep the metaphorical gun in your holster with the safety on. "My son/daughter/child (or simply by name) has been telling me that you have not been calling him/ her/them by his/her/their name at school, but I know that I do not always get the whole story about what's going on at school. Can you please shed some light on this? Is there a problem or someone I should speak to about this?"

While the teacher may indeed be ignorant, remember that ignorance does not always mean willful disregard. Perhaps the teacher doesn't understand and would benefit from some education? Perhaps the teacher has never had a student who is gender diverse? Gender-diverse kids often reach a point of exhaustion from being asked to educate the world, and sometimes parents can take that task off their shoulders. It should never have to fall on parents and kids, but in the real world it often does. When it comes to questions (and I presume teachers who aren't affirming kids have them), I use the following response technique I learned in a sex education course for parents.

How to answer sexual orientation/gender identity (SOGI) related questions:

Step 1: When asked a sensitive question relater to SOGI, the first two words you may want to say are, "Good question." This validates the question and gives you time to be thoughtful in your response.

Step 2 A: For fact-based questions, if you have the empirical answer, state it simply and succinctly. If you're at all unsure, say, "I don't know. But I can find out."

Step 2B: For values, opinions, or personal-belief questions, use this to describe the diversity or range of beliefs and experiences: "For some, For others, For you..."

This same framework can be used to respond to teachers. Some may not be honoring names/pronouns because they simply don't know how to, because they are afraid of getting in trouble of going against you as the parent, or because they forget to. This is very different from outright refusal. In these situations, respond to them with fact-based answers as if they had asked questions. In the three situations referenced the answers can change slightly:

1. That's a good point. I can understand not knowing how to use "they" as a singular pronoun. We're used to using "they" as a plural, but we refer to individuals singularly. Grammatically, we still say "they are" when referring to a single person just as we would say "she is." What other questions do you have about names and pronouns?

2. That's a good point. I can understand worrying about getting in trouble. The school board does not have a policy regarding gender identity, but I've been advocating for one. I'm sure you've called Alexander "Alex" before and thought nothing

of it. Using my child's name and pronouns should be just as seamless. The difference is that Alex is still Alexander—he might prefer "Alex," but you're not outing him or making him feel distress when you call him Alexander...

3. That's a good point... I know in the beginning I too would mess up with names and pronouns. I sat down with my child when they came out and changed their name and explained that I very much respected them and wanted to call them their chosen name, but I also had 11 years of calling them something else so I might slip up from time to time and I was sorry. I then asked them how they wanted me to handle the situation when I did.

These types of questions are very different from intentionally challenging questions. They require a much more assertive and authoritative response. "You are absolutely entitled to your values, opinions, and personal beliefs and I will respect them. For some students, they use the name listed in your attendance list. For others, they go by nicknames. And for my child, they go by their chosen name. For some situations, like when you're not at school, you can do whatever you like regarding the transgender community. When at school, you are expected to follow the school board's policy. And for [my] child, if you're unwilling to do this, I will have to speak to the principal."

The teacher may not be a member of the National Education Association (NEA), but teachers' ethics and responsibilities generally still fall under it. The NEA has gone on record publicly stating that, "Every student matters, and every student has the right to be safe, welcomed, and valued in our public schools." In fact, it has been a corporate sponsor for the Human Rights Campaign's Time to Thrive conference for several years. In 2015, the NEA Representative Assembly passed NBI 45 which called on the association to inform state level affiliates and their members about the rights of transgender students, including the "right to be called by the name and pronoun that corresponds to their gender identity" (p.3). In 2016, the NEA published *Legal Guidance on Transgender Students' Rights*, which includes guidance on how students should be treated and addressed by teachers, key actions schools and districts should take, the legal protections of transgender and sexual minority students, and how student rights apply in "particular situations" (e.g., bathroom use, records).[17] This guidance, from a reputable source that teachers are familiar with, can be cited in conversations with teachers and other staff.

The last thing to consider is that there are consequences for all actions, both positive and negative. Is your child going to want to attend school with that teacher the day after you've had a difficult conversation with them? There is no doubt that kids should be affirmed and honored in all environments and contexts, but I think a large part of our role as parents and professionals is preparing kids for the world they live in today and serving as the executive functioning/ thinking ahead that kids rarely have/do. You want your kid to be respected and affirmed, but you also want your kid to be liked. The more negative conversations you have with their teacher (even if the negativity is driven by the teacher), the less liked that kid is going to feel, and possibly be.

So even if you have to elevate your concerns to the principal or district, always go back to square one with each new person you meet (which is very hard, I know!). Assume positive intent and keep the gun in the holster: *"Dear Principal, My child is transgender and goes by...and uses...pronouns. These have not been honored in...'s class. I've tried talking to the teacher, but I am less familiar with your school district policies or how to help the teacher address my child correctly. Perhaps you could assist me? I would be glad to share any resources I have or meet with anyone I should meet with. Please just let me know how you can help and what I can do on my end. Thanks!"*

Janis Tannehill: First, know your rights and the policies of your school district with regards to respecting preferred names and pronouns (as opposed to legal name changes). In some states you will have recourse and in some you won't. Start with the teacher

17 Brown, E., Gilbert, K., Koffman, M., Moore Krajacic, S., Sheridan, G., & Wiman, E. (2016). *Legal Guidance on Transgender Students' Rights.* Legal Insight: Legal Guidance on Transgender Students' Rights. Accessed 01/05/2021 at www.nea.org/sites/default/files/2020-07/2018_Legal%20Guidance_Transgender%20Student%20Rights.pdf

and work your way up the administrative chain of command. Put as much as possible in writing. Sometimes a simple, "As a reminder, my son may be Q on the class list but his name is X and he uses these pronouns" will suffice to show the teacher that this name change is real, not some passing fancy and not a joke. People act differently when they know their behavior is being monitored. If that doesn't work, start emailing and cc'ing everyone, from the school counselor, to the vice principal, up to the principal. Schools don't like to be embarrassed and would prefer to handle things internally. Some districts go by the "principal's discretion" as to what policies they will and won't enforce, so it comes down to luck of the draw with your principal, depending on whether they are an ally or an enemy. If your principal is not supportive, make sure you know who your school board representative is and reach out to them and the district.

In my son's experience, he had one electives teacher who could not seem to understand and despite having a legal, male name on the roster, would misgender him. He didn't tell me until close to the end of the year. The teacher was counselled after my son was no longer in their class, and retired a few years later so I don't know if their behavior ever changed.

Our child's school won't let them use bathrooms congruent with their gender identity. What should we do?

Amy Cannava (NCSP): First, be familiar with what your state laws are and what the district policy is. If the policy is either non-existent or insufficient, that's where you need to start, but policy change can take time and your kid has to pee. Unfortunately, courts have ruled on both sides of this issue, and where your school stands can fall under the rules of the circuit court which it feeds into geographically. Gender Spectrum put out a report entitled *Transgender Students and School Bathrooms: Frequently Asked Questions*, which was endorsed by the American Counseling Association, the National Association of School Psychologists, the National Association of Elementary School Principals, and the National Association of Secondary School

Principals, and provides guidance for schools in implementing inclusive school restrooms.[18]

Schools generally understand binary gender, whether that is cisgender male/transgender male or cisgender female/transgender female. Where I find they are often more confused and unnecessarily fearful is with gender fluidity. *Oh no! She was a girl yesterday and used the girls' restroom but is a boy today! Whatever will we do?!?* I find their fear is usually less about gender and more about sexuality, with the false presumption that your transgender kid is going to use the restroom with someone they are attracted to.

While I wouldn't necessarily remind schools of this, as someone who has worked in high schools for 20 years, I can assure you that when kids want to do *that*, they will, and it has nothing to do with gender identity and needing to use the restroom. Schools will sometimes offer single-user restrooms which are inconvenient and, due to their locations, stigmatizing. Your kid shouldn't have to traverse the entire campus to use the nurse's restroom and be tardy to class. In fact, courts have ruled that "separate but equal is inherently unequal." This extends beyond race. Unless your child *wants* to use the restroom in the nurse's office, they shouldn't have to and asking them to do so is unfair. In some places, it is illegal. If another student feels uncomfortable sharing a restroom with your child, they don't have to; they can either pee when your child is not in the restroom, or they can use the single-user restroom down the hall.

In 2021, there was a lot of media attention drawn to a case in Loudoun County Public Schools in Virginia, in which a student sexually assaulted two girls. This case is tragic for the students involved and will be for others if it becomes a barrier to schools' consideration of trans-inclusive policies. The first thing to understand is that there is no indication that the student was indeed transgender, nor was he pretending to be. The reality is that he and the female student had previously (consensually) had sex in the girls' bathroom.

Gender-diverse youth are statistically more at risk of harassment and assault than they are likely to perpetrate such. Further, research shows that a transgender youth's *perception of safety* is strongly

---

18   https://genderspectrum.org/articles/bathroom-faq

correlated with positive mental health; are those arguing against inclusive restrooms able to justify their opposition due to the same reason? A transgender student, on the other hand, who is forced to use an isolated single-stall restroom at the far end of campus is de facto outing themselves out as transgender, which could become another safety issue.[19]

As has been noted throughout this section, if your child is unable to attend school because of inability to go to the bathroom and they are protected under either Section 504 or the Individuals with Disabilities Education Act (IDEA), the interrupted instruction may be considered a denial of FAPE, resulting in the need for compensatory services. If your child does not have a Section 504 but experiences medical problems associated with inability to void (gastrointestinal problems, urinary tract infections, etc.) they may also be eligible for a Section 504 Plan.

The bottom line is that your child *should* have the right to use the restroom of their choice, but this may not be a protected right under the law where you reside. There is, however, a delicate line between drawing attention to the issue and drawing attention to your child which can be stigmatizing. Gavin Grimm fought for the rights of transgender students everywhere and his fight made incredible differences for countless students. But not all attention is positive; the legal battle and publicity undoubtedly opened him up to cyberbullying and media attention. While you're advocating on behalf of your child or even with your child, be vigilant in ensuring that the attention you're creating remains desired. If it stops being so, it's okay to retreat to protect your child.

Finally, as is discussed in HRC's *Advocating for LGBTQ Students with Disabilities,* there is a difference between an allowance and an accommodation. Schools will often act as if you're asking for special treatment for your child, but you're not. An *accommodation* is something that is done for or on behalf of your child, such as preferential seating or providing extended time. The school is not *doing* anything by simply *allowing* your child to use the restroom. Therefore, this

---

19 Weinhardt, L.S., Stevens, P., Xie, H., Wesp, L.M., *et al.* (2017). Transgender and gender nonconforming youths' public facilities use and psychological well-being: A mixed-method study. *Transgender Health, 2*(1), 140–150. doi: 10.1089/trgh.2017.0020

shouldn't require a meeting or any kind of special plan. No one is taking your child to the restroom (which would be a service) or building a separate restroom (which would be a modification) or ensuring that no other children are able to use the restroom at the same time as your child (this would be an accommodation). Sometimes it's best to keep things simple and remind schools to do the same—making a bigger deal out of something than it is results in it becoming a bigger deal than it is.

The school is segregating some events like "family life education" by sex. How should we handle this with our trans child?

Amy Cannava (NCSP): First and foremost, does your child want to participate in family life education? Yes, schools often segregate by gender, which can be an issue when transgender students are misassigned. Additionally, is the curriculum which is being taught LGBTQ inclusive? If it's not, sitting in a room of people of the same gender may still not be desired. Therefore, there are actually two underlying issues with this question: 1) Segregation by gender and/ or misassignment by staff and 2) lack of LGBTQ inclusive sexual health education.

First, the Sexuality Information and Education Council of the United States (SIECUS) actually does not recommend segregating by gender.[20] It also recognizes that "Sex Ed should be accessible, equitable, and inclusive for all." All students of every gender need to understand puberty, development, reproductive health, and sexual health. Knowing about your own body is necessary but not sufficient. When classes are needlessly segregated by gender, the issue becomes where does a student who is transgender, gender queer, agender, non-binary, bigender, or gender fluid go? From the offset, you may want to ensure that your transgender son is placed in the boys' class, but unless the curriculum is identical across classes, will your son be taught what he needs to know about his biological parts?

---

20 https://siecus.org

I would advocate for combined classes. I know schools sometimes say that the teacher or students may be "uncomfortable" discussing sex and their bodies with the opposite gender, but my argument is that we do live in a heteronormative world where the majority of people have sexual relations with the opposite gender. If the students are too embarrassed to talk about or learn about their own bodies and sex in a classroom with people of the opposite gender, they absolutely are not ready to be having sex yet! Also, not everyone in this heteronormative world has a desire to have relationships with people of the opposite gender so separating people by gender doesn't necessarily result in "comfort" or students being more attentive because they're "less distracted" by peers of the same gender. If the school insists on gender segregation, I would ask your child what class they want to participate in or if they want to be opted out entirely. I hate that exclusion is sometimes in the best interests of LGBTQ students because the adults are "doing it wrong." If this is the case, *Planned Parenthood*, *Amaze*, *Scarleteen*, *Advocates for Youth*, *LGBTQ+ Youth Help*, and *RespectAbility* are phenomenal LGBTQ inclusive resources.

Regarding LGBTQ inclusive sex education, the National Association of School Psychologists recently published a position statement on *Comprehensive and Inclusive Sexuality Education*.[21] The following is an excerpt straight out (no pun intended) of the position statement:

> Inclusive sexuality education occurs when students receive comprehensive, meaningful, empirical, and applicable information that is inclusive of diverse sexual orientations, sex assigned at birth, gender identity, socioeconomic status, race/ethnicity, disability status, and cultural backgrounds, and provides access to accurate and unbiased information related to supporting sexuality education... Concerted efforts must also be taken to ensure inclusivity of those within the LGBTQ+ community who are historically excluded, such as non-binary, asexual, genderqueer, and gender fluid persons.

If the curriculum is not inclusive, consider volunteering for the school

---

21   National Association of School Psychologists. (2021). Comprehensive and inclusive sexuality education [Position Statement]. Accessed 18/07/2022 at www.nasponline. org/x57367.xml

board committee which oversees family life education. Alternatively, you can share information and available vetted curricula which are published. The Sex Education Collaborative's Healthy Teen Network offers free online trainings in *Building Support for Sex Education in School* and *The Teacher's Guide to Sex Ed.*[22] Both trainings are LGBTQ inclusive. There are also free school-based curricula which meet the National Sexuality Education Standards,[23] such as *Rights, Respect, Responsibility.*[24] Advocates for Youth (n.d.) who authored the *Rights, Respect, Responsibility* curriculum also has LGBTQ inclusive guidance on the *Best Practices for Youth-Friendly Sexual and Reproductive Health Services in Schools.*[25]

Janis Tannehill: I wish I had a good answer for this. Relying on the school system to adequately teach our gender non-conforming kids about sex and relationships is foolish—schools simply don't know what they are doing when it comes to orientation and gender. Frequently they're handcuffed by state-level requirements that make discussion of anything not cis and heterosexual illegal. If there are any other options open outside school, take them.

Family life education is the absolute worst and is a reflection of how broken and dichotomous our education system is. Every state has its own curriculum, and these are almost universally lacking. Abstinence-only sex education has been shown not to work, yet most states still teach it. The contributions and struggles of LGBTQ people, especially youth, are largely ignored and sometimes actively vilified. Our school district which is in a very progressive area only recently (2018) approved expanding the definition of family to

---

22 https://sexeducationcollaborative.org/offerings?field_topic_tid%5B%5D=116&-field_organization_state_tid%5B%5D=47

23 Future of Sex Education Initiative (FoSE). (2012). National Sexuality Education Standards: Core Content and Skills, K–12 [a special publication of the *Journal of School Health*]. Accessed 18/07/2022 at https://advocatesforyouth.org/wp-content/uploads/2019/09/josh-fose-standards-web.pdf

24 Advocates for Youth. (2019). *Rights, Respect, Responsibility: A K–12 Sexuality Education Curriculum.* Accessed 18/07/2022 at www.3rs.org

25 Advocates for Youth. (n.d.). *Best Practices for Youth-Friendly Sexual and Reproductive Health Services in Schools.* Accessed 18/07/2022 at https://advocatesforyouth.org/resources/health-information/bp-youth-friendly-services

include same-sex parents and slightly broadening the definition of orientation and gender to include more LGBTQ people.[26]

For my son, the in-school family life education was just another exercise in exclusion and "othering." The whole process was very triggering, from denying his existence as a transgender person to reinforcing that he went through the wrong puberty as a girl. The final straw was when the girls went in one room to learn about breast self-exams and the boys in another to learn about scrotal self-exams, while my trans son chose to stand in the hall alone not knowing where to go or where he fitted in.

We had the option through our Universalist Unitarian Church for our kids to take a program called Our Whole Lives that goes beyond the birds and the bees and explores different family dynamics and the full range of gender and orientation as part of identity and relationships. My kids found it very valuable, and I highly recommend seeking this program out if possible. I gave my trans son the choice to opt out of school family life education but he felt he was a resource for his other LGBTQ classmates who had questions about their gender, orientation, and safer sex practices. We found it both funny and ironic that he was providing more useful information to his classmates than the mandated curriculum.

How do we let the school know that our child will be socially transitioning? What do we need to do to ensure that this is respected and goes in their records?

Amy Cannava (NCSP): This is a great question and I love the wording on it! It's assertive and you should be assertive when it comes to your child's gender expression. I would start by contacting your child's school counselor and say just that: *My child is socially transitioning and we want to ensure that this is respected and is reflected in their records accurately.* This leaves no ambiguity, respectfully conveys what is happening and that their transition is not optional, and that

---

26 www.washingtonblade.com/2018/06/15/fairfax-school-board-approves-lgbt-inclusive-sex-ed-curriculum

you and your child both expect the school to adapt. If your child has been attending the school already, this should not come as a surprise as children show preference for certain clothes before "officially" socially transitioning. The Human Rights Campaign Foundation has a useful 11-page guidance document entitled *A Parent's Quick Guide for In-School Transitions: Empowering Families and Schools to Support Transgender and Non-Binary Students*.[27] Additionally, Gender Spectrum has a *Gender Support Plan* which can help you work through the process, and ensure that your child's privacy is respected and that disclosures are purposeful and only carried out as necessary.[28]

Who your child chooses to come out to is their business entirely and a student's transgender status should never be maintained in their cumulative school record. Any documentation which identifies his/her/their transgender status should be maintained in a separate file (which is not accessible to anyone in the school), such as a file kept in the school counselor's or nurse's office. While I personally like using the *Gender Support Plan* for idea-generating, I do not advocate for its use as a form which is shared with the school because it is lengthy and includes a lot of information that is privileged and may not be appropriate to disclose to everyone who might be granted access. I do, however, think using the form to guide conversations with a designated school staff member (such as the school counselor, school psychologist, or school social worker) is highly appropriate and recommended. Additionally, ask your child what questions or concerns they have about social transitioning in the context of school. How do they want it handled when they are deadnamed or misgendered? Do they want to be allowed to speak to the class about the changes or would they rather someone spoke for them? Do they want to transition without it being made a big deal or disclosed? You can help drive the train but allow your child to determine where it goes, who gets on and off, and when it stops.

As far as school records go, while not federally required, states are given the option to require legal documentation to "officially" change student records. That said, this doesn't mean you have to legally

---

27 https://hrc-prod-requests.s3-us-west-2.amazonaws.com/assets/ParentsGuideFor-SchoolTransitions.pdf

28 https://genderspectrum.org/articles/using-the-gsp

change your five-year-old's name...and then change it again when she is six and again when she is seven. Students go by "nicknames" in school all the time and student information systems allow for this to be documented. There are also workarounds for enabling teachers to download their class lists with nicknames listed rather than deferring to legal names and leaving off gender. Some states also allow you to have an "identification card" through the Department of Motor Vehicles and some states allow for these identification cards to indicate a different gender than that assigned at birth (and sometimes an "X" for non-binary) with any medical or mental health professional signing off on such, whether or not a young person has medically transitioned. You can see if the school accepts this, since not every state allows for a revised birth certificate. Remind schools that under the Family Educational Rights and Privacy Act (FERPA), and best practices, records which denote your child as being transgender are not to be maintained in a school cumulative record as this is considered personally protected information (PPI) which not every educator should have access to. For additional information, the National Association of School Psychologists has published a FAQ sheet.[29]

Jennifer See: I already had a good rapport with our school as an active PTA parent and classroom volunteer. I had a pretty good idea of who was supportive and approached those people first. The principal, guidance counselor, and classroom teacher were the main three I had to deal with. Social transition on the school side for us was pretty straightforward as the district already had a policy in place for handling affected kids. I have many friends who ended up targeted at school board meetings or dealing with individual teachers regarding their kids, but that was not my experience. I had more issues with the mental health challenges with my daughter, resulting in a lot of absences and eventually homeschool instruction.

Generally, deal with the medical professionals and therapists first. Then involve the guidance counselor once you have an action

29 www.nasponline.org/resources-and-publications/resources-and-podcasts/diversity-and-social-justice/lgbtq-youth/gender-inclusive-schools-faqs

plan with the therapist. Sometimes a letter from the therapist can be helpful to tell the school what accommodations would help the transition to be successful. Even if you still question your child's need for transition, this is where they are and what they have expressed that they need. Go all in on support for your child. The school should be directed to use their preferred name.

Janis Tannehill: My first stop was my kid's grade level counsellor, and she didn't know what to do either! Be prepared for administrators to not know the nuances of transition policy for kids within their own system—it might seem as if there are queer kids all over the place, but the overall population is very low. Give people the benefit of the doubt and the time to research policy within their school and district; lack of knowledge is not necessarily a lack of support.

Every state and school district is different when it comes to laws, policy, best practices, and accommodations. In the face of lack of guidance, best practices are generally to be supportive. Once you are armed with knowledge of the law and policies of your school, try to go in with a clear list of what you want:

- *Name changes:* preferred or legal? If the yearbook allows preferred names, when is the cut-off date for change requests? How do names show up in the roll? Are preferred names first or will substitutes continually out your kid because of the way the roll is presented? Do you need to email each teacher directly letting them know of name and pronoun changes, or does the administration of your school have a mechanism for that? My son's school allowed him to change his name in the yearbook, but not in the school records or the roll until it was a legal name change.
- *Bathrooms and changing rooms:* some schools will allow a trans kid to use whichever bathroom suits them, with some it is sex assigned at birth or nothing, some have specially designated facilities, and some use the bathroom of their affirmed gender. Know what the policy of your school is, and if your school doesn't have a policy, make them implement one that

will benefit all kids, allowing students to use the bathroom most closely aligned with their gender, or giving them an open choice of bathrooms. Changing rooms can be a little more complicated, and access to private changing areas is a more common solution. My kid absolutely refused to change at school, and he didn't want anyone seeing his body. On the rare occasion that he had to, he would change in a closed bathroom stall.

- *Sport:* this really depends on your state and district. Sport has become a hot button issue, as to whether a kid has to participate on a team of their sex, or gender, or is denied the right to participate in sport at all. Know your district's policy and look for waivers at the high school level to allow trans students to change to the team of their affirmed gender. Once you have the law and policy on your side you will have the ability to make the school adhere to its promises. Find out who your administrators are and who to complain to if they are not doing as they should.

How do we get the school to change our child's name and gender marker in the system? What if they were born in a state that won't let us change their birth certificate?

Amy Cannava (NCSP): In 2021, the US Department of Education (DOE) published *Supporting Transgender Youth in School*, which asserts that schools should be:

adopting policies that respect all students' gender identities—such as the use of the name a student goes by, which may be different from their legal name, and pronouns that reflect a student's gender identity—and implementing policies to safeguard students' privacy—such as maintaining the confidentiality of a student's birth name or sex assigned at birth if the student wishes to keep this information private, unless the disclosure is legally required.[30]

---

30 www2.ed.gov/about/offices/list/ocr/docs/ed-factsheet-transgender-202106.pdf

There is nothing in federal law that requires families to provide legal name changes in order for records to be amended, but states can choose to require such.

As previously noted, students go by different names at school frequently. Christopher may go by "Chris" and Jasmine may go by "Parrot." Especially in the latter case, no school employee will ask the student to provide written documentation that the student's name is Parrot, but they may very well be calling her/them Parrot in classes! Transgender students cannot legally be singled out for different treatment so if any other student in the school goes by a different name, the school has to allow your child to.

That said, a school can refuse to change your child's name on official school records if your child has not had a legal name change. (Refusing to change their names in school records once you come back with a court-ordered name change is illegal, however.) You can argue that in refusing to do so, they are creating a hostile environment for your child by exposing them to harassment which they will be unable to guarantee protection from, and are inadvertently disclosing federally protected and private privileged information. Not all states allow for changing a birth certificate, so some families have had better luck going straight to the Social Security Administration and changing the gender marker there, and the gender marker and legal name on their passport. Consider reaching out to your state's ACLU for support if you continue to receive unnecessary pushback.

Also, know that under FERPA, students (current or former) can also request that their educational records be revised and redacted if the records are "inaccurate, misleading, or in violation of the student's rights of privacy."[31] This can be requested to ensure that a transgender person's educational records reflect their name and not their deadname, and their affirmed gender rather than their sex assigned at birth. This will be especially important as your child begins to apply for jobs and/or college.

---

31 Family Educational Rights and Privacy Act (FERPA) (20 U.S.C. § 1232g; 34 C.F.R. §§ 99.00 et seq.). Under Section 34 C.F.R. § 99.7(a)(2)(ii)), transgender youth and/ or adults can seek to have their name and gender marker changed. Prior to the age of 18, the students' parents would have to request this. www.lambdalegal.org/ know-your-rights/article/youth-ferpa-faq

Janis Tannehill: Name changes due to divorce, remarriage, and adoption are common. Get a court-ordered name change, then bring in the legal name change to student records for this change to take place immediately.

Gender markers are more difficult since each state is different as to how, when, and under what circumstances gender markers on birth certificates can be changed, if at all. Go for the passport route. Passports can be applied for under the gender marker recommended by a health professional, not birth certificate. Since it is a federal ID, a passport should be able to be used to change gender markers on school records. If you can't get a birth certificate, there are other ways to get other ID.

The Transgender Law Center is your friend—it keeps all the laws for each state up to date and provides sample forms for healthcare providers to help with gender marker changes with Social Security, passports and the DMV.

Our trans child wants to play sports but isn't ready to use either locker room.

Amy Cannava (NCSP): When a child wants to play sports but isn't ready to use either locker room, alternatives should be provided to allow the child to play. There is no reason a child can't use an alternate restroom location, the gym, or even an empty classroom with the blinds drawn. The key is that your child feels comfortable. That said, it is important for the child to understand that there are consequences for any action. The child may be asked questions by teammates as to why they're not changing in the locker room so she/he/they should be prepared to respond with the understanding that what they choose to share is at their discretion. People change outside the locker room for various reasons, including but not limited to medical concerns (e.g., eczema, scoliosis), different pubertal changes, and history of trauma or abuse. Your child can share as much or as little as desired and their response does not have to be factual. Adults can also dissuade youth from asking personal questions, but there will always be times when young people are alone and may ask questions they've been told not to; at some point, attempts to deter attention can actually increase attention. Trans Athlete, run by Chris Mosier (a trans man and US National Team member), provides current information by state of rules and regulations as well as best practice recommendations for gender-diverse youth in sports.[32] Additional resources include *Athlete Ally*,[33] the Society of Health and Physical Educators (SHAPE America) *Transgender Inclusion*,[34] and GLSEN's *Changing the Game*.[35]

Our teachers want training, but the administration is afraid to provide or approve it. What should we do?

Amy Cannava (NCSP): So much of what is refused or refuted by a school system comes from a place of fear, so this question is an astute one. Educators are accustomed to learning; they impart knowledge and generally view expanding one's consciousness as productive and beneficial. When faced with something they do not understand, they will often ask questions and seek to learn more. Education is founded on the pursuit of knowledge. What would be the administration's reason for refusal to teach or to allow teachers to learn?

One fear comes from the misconception that sexuality is just about sex, and the incorrect conflation of gender and sexuality. The other comes from fear of how it will be perceived by the school board and parents (and as a result, the media). They may hide behind associated costs or time, but those are merely hurdles and not barriers. If teachers want to learn, the school should do everything in its power to make this happen.

There is greater concern when teachers do not want to learn. If the administration wants you to go to the school board to request training or funds, do so. If the administration asks if there are

---

32 www.transathlete.com
33 www.athleteally.org
34 www.shapeamerica.org/standards/guidelines/Transgender/?hkey=241d34b2-5445
    -4914-b863-cd4e68314e8b
35 www.glsen.org/sites/default/files/ctg/GLSEN_CTG2021_PETeachers_Mid-
    dle-High_Guide.pdf

organizations or programs you can recommend, do not pass up the opportunity to inform them.

Your state likely has both state and local resources which can provide professional development for educators. There are also national programs and frameworks, both gratis and paid, in-person and online. Here are just a few:

- GLSEN provides professional development by local chapter.[36]
- PBS Understanding LGBTQ+ Identity: A Toolkit for Educators.[37]
- PBS *Frontline: Growing Up Trans.*[38]
- HRC *Welcoming Schools* Training.[39]
- Advancement Courses' *Safe Spaces and Affirming Places: Supporting LGBTQ+ Youth in Schools.*[40]
- The National School Board Association's *Bridging the Gap: Professional Development and LGBTQ Youth.*[41]
- The American Psychological Association's *The Respect Online Course.*[42]
- The Trevor Project's *Lifeguard Workshop.*[43]
- Learning for Justice's *Best Practices for Serving LGBTQ Students.*[44]

Debi Jackson: If you have teachers in your child's school who want transgender-inclusive training, work with them to create a proposal for the school. Educators enter the profession because they like children and genuinely want them to be successful in their school careers and in life. Point out that the best way to support transgender and gender non-conforming youth is by really understanding them,

---

36 www.glsen.org/professional-development
37 www.pbslearningmedia.org/collection/lgbtq-identity
38 www.pbs.org/wgbh/frontline/film/growing-up-trans
39 https://welcomingschools.org/resources/training
40 www.advancementcourses.com/courses/safe-spaces-and-affirming-faces-supporting-lgbtq-youth-in-schools
41 www.nsba.org/ASBJ/2021/February/Professional-Development-LGBTQ
42 www.apa.org/pi/lgbt/programs/safe-supportive/training/respect-online-course
43 www.thetrevorproject.org/education
44 www.learningforjustice.org/sites/default/files/2018-09/TT-LGBTQ-Best-Practices-Guide.pdf

knowing how to create safe and inclusive spaces, and implementing supportive policies that will protect them.

There are great training programs out there that focus on LGBTQ issues as well as those that are transgender specific. If they are leery of one kind of program, the other might be something they would consider. There are also continuing education resources about LGBTQ topics from organizations like the National Education Association that schools might consider if they are worried that community members would balk at an LGBTQ organization presenting their own material because of "an agenda."

If all else fails, a favorite tactic of mine is to point to all of the lawsuits against unsupportive schools that were decided in favor of the transgender student. A helpful resource to make that point is a document called "15 Expensive Reasons Why Safe Schools Legislation is in your State's Best Interest."[45] A school might worry about community backlash, but it is more concerned about the expense of a lawsuit and potential payout with a legal loss.

How do I make sure my child is safe at school?

Amy Cannava (NCSP): Many of the questions above address variations of this question. The best things you can do to ensure your child feels safe are 1) maintain an open dialogue with your child and the school, and 2) observe your child for changes in behavior and habits. If something is wrong, you'll know through observing and listening. Remind them that they can always talk to you about anything. Reinforce to them that anyone can benefit from therapy, but there are times in their life when they may need it. This will allow your child to have access to someone they can trust and confide in apart from you as well.

Janis Tannehill: The unfortunate truth is, you can't guarantee their safety. Kids who are different have always been a target for

---

45   www.trans-parenting.com/wp-content/uploads/2014/06/15reasons.pdf

harassment and bullying. Your kids will find some measure of safety in community by discovering other queer kids to hang out with.

Since my son was dealing with diagnosed anxiety and depression (and later we found out complex PTSD), his high school counsellor gave him a "flex pass" which allowed him to leave class to take a few minutes in the hall or the clinic when he felt overwhelmed or stressed. He would also use it to avoid classmates and teachers who were giving him a tough time, or to visit the bathroom.

My son chose the path of least resistance and found ways to avoid using the bathroom during the school day, figuring out which ones were the least trafficked and at what time of the day. Girls' bathrooms were triggering, and he didn't feel safe in the boys' bathrooms unless they were deserted. Despite having open access to any bathroom he wanted to use, he never really felt comfortable in any. When touring universities, the LGBTQ climate and number of unisex (single-stall) bathrooms were huge considerations for him.

My child is gender non-conforming and their gender expression doesn't match their gender identity. What bathroom do they use safely?

Amy Cannava (NCSP): There is no "one size fits all" answer to this question but thinking about it can help you and your child to figure out what's best for your child. There's a difference between gender identity, gender expression, and gender presentation. Gender identity is a person's internal sense of being. Gender expression is how they externally convey their gender to the outside world. Gender presentation is how the world sees that person's gender. Unfortunately, these three things are not always aligned and the distinction between them can result in animosity, harassment, and dysphoria. The "right" bathroom is the one that results in the least amount of all these things for your child. This will depend on your child, how their presentation is observed by others, and the school climate itself. If they are gender non-conforming and do not present on the binary, restroom selection can be that much more challenging because present-day society in the United States divides gender into only two categories. You should think about questions your child doesn't want to have to think about, or shouldn't have to think about, such as what/how their gender will be perceived by others and where they are more likely to be physically safe as a result. This may or may not align with where your child wants to use the restroom, however, and you should support this while serving as their executive function: help them to understand how various situations may play out so that they can make an informed choice. Single-user restrooms are a possibility but only if your child wants to use them. Finally, help your child to identify at least one supportive and trusted adult at school.

Chapter 8

Culture and Religion

Each of us comes from somewhere, and the culture we grow up in and live in now affects how we see our child's coming out. Part of our cultural paradigm is religion, which often takes an unaccepting view of trans people and those who affirm their lives and experiences. Every parent comes from a different place and has their own experiences regarding religious and cultural pressures on how to deal with their child coming out and transitioning. In the end, each of them puts their child first, and all of them are the better for it.

I worry about the dishonor that this will bring to my family and lineage. How can I handle this with my family?

Marsha Aizumi: I used to worry a lot about the dishonor and shame that would befall our family and lineage when my child came out. I remember at a very early age an elder telling me, as we sat around a table celebrating New Year's Day, that our family name goes back to the samurai times. "Never bring dishonor to our family name!" So when Aiden came out, I heard this elder's deep, resounding voice echoing in my head along with my own voice saying, "How could you have let this happen? You are a terrible mother!" For months, these voices played a repeating tape in my mind. And for months, I felt a cold, sick feeling in my stomach when those voices emerged. I was so ashamed.

It took a long time for me to overcome my shame and my feelings of bringing dishonor to my family. It took me going to PFLAG meetings and understanding that my child did not have a choice because this was who they were at their core. It took time to process what I believed and what I wanted my child to feel. Asian families have faced so much discrimination historically, so we don't want to stand out and be a target.

But I decided that I would best honor my family by standing by Aiden and being a visible voice in the Asian community. This would make a statement to my son that I was not ashamed of him, and it would send a message to other Asian families that there were parents who loved their LGBTQ children and were not afraid to show up for them.

Aiden and I have made our story visible through our memoir, *Two Spirits, One Heart: A Mother, Her Transgender Son, and Their Journey to Love and Acceptance*. I have invited my family to events Aiden and I have spoken at, so they can learn. My brother has marched with me in a Pride parade and even attended a rally for LGBTQ families. My other brother donates to LGBTQ causes like PFLAG and Okaeri, a Nikkei LGBTQ community. For me, the key was to reach out to my family and encourage their support. Many times, these connections allowed discussions and questions to emerge. It has been a process. Staying calm, being patient, being respectful, listening to my family's concerns, and not reacting have been key. I am lucky that my family has in turn been respectful, kind, and open.

My family and extended family have found ways to be advocates. They are proud of us and we are so proud of them. And I truly believe that we have brought honor to our ancestors and all of our family by our courage in the face of fear and our visible voices of love and hope.

In our culture, we do not air our private matters in public. I want to get support but going to a support group like PFLAG is too public. How can I get help?

Marsha Aizumi: I completely understand not wanting to attend a support group to air in public what Asians consider very private matters. I felt exactly the same way. Initially, I did a lot of research online and ordered books, but in the end my son was being physically attacked and so I was desperate. I attended my first PFLAG meeting and it was good to get the support. However, they were all non-Asian, so they did not understand the nuances of the Asian culture. Today, there are many groups that are led by individuals from specific API (Asian Pacific Island) communities, and PFLAG has intentionally created spaces for communities of color. Here are just a few resources:

- PFLAG San Gabriel Valley Asian Pacific Islander.[1]
- PFLAG New York City: API Rainbow Parents.[2]
- PFLAG San Diego API.[3]
- Okaeri: a Nikkei LGBTQ community.[4]
- Desi Rainbow Parents and Allies.[5]
- Viet Rainbow of Orange County.[6]

Many of these groups have individuals who speak Asian languages, so families who struggle with English can communicate in a way most comfortable for them. PFLAG SGV and API and other organizations may also offer models such as one-on-one conversations, which they call Family Circles, or Afternoon Teas for Asian Parents (ATAP), which are organized around a specific API language and are only for a few families. Besides offering support, these groups can provide resources in Asian languages. The Family Acceptance Project has translated a poster which provides words and actions that can support our LGBTQ children. It has been translated into eight API languages.[7]

Clara Lee: For many Asian parents, seeking help and going to the support meeting where you do not know anyone can be scary and overwhelming due to cultural or personal reasons. When someone reaches out to API Rainbow Parents via email, I often offer to talk to them in a one-on-one setting before suggesting they join a meeting, and I assure them I will be there too.

---

1   www.sangabrielvalleyapipflag.com
2   www.pflagnyc.org/support/api
3   https://pflag.com/support-meetings
4   www.okaeri-losangeles.org
5   www.desirainbow.org
6   www.vietroc.org
7   https://familyproject.sfsu.edu/poster

When my son came out, it took me a while to seek help from others and go to a support meeting. I needed time and space to get my head around what it means to have a trans child and accept him. In Korean culture, many parents think of their children as extensions of themselves and the family, often associating their children's accomplishments with their own and as honoring the family. Having a child who does not fit into a certain picture of what the family expects often brings fear for their children's future and safety, and a feeling of shame to many parents. Because of my upbringing in a Korean American immigrant family, and the cultural values and norms I learned, I also had a limited view of how I should raise my child and what success and happiness would look like. My son being part of the LGBTQ community did not fit those expectations and I struggled to be able to shift my mind and heart.

My son sent me multiple links as resources, but at that time I was too overwhelmed to even look at them. It took me a few months to get used to the idea and search online to learn even basic information on transgender topics. I also searched online with Korean words for LGBTQ. Many online resources talked about the importance of meeting other parents through support groups.

Living in New York City and working for a big financial company with a commitment to diversity and inclusion meant I had plenty of resources nearby. Once I worked up the courage, I started attending a monthly support meeting offered by the LGBT Center in New York City and the PFLAG NYC chapter. But I would often remain quiet and just listen to others. I also noticed I was the only Asian parent in the meetings. I thought, perhaps there are no Asian LGBTQ people in New York City? Or maybe I'm the only Asian parent who struggles when other parents are doing okay? Those were questions that came to mind, but I knew this could not be true. I remember the first time I met Marsha Aizumi, an Asian mother who has gone through a journey similar to mine. It was at the book reading event in New York City for her book *Two Spirits, One Heart*, and it was a profound experience to know that I was not alone in this journey.

Jennifer Solomon: For many parents, talking about their child's gender identity or sexual preference is a very private thing. Unless you have friends who also have LGBTQ youth, they cannot relate, so getting support or advice can be a challenge. Finding a safe place to share concerns or fears is crucial to finding your way. Facebook has many different private groups with thousands of members. Because of the pandemic there are many resources now available virtually. This is one way to stay private but also have a network of resources. Organizations like PFLAG also offer support groups that are geared towards specific cultures or ethnicities. I highly recommend checking these out because I think you would be surprised to find many other families who feel the same about publicly sharing. Safe spaces are where you can be yourself and ask questions freely without feeling pressured or having to explain yourself. It takes a village to raise a child! You are not alone. Find your comfort place and let others help you on this journey.

Language is a huge barrier to understanding. How can I get help in my language?

Marsha Aizumi: Many of the API groups I have mentioned when talking about support can also help you with resources for non-English-speaking parents and family members. PFLAG has specific groups for non-English-speaking parents of LGBTQ youth.

One thing to keep in mind is that in many immigrant families, the parents and grandparents may not speak English. Their children who were raised in the US mainly speak English, so there could be a gap in communication, especially around a complex topic such as LGBTQ. We have found you have to be careful with the words you use, because many words related to LGBTQ could have very negative connotations. Bringing in bilingual support individuals who understand both languages and which words are positive, and which are derogatory, could be a very important piece in bridging that gap of understanding, and the kinds of images that are projected.

I want to highlight the Family Acceptance Project posters again for families that need something in an API language.[8] These posters

---

8   https://familyproject.sfsu.edu/poster

are not only in English and Spanish, but also in Japanese, Chinese (traditional and simplified), Korean, Hindi, Vietnamese, Punjabi, and Tagalog. There are three posters: one with helpful words and behaviors, one with unhelpful words and behaviors, and the third with helpful words and behaviors from a conservative viewpoint, which doesn't talk about dating.

I loved reading about things I could do to support my child, as well as discussing unhealthy behaviors like alcohol, drugs, and suicide. I even appreciated the unhelpful words and behavior information which gave me an opportunity to go back to Aiden and say I am sorry for the things that I did that were unhelpful. Keeping our hearts open to each other was a major goal for me, because I knew if our hearts were open, we could listen to each other better, and communicate more gently but openly. This poster information helped our family stay connected, but most of all it sent a message to our son that he would always belong in our family and he would always be loved.

Clara Lee: I am fortunate to be bilingual in English and Korean, but I am fully aware of the power of seeing resources and talking to others in one's own language on LGBTQ topics. I have been supporting immigrant parents and API LGBTQ individuals for many years and have noticed a growing number of parents' groups and LGBTQ serving organizations in our home countries, in addition to groups supporting Asian LGBTQ people and parents in the US. Some of these organizations in our home countries would often translate English materials or resources into their own language.

For example, PFLAG Korea several years ago leveraged its volunteers to translate PFLAG resources into Korean. It is also developing its own multimedia resources like books, YouTube videos and feature-length documentaries with stories of parents and individuals. Several years ago, I met several bilingual Korean American parents through my work with API Rainbow Parents of PFLAG NYC. We saw a need to offer culturally sensitive and language-specific support platforms, so we started a group chat via the Kakao chatting app and we offered a monthly virtual meeting via Zoom. We now conduct meetings in Korean and look for resources in Korean for parents. The virtual group has grown to include 30+ parents/family members.

Many parents found us online or got a referral to the Korean American Rainbow Parents group from their own children, who often reached out to us first before they came out.

Sometimes language is not the only barrier. Korean parents still retain the values from their own upbringings and experiences, including a binary construct of gender with almost no exposure to LGBTQ topics—or exposure that has created harmful or negative perceptions. Hearing other supportive parents who went through the journey by overcoming their own prejudices and changing their minds and hearts can help many parents, as they see themselves in those personal stories that other parents share.

How do we balance supporting our child with our faith?

Chester Hitchcock: While our world is full of orphans and unwanted children, the reality is that the family unit is the backbone of our society. Furthermore, although Christianity is decreasing in North America, families who are connected to a church generally identify this as one of the most important factors in their life.

With each church, there is commonly a set of doctrines that are upheld and promoted for generations without much questioning of their strengths and weaknesses. Nevertheless, most Christians have, on occasion, needed to rethink some of their beliefs due to events and circumstances going on around them. Frequently, the rethinking of certain beliefs results in a strengthening of faith rather than a loss of faith.

Parents whom I have talked with regarding a child that comes out to them as transgender, or any other part of the LGBTQ community, have told me that by keeping their eye on the love of God and maintaining and declaring that love clearly to their child, their faith has grown by leaps and bounds.

This is because we live in a time when many have gone before us to do the research that balances our faith with the LGBTQ community. In addition to the book that you are holding in your hands, there are great books such as: *Mom, I'm Gay—Loving Your LGBTQ Child and Strengthening Your Faith* by Susan Cottrell. Susan is founder of FreedHearts, an organization where Christian parents of LGBTQ children can connect to support one another.[9]

Additionally, while there are plenty of books and sources of internet information that condemn transgender people, there are also various YouTube channels like mine where you can find short videos that cover the Bible passages that have been misunderstood regarding those who are LGBTQ. My series on YouTube is titled: *God Loves the LGBTQ+ Community.*[10]

To put it simply, no one needs to sacrifice their faith in order to support their LGBTQ child—or vice versa. Our faith can grow stronger as we love our child with a Christ-like love.

Marsha Aizumi: I did not feel I had to balance supporting my child with my faith, since I had already lost confidence in the Lutheran (Missouri Synod) church we were attending. At one Bible study, I heard people talking about intolerance for homosexuality. I never went back to church after that, but Aiden was close to friends from school at this church, so I just let him continue to attend their Sunday School.

Little did I anticipate that a visiting minister would ask Aiden to leave the church until he found himself. In other words, Aiden could return when he was not LGBTQ. In retrospect, I wonder if I should have pulled him away from this church when I heard their negative stance on LGBTQ, but I did not want to pull him away from his friends who knew he was identifying as lesbian at the time and were so accepting. He needed a place to feel that he belonged. But in the end, the church told him he was not welcome.

Even though I did not have to choose between my child and my church, if I had to make that choice, I would have always chosen Aiden. However, many families are very connected to their churches. After World War II, when Japanese Americans were released from concentration camps, the church was their community of safety and belonging. And I know that many religious parents, out of love, do not want their children to go to hell or be an abomination, so they try to make them straight.

---

9   www.freedhearts.org
10 www.youtube.com/watch?v=vT8GckgexVo

In the end, I believe as parents we must make a choice, if we want to support our child and our church is not supportive. I chose to leave the church to be true to myself and my child. I have heard of others who have moved to a church more open and affirming. And I have seen parents who have stayed and try to educate their church. These are the brave parents. I was not so brave. I was still fragile, and I did not have the strength to fight that fight.

I once heard a mother say, "If my LGBTQ child goes to hell, because of who they are, then I will go to hell with them...because I am their mother." That statement always choked me up because it represented a mother's unwavering love. At the same time, I wondered why she had to make that choice. One day I hope *all* churches are seen as loving, inclusive, and welcoming spaces, free from judgment, exclusion, and closed hearts. When that happens, we won't have to choose, and we can have both.

Debi Jackson: One reason a lot of parents find they struggle to support their transgender child is because of what they have been taught in their church. This can be true regardless of what faith they follow. I grew up as a Southern Baptist, going to church at least four times a week, and I was even my on my high school's student council as our chaplain. Yes, in Alabama, we had high school student chaplains. To answer this question, I think it's important to separate "faith" from "religion."

My answer a decade ago when Avery told us that she was a girl was very different from what it is today. Back then, I was still living within a very conservative bubble, and being a Southern Baptist was a core part of my identity. Even though I could logically pick apart quite a few Bible stories and reconcile them with science (hello dinosaurs—I started school as a geology major and I can justify Biblical time vs geological time because of literary license), I struggled with the creation story and God making man and woman. But then I read a beautiful passage in *Trans-Gender: Theology, Ministry, and Communities of Faith* by Reverend Justin Sabia-Tanis, a transgender clergy member.[11] It

---

11   Tanis, J. E., Schlager, B. S., & Perry, T. D. (2018). *Trans-Gender: Theology, Ministry, and Communities of Faith.* Eugene, OR: Wipf & Stock.

reminded me of the amazing diversity in the world and taught me not to think God suddenly wasn't very creative when it came to creating people. I have faith in a creator who celebrates diversity.

Today, I recognize how much religion has been weaponized against the LGBTQ community. I know the truth about how social issues—such as LGBTQ people wanting to be recognized with equal rights to marry and have a family—have been used as divisive tools for political gain and to win votes. I can separate the words of the Bible from the twisted way that those words are interpreted and taught by people who really just want to maintain power over others. My faith has nothing to do with what I was taught as part of a religion.

I'm known for quoting one Bible verse in my first speech about being the parent of a transgender child, and I stand by that quote. The speech is called "That's Good Enough" and this is what I said: "Jesus sought out those who others rejected. Some people choose to embrace Biblical verses that appear to say being transgender is wrong. I choose to focus on verses like 1st Samuel 16:7 which says 'But the Lord said to Samuel, "Do not consider his appearance or his height, for I have rejected him. The Lord does not look at the things people look at. People look at the outward appearance. But the Lord looks at the heart."' My daughter is a girl in her heart. She knows it. God knows it. And that's good enough for me."

Janis Tannehill: My born-again Christian mother said, "God don't make junk." What she meant by this is that everyone is made the way they are for a reason and should be accepted as such. When you go to your faith leaders and tell them about your kid asking for their guidance and the first words out of their mouths are about sin, over-coming sin, crisis of faith, or falling from God's path or graces, this is a good indicator that your church is not an affirming one. Despite my mother asking how her church felt about LGBTQ people and them starting in on sin, she still chose to go there because that's where her friends were. This really hurt me because she was actively choosing to put her soul in the hands of people who would not do the same for her grandson. Whether she understood it or not, this created a rift between us. Although she said that her God had a place for my kid as he was, she chose to go to a church with those who didn't.

The purpose of faith is to sustain you and your soul's journey in a community, not the other way around. Any church that requires your allegiance no matter the cost, as a price tag for your soul getting where you want it to go, requires scrutiny. Any church that changes their acceptance of you and your family from one week to the next based on your child's identity doesn't care about your family. Welcome to America!

There are lots of churches to choose from, so choose a church that accepts every member of your family as they are. Unitarian Universalist churches have been great for us through transition. Any place of worship with giant Pride flags out front may be worth a visit to see if they are a better fit.

My child keeps asking why God put her in a boy's body when she is a female. What should we tell her?

Chester Hitchcock: I don't want to minimize the pain that transgender kids feel when they are not comfortable in their body. No one can comprehend what they are going through unless they have experienced it themselves. Therefore, I look for ways to shift the paradigm that can both comfort as well as encourage them to follow their path in a way that gives them strength and hope rather than shame and despair.

Though for thousands of years, God has been defined as male, the Bible gives us glimpses of the feminine side of God. In Luke 15:8–10, God is portrayed as the woman with a lost coin (see also: Matt. 23:7; Deut. 32:18). Genesis 1:27 tells us that God created both male and female in God's image. Since binary means there are only two choices, if we limit creation to binary, we lose an understanding of the essence of God being both male and female. Therefore, it stands to reason that God was not and is not limited to binary creation.

Jeremiah 23:6 and 33:16 both speak prophetically of Christ with the words "The Lord our Righteousness" using the pronoun "he" in 23:6 and the pronoun "she" in 33:16. Perhaps sharing these and other similar examples may not satisfy their longing to make their body match who they are inside. However, if it helps them in their journey until, or if, that time becomes possible for them, maybe they will get a better picture of who they are in God's eyes and ultimately gain courage rather than shame.

Possibly one of the greatest needs of a transgender child is positive Christian LGBTQ role models. In her book *Walking the Bridgeless Canyon*, Kathy Baldock,[12] founder and Executive Director of Canyon-Walker Connections, states that she knows "hundreds of remarkable young LGBT Christians who are leaders in their denominations, churches and communities, and who are working toward inclusion in conservative Christian environments" (p.388). She mentions six of these role models by name and gives a little background on each one.

With biblical examples of a God who is less concerned with gender than are many churches, and with multiple LGBTQ role models faithfully serving that God, transgender children can find hope, courage, and purpose in their life through their religion.

Noah Berlatsky: My family isn't religious, so I'm not speaking about this from a theological perspective. But it might be helpful to tell your child that she isn't in a boy's body. If she's a girl, then she's in a girl's body! Bodies of every gender come in all shapes and sizes and with all sorts of differences.

Just about everyone feels uncomfortable with some aspect of their body at some point. That's often not because there's something wrong with their body, but because people have narrow and harmful ideas about what bodies should look like or be. You should absolutely do what you need to in order to make yourself feel comfortable with your body, whether that means hormones or other procedures. But none of that means someone put you in the wrong body. Whatever gender you are, and whether you're cis or trans, your body is the right one for you.

Debi Jackson: When Avery was four and angry with God, her concerns centered around the idea that she was "in the wrong body"

---

12 Baldock, K. (2014). *Walking the Bridgeless Canyon: Repairing the Breach Between the Church and the LGBT Community*. Reno, NV: Canyonwalker Press.

and that "God got things wrong." I assured her that nothing about her body—or any other part of her—was "wrong." The Bible tells us that God knows each of us before we are in the womb. That means God knows our soul, our spirit, completely outside any body. And because God created the world full of all kinds of living creatures, we know that He's pretty darn creative. Just because some people—those imperfect people who seem to get a lot of things wrong in Bible stories—don't understand that God also created transgender people, it doesn't mean that God didn't create them. It does mean that God cares more about who they are on the inside, in their soul, than what they do with their bodies. Some people get tattoos. Some people color their hair. Some people have surgery to change their nose. God doesn't judge that or love them any less, because their spirit isn't affected by those things. So trans people can adjust their bodies however they want and God isn't going to care.

Family members are using religion as a reason for refusing to recognize my child's identity. How should I approach this?

Chester Hitchcock: Families can be the greatest source of strength when we are in times of need. Unfortunately, this is not always where we find strength. Genesis 2:24 states: "Therefore a man shall leave his father and mother and be joined to his wife, and they shall become one flesh." This verse makes it clear that adding a new member to the family sometimes causes division, and one must make a decision to separate from part of the family, even in heterosexual relationships.

Matthew 19:29 gives a similar scenario that reflects the tragedy of sometimes parting with family when circumstances require it. A family that doesn't recognize a child's sexual/gender identity can be more than hurtful, it can be devastating. From a biblical perspective, tough extended family decisions need to be made in favor of the health of the immediate family.

But before severing family ties in a way that deepens the pain, I would suggest pleading with your family to consider reading some of the research on the topic of LGBTQ and the Bible. There are many books available, but one that I would highly recommend is

UnClobber by Colby Martin.[13] This book breaks down the six biblical passages that are generally used to condemn the gay community. It is an easy read that Rob Bell, a *New York Times* bestselling author, says is "Funny, smart, and brilliantly paced! ... Colby shows what the Bible actually says—clearing up all sorts of confusion along the way."

Jan Morris, a transgender woman (1926–2020) and an acclaimed British journalist, travel writer and historian, wrote more than four dozen books. In her autobiography titled *Conundrum*,[14] she writes, "I was three or perhaps four years old when I realized that I had been born in the wrong body, and should really be a girl. I remember the moment well, and it is the earliest memory of my life" (p.3). Jan's success as a renowned writer is a reflection of how a transgender person can rise to their greatest heights when surrounded by a supportive family.

If religion really is the excuse a family member uses for not accepting a child's identity, they should be willing to defend their belief when a biblical perspective is presented that is more accurate, or accept that *their* behavior is causing division in their family.

Janis Tannehill: Make sure your family knows they are making an active choice between their religious expression and the health of your child. Let's be plain here, it is religious expression and not religion that is the problem. Plenty of religions and individual denominations have space for LGBTQ people. Churches that choose not to accept all people are making a choice to exclude people they don't understand and can't control. Refusing to use your kid's chosen name and pronouns actively hurts them; what kind of god advocates harming a child and pushing them towards suicide? Any family member who is actively hurting your child is not your family. Be prepared to cut out family that hurts you, and choose your kid, always.

---

13   Martin, C. (2022). *UnClobber: Rethinking our Misuse of the Bible on Homosexuality.* Louisville, KY: Westminster John Knox Press.
14   Morris, J. (1974) *Conundrum.* New York, NY: Harcourt Brace Jovanovich.

I have been a member of my church all my life, but they are not supportive of the LGBTQ community. Is there a way to support my child and still be a member of this place I have grown up in and where I have so many friends?

Chester Hitchcock: As I have explained in response to a previous question, for the health and well-being of the immediate family, there are times when it is necessary to separate from those whom we love for the sake of another. There are several places in scripture where this is acknowledged, such as Genesis 2:24 and Matt. 19:29. However, some have been quite successful in maintaining relationships with those who have different views. Unity in diversity is possible if there is respect on both sides.

I have had members in my church who attended another church because of a spouse or loved one and split their time and commitment between the two. I was never opposed or threatened by this, but I know of other pastors who were. Some churches are strictly opposed to their members being a part of a different denomination. My position is that no one has the right to tell another where they can worship, and people should be free to be members of multiple churches. It can be a challenge if you or a loved one is LGBTQ and try to remain involved where the gay community isn't seen as equal. Trying to attend one church that is open and affirming while keeping a relationship with another because of lifelong history can be a struggle. For that reason, some LGBTQ people and their families have found it necessary to break lifelong ties with their church while maintaining personal friendships with supportive members from that congregation.

Lifelong membership in a specific congregation can be extremely painful to leave behind. One must choose which pain is the least difficult to endure: leaving, or facing constant criticism and judgement for the rest of one's life. Each situation is unique, and no single answer will fit them all. Fervent prayer and constant love for the person who is LGBTQ are essential.

God is not anti-gay or homophobic! Churches that are anti-gay impede those who are LGBTQ in their desire to worship and serve the One who created them.

List of Additional Resources

American Civil Liberties Union (ACLU) (www.aclu.org)

Family Acceptance Project (https://familyproject.sfsu.edu)

Fenway Health (https://fenwayhealth.org/care/medical/transgender-health)

Gender Odyssey (https://genderodyssey.org)

Gender Spectrum (https://genderspectrum.org)

GLSEN (www.glsen.org)

Human Rights Campaign (www.hrc.org)

Lambda Legal (www.lambdalegal.org)

National Center for Lesbian Rights (www.nclrights.org)

National Center for Trans Equality (NCTE) (https://transequality.org)

OutYouth (www.outyouth.org)

PFLAG (https://pflag.org)

Stand With Trans (https://standwithtrans.org)

The GenderCool Project (https://gendercool.org)

The Trevor Project (www.thetrevorproject.org)

Trans Family Support Services (https://transfamilysos.org/services/support-groups)

Trans Lifeline (https://translifeline.org)

Transgender Student Educational Resources (TSER) (https://transstudent.org)

University of California San Francisco (UCSF) Center for Excellence for Trans Health (https://prevention.ucsf.edu/transhealth)

Index of Questions

Social Transition

Family Matters

Mental Health and Medical Care

Schools